SEATING MATTERS

State of the Art Seating Arrangements

Other Books By Dr. Paul O. Radde

Supervising:
A Guide for All Levels

Austin, Texas
Learning Concepts
1981

The Supervision Transition
An Employee Guide to Choosing and Moving Into
a Supervisory Position

Fort Washington, Maryland
Thriving Publications
1991

Thrival!
How to Have an Above Average Day Every Day

Austin, Texas
Path Lighter Press,
an imprint of Thriving Publications
2003

SEATING MATTERS

State of the Art Seating Arrangements

Paul O. Radde, Ph.D.

Thriving Publications
A Division of Thrival Systems®

The Thrival Institute
3873 Florentine Drive
Longmont, CO 80503

www.Thrival.com

SEATING MATTERS
State of the Art Seating Arrangements

Copyright © 2009 by Paul O. Radde

All rights reserved,
Including the right to reproduce this book or portions thereof in any form without prior written permission of the author or granting agency. This also precludes placement on or transmission via the internet by wireless or wire transmission. Licensure is granted for local use or within one meeting facility for which this publication is purchased.

For permission: DrPaul@Thrival.com (303) 818-8795
www.Thrival.com

Thrival Systems® is a service mark of Dr. Paul O. Radde
Manufactured in the United States of America
Library of Congress Cataloging-in-Publication Data

Radde, Ph.D., Paul O.
SEATING MATTERS
State of the Art Seating Arrangements
Thriving Publications

1. Innovation 2. Spatial Arrangement 3. Meetings

ISBN 13: 978-0-9625872-2-1
ISBN 10: 0-962572-2-2

Permission for use of illustrations from Mastering Meetings, courtesy of 3M Visual Systems.

Except in the United States of America, this book is sold subject to the condition that it shall not, by way of trade or otherwise, be lent, resold, hired out, or otherwise circulated without the publisher's prior consent in any form of binding or cover other than that in which it is published and without a similar condition including this condition being imposed on the subsequent purchaser.
The scanning, uploading and distribution of this book via the Internet or via any other means without the express written permission of the author is illegal and punishable by law. Please purchase only authorized electronic editions, and do not participate in or encourage electronic piracy of copyrighted materials. Your support of the author's rights is appreciated.

This book is dedicated to:

Mercedes Rosalind Morris, Dean Emerita of the
North Dakota State College of Science,
my aunt, parent, English teacher, and a
continuing inspiration in my life, who
put on many special events.

Michael Paul McKinley, CSP, CPAE,
friend & colleague, with whom this quest for
optimizing the learning environment was rekindled,
for his ongoing support and efforts
to improve the meeting environment.

Table of Contents

Foreword	xi
Introduction	1

Part I.
Current Seating Practices — **9**

Chapter	1	Why People Attend Meetings	11
Chapter	2	Straight Row Seating Undermines a Meeting	17
Chapter	3	Criteria to Optimize Your Meeting	35
Chapter	4	Room Set Function Trumps Form	43

Part II.
Five Principles To Set or Troubleshoot Any Room — **47**

Chapter	5	Principle 1. Set to the Long Side. No Bowling Alleys	49
Chapter	6	Principle 2. Face Each Chair Toward the Presentation. No Straight Rows. Curve the Rows	55
Chapter	7	Principle 3. No Middle Aisle. Flare Aisles Off at 45 Degrees	67
Chapter	8	Principle 4. Cut Single Chair Access Lanes into Section	73
Chapter	9	Principle 5. Place the Last Row on the Back Wall	83

Part III.
Application of Principles and Refinements — **87**

Chapter	10	Accommodating Participants in the Smaller Meeting	89
Chapter	11	Fine Tune the Room	105

Part IV.
Influence: Gaining Acceptance for Your Room Set-up — **115**

Chapter	12	Influence Issues: Overcoming Resistance	117
Chapter	13	Optimizing the Meeting Facility Experience	129
Chapter	14	Dealing with Resistance to Change	143

Appendix A
Licensed Folio of Large and Small Room Seating Arrangements — **156**

Acknowledgments	177
Author Bio	179

Foreword

As a pre-kindergartner, my first experiences with education came when I 'played school.' Even though I was in nursery school (now called "Pre-K(indergarten)") and loved play (structured and unstructured), I somehow knew (did someone tell me?) that chairs were to be put in rows and you were to sit in those rows and behave. Worse, none of my 'pupils' objected!

It has fascinated me for years that – although I've been unable to uncover why - meetings look like the worst grade and high schools any of us ever attended. Worse, meetings even resemble one's worst college or university experience! Think about the structure: it begins with a continental breakfast (think: playground before school or a dinner with friends before heading in), a general session ('home room'), and then short breaks which allow barely enough time to stand up, say hello to a colleague, use the restroom, get a cuppa coffee and move to the next session. There may be a lunch with a speaker (no time for conversation or even 'down time') and then it all repeats, sometimes with an afternoon general session with a motivational speaker (pep rally?) and then the 'networking reception' (after school activities or perhaps a sporting event) at which it is too loud to hear anyone or where there is such limited seating, you are forced to hold a plate, a beverage, eat and talk!

We spend most of our time at meetings sitting on our tushes on chairs set in straight rows with no room for comfort and sight-lines that allow us to see not much more than the back of the head of the person in front of us. (Think coach airplane seating.) Some of us are bold enough to pull a chair out from a row and put it against a wall. Others, understanding the fire laws, realize that unhooking a chair from its compatriots will be unsafe. So, by our presence, we sit there, "cheek to cheek", no matter our size, comfort level, need to see and hear and participate.

The Foundation of Meeting Professionals International (MPI) did two studies some years ago about why people attend association annual meetings and what makes (corporate) meetings work. In those studies, it was confirmed that the reasons people attend meetings are to
- interact with peers (sometimes referred to as "networking") to gain insights and knowledge and solve problems.
- receive education they can put to work immediately.

What participants want from the meeting sponsor are:
1. well-prepared, appropriate and knowledgeable speakers.
2. presentation materials available and in sufficient supply.
3. an agenda that acknowledges participants' needs and is covered as promised and on schedule.
4. comfort.

"Comfort" is different for each of us and yet there are, I've learned in years of training people about meetings, some commonalities. In the words of those who have been trained: temperature (not too hot or too cold), seating (back support, not such hard surfaces), sight-lines, clear audio.

Some of us knew this information from observation and perhaps common sense, looking at our own motivation and our successes and failures as meeting participants and those who arrange meetings. Even with these studies, and Paul's work and sessions, little has changed and little is, still, changing. This book, and a wider readership and willingness to change meetings, is another step in the right direction.

There are plenty of excuses about why seating is not done well: more people can fit in a smaller space if the chairs are set in straight rows; chairs are designed for discomfort; hotel and convention center carpet is still designed for chair placement – and that placement is tight; hotels (their owners and management companies) want to make money and to do so, they want to fit as many people as possible into small(er) spaces to be able to sell other rooms for other functions; meeting space and labor have a cost to the provider and the consumer; etc. Here you will get solid arguments to counter some of these entrenched and unquestioned misperceptions about room set and capacity.

It is also because hotel sales and marketing people, convention services staff and those who set up rooms (usually known as 'housemen') have not been informed of or educated about the impact of seating and meeting outcomes. Come to think of it, neither have those who plan meetings! Look at a textbook or meeting guides in the meetings and hospitality industry and you will rarely if ever see any discussion of the impact of seating on outcomes.

Paul's terms for the only useful applications of straight row seating styles – Puritan Meeting, Jury, Egg Carton, Police Lineup and Public Health Clinic – are so apropos for what we experience and what is not best practice. Think too about movie theatres and how so many have changed from straight, one level seating to 'stadium' seating, with more comfortable chairs, tiered, for better viewing. Think about where you sat or wanted to sit at the last meeting you attended or at a movie: the aisle, in the center section (if in fact there were sections with aisles!) for comfort, for sight-lines and for easy access.

Seating matters. Did you know that before you picked up this book? Oh you will think so much more before you finish!

We've not come far enough in moving people into comfortable seating to accommodate learning and participation styles. Dr. Paul Radde's book will help you move this process along much more quickly. Read it now. Practice the principles now. Then let Paul know your experiences c/o DrPaul@Thrival.com (put "SEATING" in all caps in the subject line) so that he (and those of us who strongly support him) can continue to improve the experience.

Joan L. Eisenstodt
Eisenstodt Associates, LLC

SEATING **MATTERS**

Introduction

> *First we shape the seating, and then the seating shapes the dynamics of the meeting.*

Once you read this book, you will never again enter and view, or set a meeting room the same as you do today. You will be knowledgeable, skilled, and empowered to improve the room arrangement and make it a more functional meeting or learning environment. And you will gain rationale and skills in persuasion required to influence decision makers in seating matters.

The meeting environment is impacted by room setups that influence:
- How participants will experience the meeting events and learn.
- Their relative degree of physical comfort during the meeting, and the
- Quality, type, and frequency of contact, degree of involvement, and relationships developed with colleagues or fellow participants.

Physical arrangements impact meeting and event interaction and dynamics.

Room Set: The Hidden Element in Meeting and Event Success
Even before participants arrive at a meeting or convention site, the seating arrangements

State of the Art Seating Arrangements

have already predisposed them to some degree of the benefit they will derive from the meeting interaction – what they will see, hear, learn, and with whom they will connect, involve themselves in the event, and network

This book provides a straightforward approach to optimizing the learning environment. It is divided into four parts:

Part I. Current Seating Practices
   The second chapter, Straight Row Seating Undermines a Meeting, includes a portion titled Chevron is Even Worse Than Standard Straight Row Sets, which thoroughly explores what is problematic for the audience member about the current standard straight row room sets offered in most meeting facilities. Those include: traditional straight row theatre style set to the narrow side of the room, as well as the chevron or herringbone set. The U-shape and the box shape set-up and the classroom style set at rectangular tables, each of which also prominently feature straight rows (the latter being generally for groups and boards under 50), will be dealt with in Part III. Chapter 10.

Part II. Five Principles To Set or Troubleshoot Any Room
   These five seating principles can optimize the learning environment, when used to troubleshoot or design and set any non-dedicated room. Each principle is accompanied with illustrations and rationale for setting the large general session. The smaller board or committee meeting set-ups, once again, are found in Part III, Chap. 10.

Part III. Optimize and Fine Tune the Meeting Environment
   provides numerous points toward accommodating participants of the small meeting, as well as how to fine tune the room in such a way as to optimize the learning environment – safety, comfort, line of sight, access, and networking.

Part IV. Influence: Gaining Acceptance for a Productive Room Set-Up
   addresses how to introduce and gain acceptance for the Audience Centered Seating™ approach with tips, tools and techniques to influence those stake holders and decision makers in position to optimize your meeting environment.

Appendix A. A Folio of Licensed Illustrated Room Sets
   offers diagrams of Audience Centered Seating™ and arrangements for large and small meetings, convention general sessions and boardrooms. Authorization is granted to the owner of this book for specific use within one's contracted for or local organization.

Who Should Read This Book?
If you have anything to do with the policy, process, procedure or decisions in placing, spacing, or the arranging of chairs for a meeting, large or small, this book is for you.

SEATING MATTERS

You will gain principles, and rationale plus understand the value of what you do. You will acquire a "certain authority" in room seating based upon your own personal experience of room set-ups.

Four Major Factors in Room Set-Up
Four major factors are involved in developing a room set that optimizes the meeting and learning experience. Three play roles while the fourth is the space itself:
1. Meeting Planner: the person in charge of facility logistics execution
2. Speaker/Presentation: presentation methodology and platform practices
3. Meeting Logistics includes available space, shape, ceiling height, columns, A/V.
4. Audience Member, whose comfort, safety and beneficial outcome is the central consideration and driving force for this work and the choice of seating set-up.

In addition, there are other players, including the meeting facilities staff, starting with the sales department, right on through to the set-up foreman and crew. Often there are interdepartmental communication issues within meeting facilities that may require you to go the extra mile in getting the room arrangement you want. Guidance is offered on how to ensure follow through from sales to operations set up staff.

Audience "Focused" Seating
The audience member participant, is the ultimate and main meeting customer. The participant should be a major driving force and the central focus for a meeting. That person's interests, well-being, and earned and learned outcomes come first and foremost in determining optimal seating arrangements.

Improved Seating Provides Customer Service for the Participant
This book is written for meeting planners, speakers, meeting facilities sales and marketing personnel, meeting services and convention operations, educational specialists, school facilities planners, and architects to optimize the learning, meeting and event experience provided by their organizations, indeed everyone who will attend a meeting. Even when your connection with the industry is tangential, everyone is seated by someone. You will find uses for what you will learn in the following pages. It all constitutes good customer service.

For Non Meeting Professionals as well as Professionals
You will be attending meetings and presentations for the rest of your life. Even if you are a late arriving participant, you still have choices. You can still influence how the meeting room is set up, better understand the impact seating is having on participants, and the message that is sent by setting the seating as it is. And you can at least select or adjust your own chair in such a way that you improve your own participation, relieve personal discomfort and make yourself more comfortable. So, even if you have been uninvolved, or a passive recipient of past seating arrangements, this book will make you aware of specific things you can do to improve your future learning experiences.

SEATING MATTERS

Once You Finish This Book
When you finish reading this book, you will be able to set and troubleshoot any non-dedicated meeting room knowledgably and with confidence in the outcome for your audience. Numerous illustrations have been provided so that you can demonstrate to the meeting facility crew exactly what you want. Appendix A provides various diagrams which you can use as templates or examples to request the precise design you want on the room diagram you receive from the meeting facility.

Extend Your Impact
If you are a meeting professional, speaker, meeting facility professional, or the chairperson of an event, the likelihood is that you impact participants with anywhere from thousands to millions of seated hours a year. You have a responsibility in determining a range of meeting room options that contribute to the degree of pain and discomfort, or to the relative ease with which your audience members have access to the entire breadth of your program.

On occasion you may be restricted by some factor such as "set-up cost," the inexperience of the set-up crews, or a particular turn-around time required for use of space. We will anticipate and guide you through these impediments and the resistance to getting the state of the art seating arrangements you request when possible.

You will learn five audience centered seating™ principles and numerous factors for setting, trouble-shooting, and fine tuning any room. *The exception, of course is the dedicated meeting room that has permanently set seats screwed to the floor. We deal here only with moveable, arrange-able space.*

In many cases you will have input into the original design of a room, or you might be in a position to advise how to re-set those chairs in a better configuration for each group that follows. You will understand very well what you are doing.

Italics are used for three purposes in this book:
1. *Emphasis for several words up to sentences within a paragraph.*
2. *Directions given for an exercise that you will find directly below.*
3. *Examples of real life situations that illustrate points throughout the book.*

Call to Action
Your involvement begins now. Determine how many seated hours you could impact in the course of one calendar year. First calculate the number of seated hours that you currently do impact. Begin with the number of participants you have in a single group that you convene, and multiply that number times the number of hours each person is seated in a meeting or group learning experience. That your combined group totals give you the seated hours you impact in one year. *Banquet seating is not the concern of this book, so count refreshment events only if there is a speaker or educational program.*

State of the Art Seating Arrangements

SEATING MATTERS

Next add in the seated hours you could impact. *For example, if you run the local PTA meeting for your children's school that meets 8 times during the school year for 2 hours with an average attendance of 36 parents and teachers, then your total would be 576 seated hours for that group alone.*

Our focus runs the gamut from training room, community and civic meeting, group discussions, keynotes, general sessions, seminars, board of directors, meetings, concurrent and breakout sessions. Calculate two totals: how many seated hours you are <u>professionally responsible for</u> having set in a year, as well as how many seated hours you <u>could be influencing</u>, personally or professionally in a year.

List all your meetings (add more if needed):

Participants_____ X # of Hours Seated_____ =_____# Seated Hours

Participants_____ X # of Hours Seated_____ =_____# Seated Hours

Participants_____ X # of Hours Seated_____ =_____# Seated Hours

Participants_____ X # of Hours Seated_____ =_____# Seated Hours

Total Number of Seated Hours You Do Impact per Year_____

Total Number of Seated Hours You Could Impact per Year_____

Speakers, multiply the length of each of your programs times the number of audience members in attendance. If you manage a convention facility, arena, or hotel, add up all the meetings contracted for in order to get your yearly total. That can range from thousands to as many as millions of seated hours per year.

There are Two Main Assertions that led to the writing of Seating Matters:

Assertion #1. Participants Should Not Have to Suffer –
 It's a meeting room, not a torture chamber.

A member of your Board of Directors is given a front row seat at the opening keynote of your corporate [or association] meeting. She sits on the outside aisle seat because she will be participating in an awards ceremony on the platform. Within 15-18 minutes a camera panning the audience shows her shifting uncomfortably in her seat, trying to angle her body so that she can look directly at the keynote speaker. After a few more minutes she seems to have given up paying attention, and is perusing her program. Curiously enough, individuals sprinkled throughout the outside of the front row seating are doing the same thing. They have checked out. And these seats are supposed to be the high status seating section.

State of the Art Seating Arrangements

SEATING MATTERS

If it were not for the fact that this Board member is heavily invested in the organization or required to be there, she might not make a return appearance. How many participants will unconsciously file away their discomfort and the difficulty they experienced, as one of the reasons they do not return to next year's meeting, while trying to watch this year's opening general session?

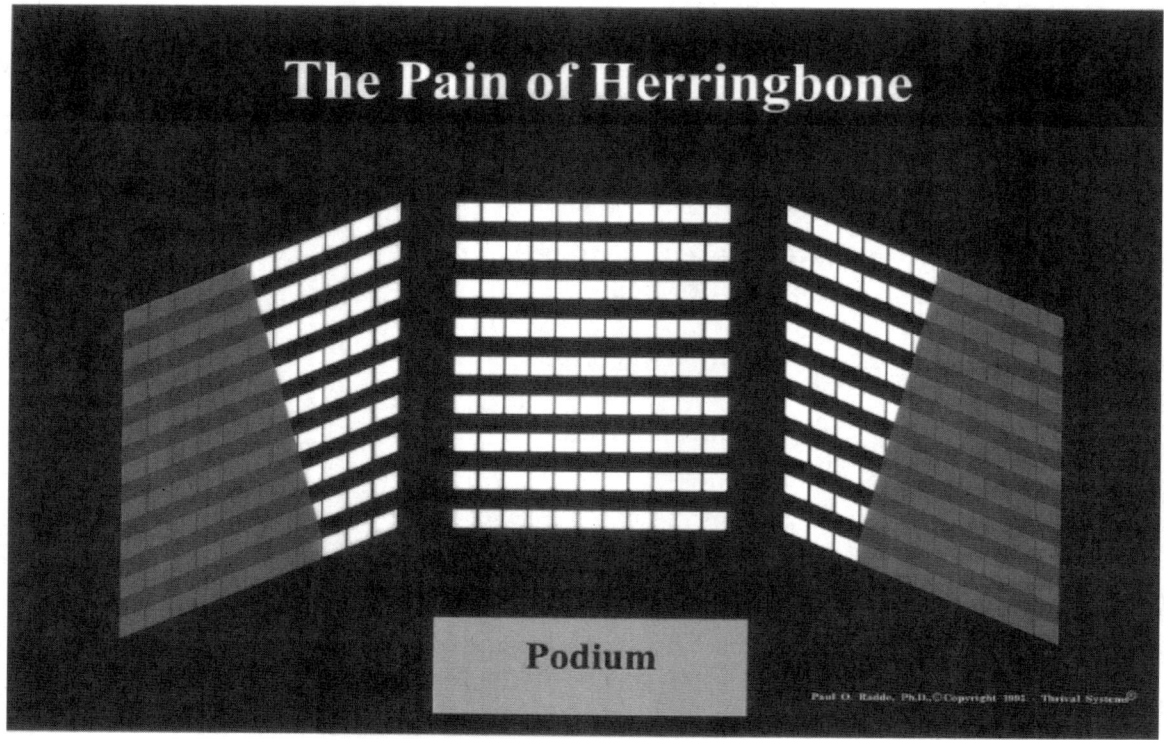

The *shaded section* in the "Pain of Herringbone" illustration, above, demonstrates those participants who acknowledge being in pain within 15-20 minutes of settling into one of those chairs in this configuration.

If you are a corporate executive, speaker, or meeting planner, you want all of your participants, especially your Board members, to be comfortable, engaged, and learning for ROI, take home value and application. If you are an Executive or Education Director, you want your members to realize direct benefit and continue attending meetings by enhancing their experience. If you are a speaker, you want to give your audience full access to your session without requiring that they tolerate the pain of a poorly set room, and you want to optimize the audience dynamic.

Assertion #2. Participants Should See the Presentation and Each Other.
Straight row seating essentially limits line of sight and networking.

One ROI: Increasing Participant Retention
You did not travel across globe, nation, state, or town to then struggle to see, hear, and engage with the presentation or your colleagues. Your benefit and your likelihood of return

to the next meeting may depend upon how the room was arranged, i.e., it was predisposed for your learning long before you entered the room, comfortable, readily accessible. So, one measure of ROI is the number of participants who, on their own initiative, return to meetings year after year.

Seat them Better than your Competition
Seating can impact ROI and return registrations in other ways. When participants have a choice about laying out their own money, getting approval to go to a particular meeting, or choosing between two professional organizations; learning and networking opportunities may be the major considerations. The date, location, price, and program content constitute major decision criteria for a relatively unseasoned attendee. However, over time, the criteria may narrow regarding whether to attend that meeting in the future.

For example, your members may have been compelled to choose between their mother association, and an association that is splitting off and is more focused strictly on their needs. If that split off association does not demonstrate high professional, state of the art practices, it may send a signal to it's members, already conflicted over loyalties, that they were better off with the mother ship association, or vice versa. Seating matters here too.

> *"We shape our buildings, and then they shape us."*
>
> — SIR WINSTON CHURCHILL

Out of appreciation for my friend, the late Frank Martineau, CAE, APR, founder of Association Trends, "participant" and "audience member" will be used throughout the text rather than the improper and dreaded word, "**attendee**: someone attended to."

SEATING MATTERS

The end point and bottom line for the success of any presentation or meeting design and delivery lies in it's impact and lasting effect on the audience. The audience member is the ultimate customer in the meeting industry. Serving the audience member is the joint responsibility of planners, suppliers, and presenters working in partnership. One of the hidden dimensions in meeting professionalism has been room design and seating. This Audience Member's Bill of Rights recognizes and addresses the impact the professional meeting facility can craft for each individual participant through preparation of the meeting environment.

Audience Member's Bill of Rights

Each person attending a meeting contracted by a meeting professional with a professional meeting facility is entitled to:

Sightlines
Have a clear, close, and unobstructed view of the presentation. This includes professional illumination to clearly light and display the face of the presenters to allow for lip reading if necessary, and for later off stage recognition.

Comfort
Be seated comfortably with regard to chair height, back support, padding and fabric, the chair facing straight toward, within 5-12 degrees of the main focal point of the presentation. Set the temperature, air circulation, and ventilation to maintain comfort and stimulate alertness.

Ease of Access
Easy access to and egress from one's seat, water, refreshments, breaks, and comfort facilities.

Safe Exit
Quick, clear, lighted, well marked and safe exit from the meeting facility.

Sound
Articulate, clearly pronounced, enunciated, and amplified words directly presented in local vernacular, translated, or interpreted to reach the vast majority of the audience, including sign language.

Meeting
Convened in a manner that provides a view of the faces of a large portion of the group in order to determine non-verbal cues, identify individuals, and decipher their response to the presentation.

Networking Opportunities
View and hear one another in order to determine common ground for meeting, conversing, supporting and challenging one another.

Special Needs and Requirements:
Fully accommodate ADA requirements and personal challenges, to provide each participant the full advantage of the meeting objectives, presentation offerings and opportunities.

State of the Art Seating Arrangements

SEATING MATTERS

Part I.

Current Seating Practices

This section presents the current reality regarding the state of meeting and event seating and room arrangements, especially factors such as straight rows that create a deterrent to meeting.

1. In **Chapter One** we look at what prompts people to attend meetings in the first place together with the main outcomes they hope to derive from their attendance.

2. **Chapter Two** spells out the spatial, dynamic, and physical challenges posed by straight row seating. This is framed within the industry mind set that maintains that straight rows are the best way to maximize the capacity of a meeting room. We beg to differ.

3. **Chapter Three** begins making the case for alternatives to the straight row room sets. Illustrations are provided throughout to complement the written text.

Chapter One

Why Do People Attend Meetings?

Seasoned association, corporate, non-profit, and national organization members have stated that they attend meetings for two reasons:

1. **To learn one new idea that they can apply in their lives or organization.**
   Most seasoned participants look for real results they can attribute directly to having attended a meeting. If they can learn just one new point to apply in their business or profession, they have met their needs.

2. **To meet one new person of interest.**
   If they make just one new acquaintance or useful contact out of their meeting contacts, that meeting constitutes a worthwhile expenditure of time, effort, and money.

Realize Meeting Goals → Retention
If seasoned participants get both content and contacts, the meeting has more than fulfilled their expectations. That is the statement of those who long ago have gained most of what the formal educational program has to offer. What keeps them coming back is the chance that they will learn something new or meet someone interesting. The more you can facilitate that happening, the better your chances of their continuing involvement.

People new to a field, meeting, or industry, may go to a meeting to accelerate their learning curve by soaking up every crumb and morsel of knowledge on the program. The more seasoned meeting attendees are the more discerning and more difficult to woo back.

Additional Reasons People Attend Meetings

Recognition: Seeing and Being Seen
Whether attendance is required, expected, or voluntary, those who attend benefit by being seen and renewing their relationships. If they are paid to go and it is part of their job, they still benefit by being seen. When attendance is not required it still may be expected, such as for those seeking office, those for whom it is politically smart to be there and be seen, those on the hierarchy, formal and informal, or wishing to be.

SEATING MATTERS

Responsibility
Many get involved through service to the organization, taking on volunteer work or by formally representing others. Still others may be presenting information, training, or entertaining participants. They have a role to play.

Challenge
Those who are newer may be required to attend in order to come up to speed, to stay current on industry information, or to acquire continuing education units as part of obtaining professional certification and maintaining currency, legitimacy and credibility. They still have a steep learning curve within the industry, so they expect to gain more than the one new take away that satisfies the seasoned participant.

Learning
The formal educational program is available to everyone who signs up and attends, or purchases the CD's or DVD's. However, the development of a personal network of professional resources, together with maintaining those relationships through intentional and deliberate contact, is a major benefit and offshoot of meeting or coming together.

Confirmation/Validation: Reinforce/Update Practices
Many want to know that they are doing their jobs about as well as they can be done. So they are seeking validation or confirmation of their performance. If they find that they indeed are off track or there is a more expeditious, efficient, or economical way of doing it, they are there to learn how.

Networking with Relationship Resources
It definitely facilitates interaction when meeting events, starting with registration, welcome, refreshments, evening events, the banquet and program seating arrangements are intentionally designed to maximize participant contact. Formalized exchanges can be based on stated interests. Formal and informal networking are based on shared background variables and characteristics, e.g. size of city or organization. Each and all help to create the common ground upon which connections are made, relationships are initiated, maintained, and sustained.

Reconnecting: Renewing/Sustaining Relationships
Renewing relationships may be the reason participants come across state, across the nation, or around the world to meet and connect, and gain value from that interaction. They are counting on seeing and renewing acquaintances. And distance relationships may not require much contact to be sustained, but at least a greeting and passing glance will do more to keep it going than not seeing each other at all.

Intentional design of time and space promotes deeper and extended contact at the meeting. And room set can be one programmatic factor, an intentional aspect of making sure that those at the meeting actually meet. Since room sets can increase or decrease participants' chances of finding each other in the audience, one should take charge of putting people together, predisposing them to meeting each other, recognizing old acquaintances. Do not rely on pure happenchance, intuition, or the low probability of finding each other on refreshment breaks, running into each other in the halls, or a last chance encounter on the bus on the way to the airport.

The meeting has to deliver, facilitate learning and networking. It is required to live up to the intention of the conveners, the marketing claims to participants, hype, and developed participant expectations and requirements.

Growing Expectations and Meeting Success to Match
The formal program may continually have to stretch and innovate to meet a continuing and evolving range of needs, skill level, and experience. It may also have to meet, match, or exceed other organizational meetings, competing organizations, and other methods of obtaining continuing education units, as well as idea dissemination and distribution. However, the more subtle points of a learning environment, such as one's comfort and ease of viewing and hearing the presentation may escape the meeting planner's attention to details.

Session Tolerance
Physical arrangements impact meeting interaction and dynamics. They also impact the health, well-being, and disposition of participants to learn and benefit from their experience. For one thing, if the given set-up is uncomfortable, individual participants are less likely to remain in the room for the entire presentation. End of session.

Older, more seasoned attendees, for example, are less likely to tolerate a spine bending, neck twisting room set, especially if they have lower lumbar or other back problems. And if they are over 40, they may have more likelihood of such ailments. After a buildup of pain, they will be out roaming the halls, looking for a firm couch, a good conversation, or a stiff drink.

One exception may be the continuing education session with tightly controlled attendance. But even then, return engagements or registrations are reduced when participants have to get beyond the physical discomfort. Those more seasoned in the organization and those who have less tolerance for pain or slow moving sessions due to years of attending, or who have lower back pain, are more likely to seek relief in the corridors of the facility.

Ramp Up Learning Curve and Future Registrations
You can facilitate comfort and learning. You can also increase the likelihood that each participant will look forward to returning to meetings in the future. That is ROS, return on service, that you provide.

SEATING MATTERS

> ### Two Recommended Meeting Services
>
> **1.) Lumbar Support:** For those more seasoned participants, and indeed for those who simply have back problems, provide or make available lumbar supports. The lumbar supports could even be monogrammed and sold through your organization, book or gift store. Meeting facilities of the future will either provide seating with enhanced lumbar support, or make it available on request.
>
> **2.) The Leg Length-Challenged** are those whose legs are too short to touch the ground from their chair. In recognition of this difficulty, devices similar to "kneelers" used in churches, could be attached to the back legs of the chair in front. Then, once the audience is seated, the short legged person simply lowers the leg rest.

Room Sets Provide the Tone
Relative degree of physical comfort during the meeting, the quality, type, frequency of contact and degree of involvement with colleagues or fellow participants are directly impacted by the way the room is set up. Room arrangements impact whether people can focus on and optimally learn from the presentation, as well as whether people can see each other early on and during the general sessions of the meetings.

Room setup can spur specific interest group formation and networking events. Participants pay attention to determine who is responding to the issues they resonate to. They will then seek out those like responding individuals to check out a potential on-going relationship.

Keep the Seasoned Participants Coming Back
The wise organization finds meaningful ways to involve their veterans and continue to harvest their experience to the benefit of everyone. The seasoned attendee can provide a wealth of information to newer members in your meetings through chance or incidental encounters, informal mentoring, personal participation in the learning experience themselves, including questions posed, and more formal involvement on panels and in presentations. Continue to attract and involve seasoned or veteran participants as **a rich** resource for everyone else in the meeting.

Archival Knowledge and Wisdom
Another major benefit from the continuing involvement of veteran participants, whether association or corporate, is the fact that they provide archival background and information about the organization and its evolution. Founding, veteran, prior board members, and seasoned members can provide insight into earlier times and the context under which rules, policy, and programs were developed. They provide perspective and rationale for earlier decisions and for the development of an industry or the organization. So maintaining participation of veteran members has its advantages for everyone. And seating can provide a major assist.

State of the Art Seating Arrangements

SEATING MATTERS

> *Those who fail to learn from history, are doomed to repeat it.*
>
> — GEORGES SANTAYANA

Matchmaking – If for No Other Reason Than This…

Matchmaking can be both professional and personal. For the busy single parent, one of the few unfettered times they may have to meet a similarly directed new love interest is at a professional or volunteer meeting. The value of meeting someone in one's own field of endeavor, profession, or area of interest could be one drawing card to get them to meetings. And repercussions when word gets out that "Jenny met her soul mate at the annual meeting" will add incentive to those who wish to do likewise. It also adds loyalty to the organization for those whose lives or impacted in this way. Innovative seating design helps people to see each other, realize an attraction, approach, meet, and acquaint.

Converge, Validate, and Challenge

A tree can fall in the forest and not be heard. And you may fill a professional position and not be understood or appreciated. Hence, the importance of organizational or association meetings where validation occurs through observing, listening to, sharing with, and rubbing elbows with one's peers and colleagues.

Professional colleagues may provide you with a level of validation that can come from no other source. They understand what you do, and often collaborate with you in your endeavors. Your spouse may provide tremendous emotional support, but unless you have similar professions or are in business together, your spouse may not understand or fully appreciate, support nor fully challenge you in ways that a professional colleague can. In an increasingly specialized and diversified world, one place where you can truly get professional support and challenge is in a meeting of your peers or colleagues.

A Chamber of Commerce executive has responsibilities within her home community that do not allow her to discuss her role in certain issues or seek counsel nearby. The position

SEATING MATTERS

holds too much potential for seeming conflict of interest, breach of confidentiality by discussing sensitive issues, indiscretion by uncovering community dynamics, or charges of favoritism by seeming to favor one side of an issue.

No one else occupies that precise position or can appreciate that perspective easily in one's home community. Yet, when that executive attends a residential summer leadership institute, meets a variety of executives facing similar and even identical problems, she encounters a resource pool that is extraordinary in her line of work. Their relationship starts with a depth of understanding of the issues each faces, together with an appreciation of these challenges.

Meeting face to face, or in sessions geared at "best practices" and problem solving, can open up additional insights through conversations that go deep into the night. The higher the quality provided by the learning environment and the opportunities to network, the more opportunities to nudge each other through fears and down the road of professional skill to maturity.

Challenge and Support

In the short run, people seek support in relationship. However, challenge may be even more important than support. Who else can understand what you do sufficiently to assess how well you are doing it, hence what you have to do to improve? Well-meaning coaches associates, motivational speakers, even your spouse, might encourage you to "do your best," but they do not have the experience or knowledge to be more precise, specific and detailed in their encouragement. Specific knowledgeable guidance is lacking. That is where your professional colleagues can provide essential input with targeted challenges.

The growth of an entire field of endeavor, or a profession; indeed the professional development leading to the enhancement of our civilization, can depend upon the range of consideration to foster an optimal environment by meeting planners and meeting facilities when they convene a group.

A meeting participant should be able to legitimately expect that his interest in learning, colleagueship, and networking will be promoted throughout the formal programming in many ways. "If you bring us together, then facilitate our networking."

Coming Up...

The next chapter explores the current state of seating practice and points out the difficulties of these practices: **Straight Row Seating Undermines a Meeting.** What follows then is an exploration of <u>five seating principles</u> that form the foundation for Audience Centered Seating™, together with <u>designs</u> and a <u>rationale</u> for the application of each principle.

Interspersed throughout the elaboration of each principle will be several of the <u>15 factors</u> that play into the "fine tuning" of the meeting room and that create the most productive meeting environment.

State of the Art Seating Arrangements

Chapter Two

Straight Row Seating Undermines a Meeting

> *How you set your audience's bottoms can affect your bottom line!*

If it's your job to get key attendees to the meeting, engage, entertain, inform or educate them during the meeting, keep them in the meeting room, and get them to return for the next meeting; you need to optimize that meeting environment. Seating is key to that endeavor.

This chapter lays out the basic case for improving upon, if not eliminating, straight row seating wherever you find it. Here we will acknowledge those few instances in which straight row seating is appropriate. And we will challenge the core mindset behind straight row seating – that it is the only way to maximize the body count in a meeting room. This chapter deals with the larger general session room sets. Chapter 10 deals with the use of straight rows in the smaller meeting, such as a board of director meeting at a rectangular table. You will arrive at the end of this chapter ready to redesign any future room set that employs straight rows as your contribution to improving the learning environment.

SEATING MATTERS

Rather than accept anything on faith, be prepared to test out what you read here. It's easy. Follow recommended exercises and your own experience to establish your basis in experience, past and future. Gain your own authority for judging the values and benefits of straight row seating. Once you do, your audience should never again have to suffer because of that seating arrangement.

But only when you have experienced or become aware of the pain which straight row room sets inflict on your audience will you take the necessary steps to ensure that innovative room sets provide a tangible service to the event. Basing those room sets on the five principles you will learn in Chapters 5 through 9, will provide your audience with comfort, safety, access; clear, direct sightlines to the presentation; and the ability to see each other.

First, The Few Appropriate Uses of Straight Row Seating

The only instance in which straight row seating might serve a useful purpose is in the larger gathering in which lights are down and the only place to focus is on projection screens set dead ahead. Not unlike a movie theatre, there is no pretense of promoting a psychodynamic. However, the lights do not stay off completely. There usually is a lighted opening to the session during which the audience could see each other.

Large General Sessions with Video Screens
A straight row set serves one very large general session or keynote session quite well. Typically, these sessions are high production presentations, carried on in a partially darkened auditorium with two large video screens mounted mid-wall or higher, book ending the stage and the live presentation. Here the straight rows hinder networking, as they do in most cases. However, when the accommodation is simply to view this high production number on screen or a live presenter, the straight rows are set directly toward the screen or the stage serves that purpose.

This large session straight row seating technology so far has been focused more on accommodating numbers rather than on deepening the face-to-face, human aspect of the meeting. In most cases, the rows in the large sessions are too long for easy access anyway as shown in facility ads with rows of as many as 15-25 chairs straight across. The setup is all about massive numbers. However, even then, those straight rows facing the straight ahead screens draw attention away from the live human action on stage.

The following diagram is a quick remedy to that big block set, putting the presenter in view of all. Improve that straight row set with a curved row approach in which a two-screen placement would be lined up facing each opposite seating section. The right side of the audience watches the left screen; the left side watches the right screen.

State of the Art Seating Arrangements

SEATING MATTERS

The illustrated design below directs more attention toward the live presenter, with the screens placed above and off to each side, so you would look at the <u>person and the screen</u> you are facing more directly.

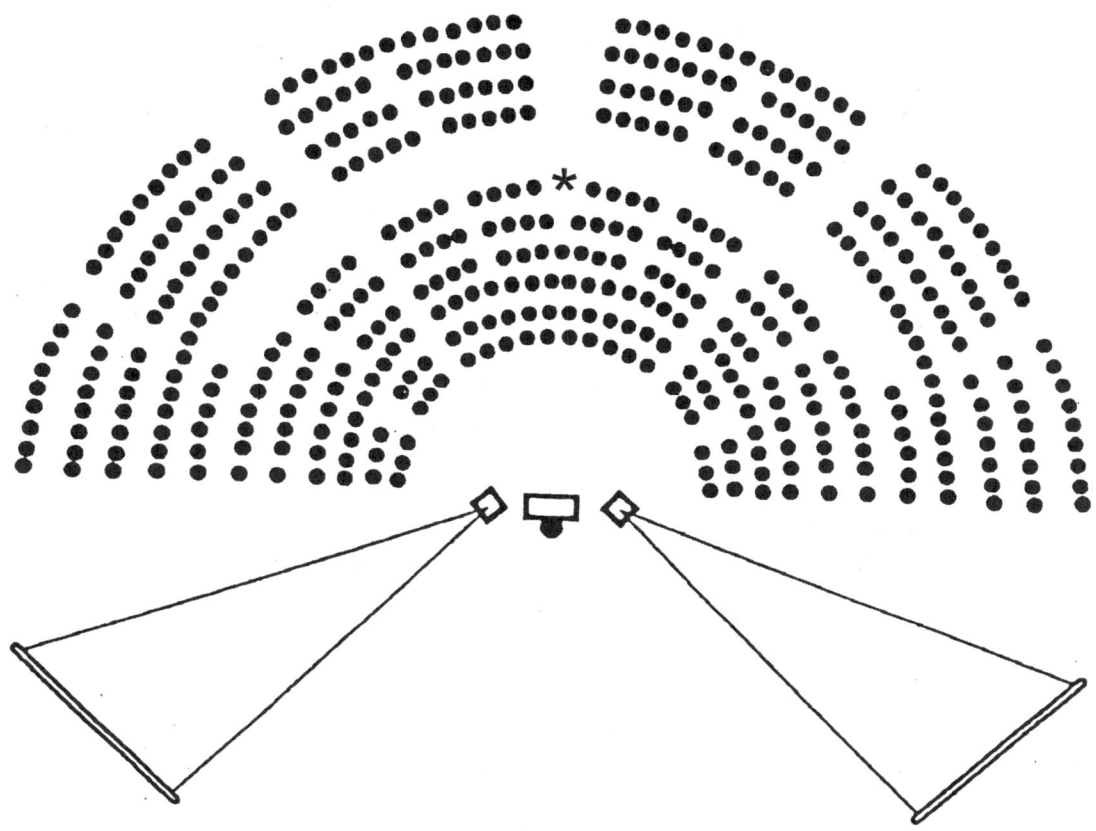

Straight rows are appropriate and serve a useful purpose in the situations enumerated below. These each involve separating people from direct face to face contact, or eye-contact in an area where they come together. Yet, they are not intended to meet or experience each other in those environments. These include:

Jury Seating
In each of these situations, the jury member is required to take in the evidence and the trial interactions and disclosures independently of other jury members. While final deliberation will be as a working group, the information intake is a single solitary responsibility. Straight rows provide the separation for each individuals' "take" on the evidence presented.

News Conference
While there may be competition to ask a question and elicit information, each newsperson is present to take in the information individually, provide his own perspective and emphasis, then write it up according to his own take on it.

State of the Art Seating Arrangements

SEATING MATTERS

Puritan Meeting
The old time Puritan meeting often took place for most of a Sunday with hellfire and brimstone preaching. The main source of inspiration, focus and control was the preacher. No input was allowed from the congregation. Salvation of one's soul was the direct goal. And a feather was suspended from a stick to awaken anyone who dozed off.

Police Lineup
The line-up provides a direct line of sight viewing of suspects by witnesses or victims of a crime. The straight row separates those within the line-up, preventing signaling or communicating with each other.

VD Clinic Waiting Room
Whether you are coming in to a public health facility for testing or awaiting your results, this is not typically a place one goes to be seen, notes Carol Weisman, once a psychiatric social worker, now a professional speaker. One would rather be out of sight. The straight rows ensure minimal contact with other patients similar to the waiting room of a bus or train station.

Egg Cartons
An egg carton is designed to contain, cushion, and separate the shells of eggs, for which the straight row configuration works perfectly.

Debunking The Mind Set and Myth of How to Max a Room

In the meeting industry, there is a widely held belief that the way to maximize the room capacity, the number of chairs you can get into a given meeting space, requires using straight row seating. This generally held belief even includes funeral directors, who think that pews or straight rows are the way to maximize their viewing rooms and memorial services. For most traditionalists this comes from their experience that "it has always been this way."

A mindset is a single assumption or a bundling of assumptions that provide the basic and underlying beliefs upon which a group operates. Similar to a belief that the world was flat, before explorers proved differently, the mindset has to be overturned before most in the group will begin to operate differently. This means experiencing the benefits of the innovative set as well as the dysfunctional outcomes the established straight row set.

SEATING MATTERS

In the meeting industry, there is a widely held belief that the only way to maximize room capacity is through straight row seating.

This is Simply Wrong!

How can this myth persist among meeting professionals?
Typically, those who design and set the room are the last ones to sit down. They are the ones you observe with the clipboard or meeting manifest checking off items, hosting or managing the event, and roaming the halls to make sure the meeting logistics come off without a hitch. Neither meeting planner, nor hotel sales and marketing, nor room set-up personnel actually get the tush-on experience of the room set. Speakers and presenters certainly do not.

None of them typically takes a seat with the audience during a meeting for any amount of time. Even when she does sit down, the meeting professional is so focused on other aspects of the meeting, she is usually so distracted by other concerns, that her seating experience ends up low on her concerns, if at all. If her meeting "looks like" the other meetings, she feels satisfied and safe.

State of the Art Seating Arrangements

SEATING MATTERS

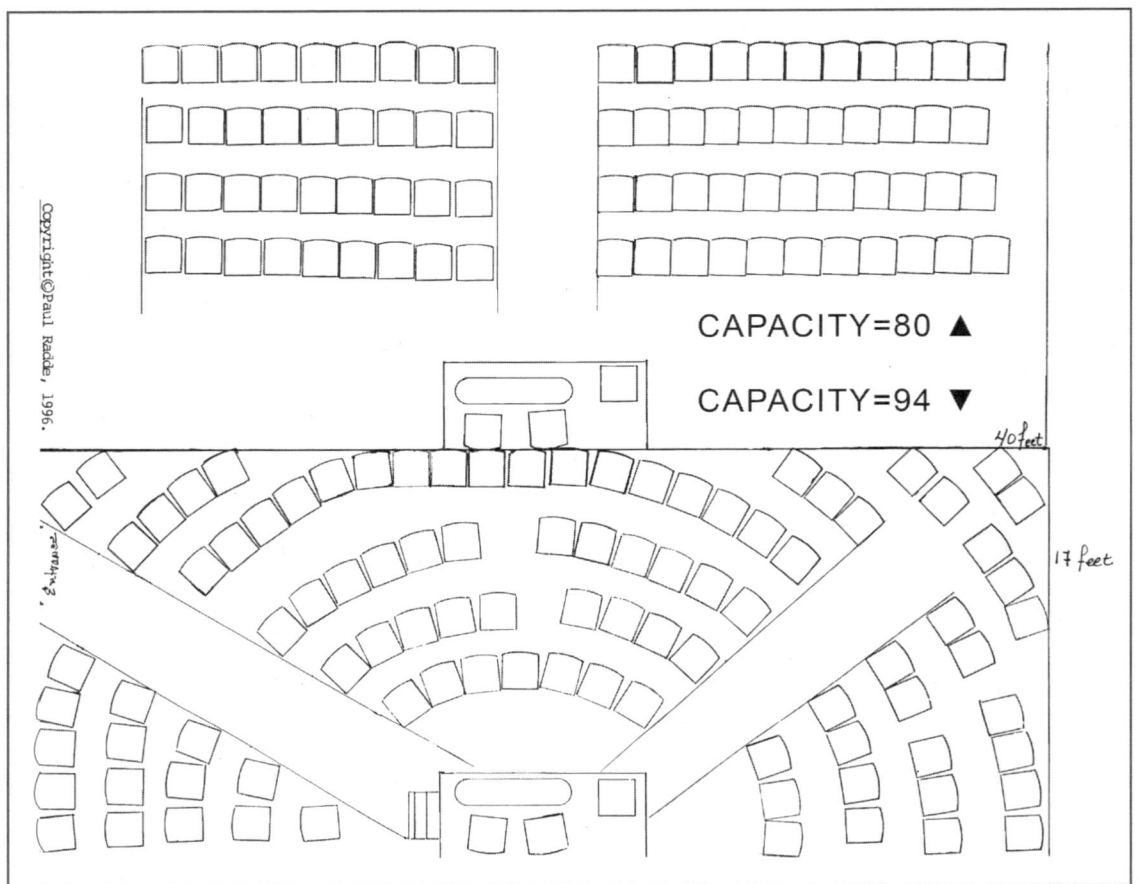

Curved Seating Meets or Exceeds Straight Row Capacities

There is a generally held and accepted misconception about straight rows "maxing" the room that is followed without question. In the illustration immediately above of a 40 x 17 foot meeting space, the straight row setup requires 8.5 square feet per participant, while the curved row setup requires 7.23 square feet per participant. The straight row set above seats 80, while the curved row set seats 94…and has superior traffic flow. That is a 14 person, 17.5% gain in capacity in the same space.

In fact, in every meeting room that I have set utilizing the five principles that follow, I have, without exception, been able to at least equal if not exceed the room capacity of straight row seating. [Occasionally the fire code restricts allowing more chairs in the room so you cannot increase capacity without the agreement of the fire marshal.]

SEATING **MATTERS**

The Opryland ballroom in Nashville was set up traditional theatre style straight rows, set for 1800 members of the National Speakers Association opening general session. The convention chair explained that they "could not" accommodate our numbers with my room set. That evening I went into the room with the Opryland setup crew and reset for curved rows, expanding aisles, essentially fine tuning the room. Not only did we reset for the 1800 attending the general session next day, we also had floor space left for at least 300 more!

In every situation I have been able to exceed the straight row capacity of that room space by 6% to 17%. That increase in capacity gains commensurate and vast improvements in safety, access, comfort, line of sight, hearing, and even general audience closeness to the presentation.

Disadvantages of Straight Row Seating

Meeting Facility: An Oxymoron?
After more than 25 years working on seating, the way most facilities set rooms throws into question whether meetings actually occur there, or are truly facilitated in their space. *Meeting facility could be considered an oxymoron in many quarters.*

> *Does a Meeting Take Place if Participants Cannot See Each Other?*

Does a meeting occur if people cannot see each other?
Straight row seating restricts interpersonal contact at a meeting. **Anytime you have three people in a straight line, visual contact is limited or strained.** Not only are you limited in the number of participants you can see, you cannot see the faces of many of the audience members. You then miss a great deal of the non-verbal communication that is available, yet not accessible. A curved row set makes non-verbal cues and gestures accessible. And, in this case, form needs to be subservient to function.

State of the Art Seating Arrangements

SEATING MATTERS

Losing Non-Verbal Cues
For example, if the head of the person seated in front of you drops forward during a presentation, you have no idea what s/he is doing. She may be dozing off, taking notes, or checking a text message on a cell phone. If she is taking notes, you might benefit from her response to what is being said by using her non-verbal as a cue to pay attention. But, not seeing what the "head drop" means, you may miss the point being made by the speaker.

Three oncologists attend an international medical conference. The Indonesian oncologist is making a presentation of her most recent research on bone marrow transplants. The other two are seated in the same straight row, with only one person seated between them. At one point, the seated oncologist from UC Berkley visibly jerks his head up at a comment made by the presenter. The other oncologist, just two chairs away misses that movement, blocked by the one person in between them.

Had the other oncologist, from Switzerland, only seen that head movement, she would have gotten his attention and spoken during the next break. Then, gathering momentum, the two of them would have contacted the presenter to discuss a key point in her presentation. Next stop would be the meeting planner. They would, all three, request that 30 minutes of the cocktail party planned for that evening be set aside for a quick panel discussion among the 3 of them to clarify the disputed point. That evening they convene the entire group, discuss the point, and get a consensus on a new direction in bone marrow transplantation. Rather than delay months while an article is written for their journal, everyone at the meeting flies back home with the most current information regarding the procedure and lives are saved.

While every missed communication in a meeting that is attributable to straight row seating might not have such life and death implications, it is not ours to judge the gravity of a potentially missed communication. Rather it is our responsibility to ensure that verbal and non-verbal messages are facilitated, not impeded, by the room setup.

A Video Conference Might Have Been Better
If you come across town, state, region, country or ocean in order to attend a meeting with friends, colleagues, peers, communities of interest, are you really gaining the benefit of meeting with them if you cannot see them? Perhaps in a large audience you would not be concerned, but in smaller and board meetings where direct interaction is essential, you are greatly restricted by being placed in a straight row, such as around a rectangular table, at a U-shape, or a hollow square set-up. If you knew in advance you would be so restricted by straight row seating, you could have seen and observed more people in this very meeting by staying home and watching on a video conference.

This chapter is devoted to make you aware of how dysfunctional straight row seating is for the participant. It is hoped that once your grasp just how bad straight row seating is, that you will not inflict straight rows on anyone ever again.

SEATING MATTERS

While the straight row mindset that "it maximizes the room capacity" is dead wrong, it continues to be the glib throw-away line or easy dismissal comment when someone questions the straight row set. Hence, the discomfort and dysfunctional design of straight row seating remains unchallenged, fostering ignorance. This institutionalized practice continues largely from people accepting the mindset without challenging the assumption themselves. Or, they do not know how to take on the established practices.

Those who do not know better need new information and perspectives. Beginning in Chapter 5, you will get both principles for troubleshooting and improving any meeting room. You also can collect insights into influence and persuasion skills beginning with the Introduction, to gain acceptance for the sets you will propose or promote.

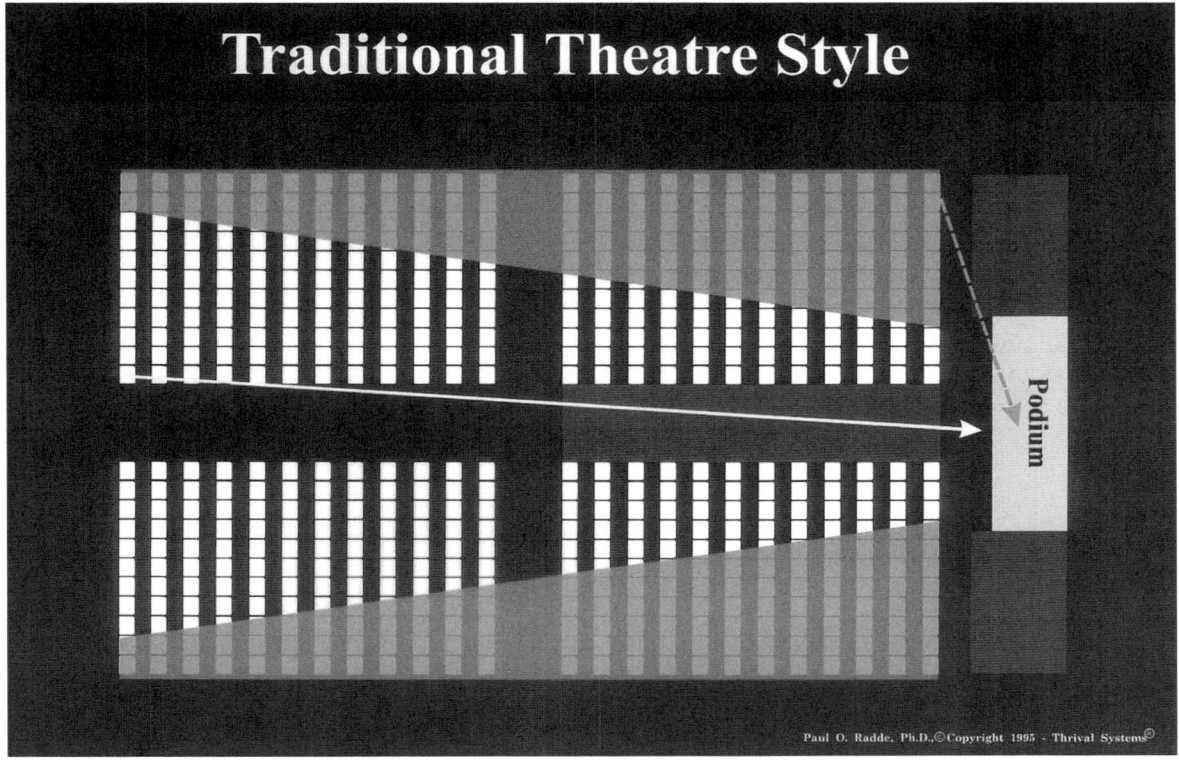

Look at this diagram. Pay special attention to the shaded areas (above) angling off from the podium. This graphically depicts those who report pain just from watching the presentation in that straight row set. Those in back are farther from the presentation than they would be in a set to the long side. When you add pain to the distance from the podium, it diminishes the value of the set to begin with.

Space Wasted and Capacity Lost

Bruce Harris, former CEO of Conferon, notes that "straight rows have more dead space in a room." The space that is wasted or dead, and the capacity that is lost with the traditional straight row theatre style to the narrow side of the room, includes those areas marked by the wavy lines below.

SEATING MATTERS

1. **The Center Aisle.** This is the only space in straight row sets from which anyone placed in a chair would be facing the presentation directly. The only space in which one would be facing the presentation dead on is not set with chairs. It's an aisle! What could be the best seats in house are not there. This is the space allotted for getting in and out of the room. That center aisle also drains energy from the presentation according to Doyle and Strauss in <u>Making Meetings Work</u>.

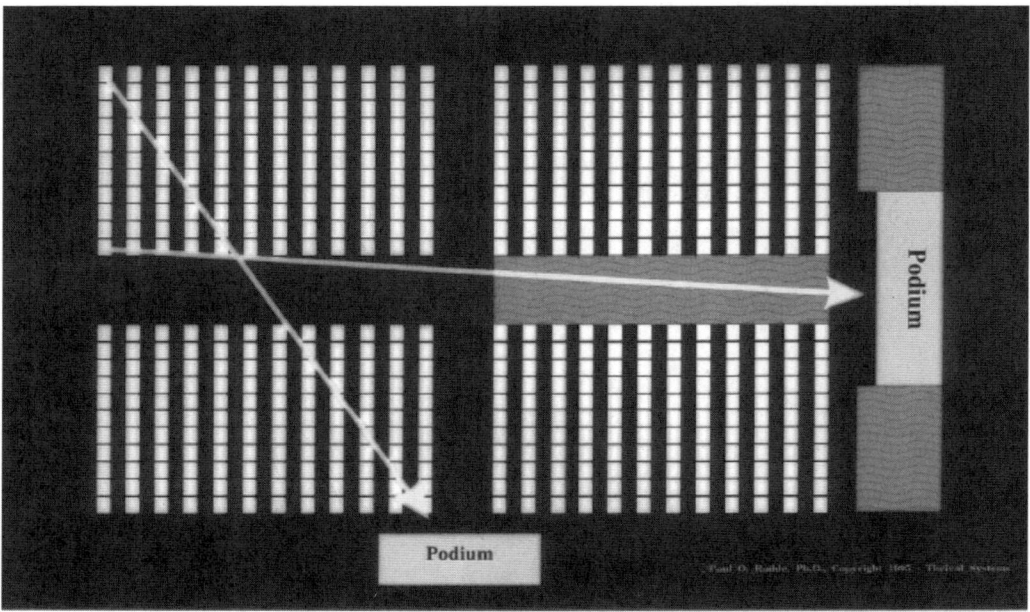

2. **The Orchestra Area** between the front row and front of the stage (in black above where the arrow ends) is usually larger than needed and underutilized for seating. Distance from the stage, even for large groups need only be 6-9 feet, not the 12-20 feet sometimes allotted. Only if there is some opening ceremony requiring a presentation of the colors by a marching unit might such an increase in distance to the stage be required. Even then you can bring the color guard up on stage. The presentation of the colors is better done on stage for visibility anyway, unless the ceiling is too low for the flag staffs. Use the close in seating for your board of directors, new members, veteran members.

3. **Off Stage** front of the house, the areas on either side of the stage or podium when not set, also eliminate some of the best, most intimate seating in the house. Until set, it is totally lost space. See the comparative straight row vs. curved row set above for the better space utilization of curved sets. Would you rather be seated in the 24th row back or here around the podium (wavy lines)?

State of the Art Seating Arrangements

SEATING MATTERS

Make It a Tush-On Experience

In my workshop on seating arrangements, I make sure that speakers, meeting facility, and meeting professionals do get this experience of straight row seating right up front. That actual or empirical experience becomes the "basis in experience" upon which they develop their own "authority" on seating.

You Can Typically See Only 2 Persons In Your Row

Typically you can see only the person on either side of you without leaning forward or back, looking behind the person next to you. In addition, most people's faces are asymmetrical. That means that unless you look at this person "head-on," directly in the face, you might not necessarily recognize him out in the hall during a refreshment break. And that person next to you, unless very short or small, will be blocking your view of the next person over. So, when you are seated on the outside of a 10 chair straight row, as in the illustration below, you can only see the person next to you, and cannot see the remaining 8 people in your row. Sitting in an aisle seat of a longer straight row simply means there are more people whom you cannot see in your own row.

The illustration also graphically depicts the degree one's neck must turn in order to see a presenter on stage (45 degrees) or in front of the stage (80 degrees).

The ad from a leading five star property showed one photo recently of traditional straight row general session seating, in which those on the outside of the front row are twisting and turning their bodies toward the presentation by crossing their legs, putting their arms behind the chair next to them, and other adaptive gyrations. The ad ran for months, showing that the ad firm and the property itself had no idea that they were showing how uncomfortable the set made the participants.

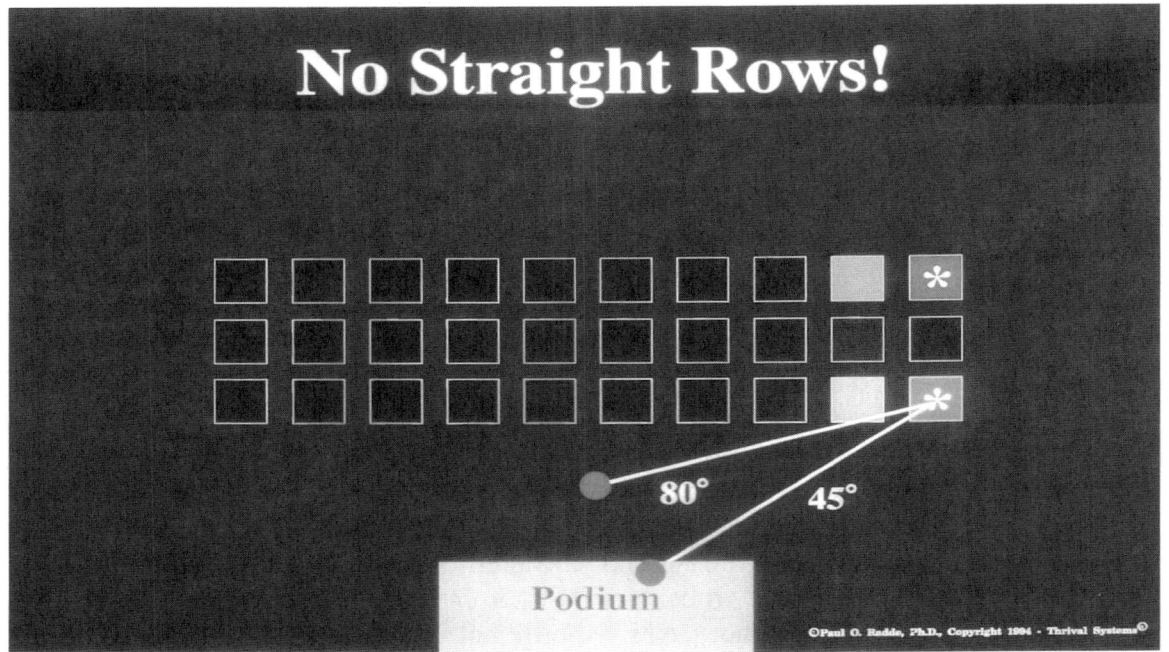

State of the Art Seating Arrangements

SEATING MATTERS

You may try to adjust your posture by shifting your weight from both *glutei maximum* to the *gluteus maximus* facing the presentation. But in a short time, you will find the pressure uncomfortable and want to shift back. Now you have one leg that has gone to sleep, and your focus is on getting blood flow back into your leg, not **on** the presentation.

Do Your Own Research
There is nothing here that I expect you to accept without checking it out for yourself. Explore straight row seating. You do not have to be at a meeting. In fact, within the next 24 hours, you will probably have the opportunity to sit down in a straight row where people are lined up directly next to you. This could be at a dinner table, church pew, meeting, or even on a couch – whatever amounts to a straight row.
- Pay attention to the following things:
- Look to your right and left without leaning forward or back.
  How many people in your straight row can you see?

Why Do Audiences Put Up With The Way It's Set Now?

Cultural Practice: Sit the Way The Room Is Set Without Complaint
There seem to be a number of cultural practices in the United States around seating. One norm consists in not moving one's seating no matter how uncomfortable or non-functional. You sit <u>where and how</u> you are placed. Most audience members will at best adjust their position a little, but certainly not to a point of complete comfort.

What keeps the audience member frozen in place, accepting whatever they are given?
During a presentation by the Capitol Steps, a D.C. based satiric review that makes fun of contemporary political figures and events. The venue was a restaurant in Annapolis, MD., set up for dinner theater. When the presentation started, I noticed a very prim woman in her 70's whose back was turned to the stage. I pointed out that she might enjoy the performance more if she turned around. I offered to move her chair for her. She declined and sat with her back to the presentation for the first half with only her head turned toward the stage and a tightly posed smile on her lips. At intermission, I once again offered to move her chair for her. At this point her response was, "Well I believe I will. Thank you." It took a lot of discomfort, and time, for her to reconsider and finally allow herself to simply have her chair turned toward the show.
When someone is seated at a round table with her back to the after dinner speaker, she may require permission in order to place herself and her chair in a comfortable position.

Giving Them Your Back is Rude?
I have had meeting planners as participants who adamantly refused to face their chairs toward the presentation when it meant showing their backs to those at their table. Even those seated at rounds thought it "rude" to turn their chairs in such a way as to offer their backs to others. It would have been entirely different if the chairs had already been set facing the presentation to start with.

State of the Art Seating Arrangements

SEATING MATTERS

The master of ceremonies has to make an explicit, firm request or demand that everyone turn around. It can be phrased as follows:

> **MC:** *"We will be starting our after dinner program in a moment. Once you finish your dessert, those of you with your backs to the stage, please take a moment to turn your chair completely around to face the presentation." And since this is a request that requires action, <u>it bears repeating</u>. Not everyone was paying attention. Not everyone had finished his dessert yet. So, there is a second request when the MC comes on to start the program. "I notice that some of you have not had time to turn your chairs around to face the program. Please take the time now to turn your chair to face the platform. We will wait." Wait, and then thank them.*

PCMA Space Verification Program

There is often a discrepancy between what is designed by an architect for meeting space, and the actual finished space. Noting this, the Professional Convention Management Association at one point, undertook a program to rectify this discrepancy so that facilities could offer, and those booking meeting space could rely upon, the accuracy of the property's room diagrams. The space was then verified, both square footage, room shape and size, and also ceiling heights. The space was then rendered with specific room designs to determine capacity while complying with fire and safety regulations.

Based upon one such sample from the space verification program from the "maple leaf room" of a fictitious XYZ Hotel, a 1,647 square foot space was set in a U-Shape schoolroom design. Forty-four chairs were included in the set together with 14 tables. However, using the audience centered seating perspective, on one side of the U-Shape alone, 19 participants are seated in a straight row. That means that the person seated at the end of that row could see the person next to her, and could not see the remaining 17 participants in that row without some extraordinary movement. Thirty-eight percent of the participants were not visible to her, 17 of 44. What an example! And this is how straight rows get entrenched in planner and facilities thinking as " the way" to set a room.

Straight Rows Stifle Audience Dynamics

When participants cannot see each other, they not only lose non-verbal reinforcement of learning, networking opportunities, but also audience bonding. More in Chapter 6.

Tom Antion, humorist and internet guru, observed that audiences in straight rows tended to laugh less since they could not see each other as easily and "share a laugh." Eye contact helps laughter to spread in a group, even becoming infectious.

"Oh, we do the most advanced sets," said the hotel brand VP of Marketing with a great deal of pride5

"We use the chevron design."

State of the Art Seating Arrangements

SEATING MATTERS

Chevron is "Even Worse" Than Traditional Straight Row Sets

I have been told by vice presidents of marketing from several hotel chains, meeting professional, meeting facility salespersons, conventions operations, and association officers, in very proud tones, that they have incorporated "modern" seating designs into their meetings. When I ask for details, they mention that they use the chevron set.

The simple truth of this highly touted approach is that it <u>actually is worse than regular straight row seating</u> in terms of being able to see the presentation as well as the ability to see those in the center section.

Chevron/Herringbone Design: One Permutation of Straight Row Seating
Chevron general seating usually consists of a standard straight row theater style center sections with two straight row sections divided by an aisle on either side of the center section in the illustration immediately below. The distinguishing feature from traditional theatre style set is that each outside seating section is slanted toward and more or less facing the presentation at an angle. Chevron and "herringbone" are identical for the purposes of this book.

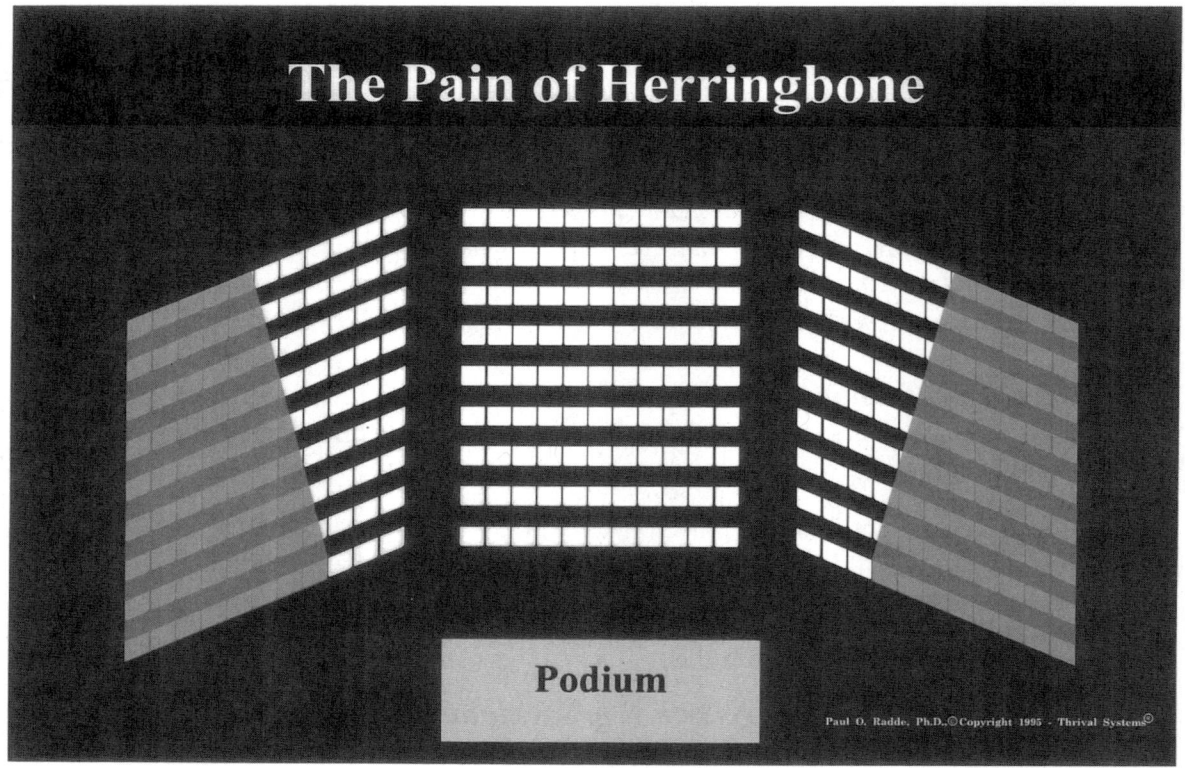

State of the Art Seating Arrangements

SEATING MATTERS

Ganged chevron or herringbone sections have all the problems attributed to regular straight row ganged seating, and then some. The additional problems posed by chevron are the following:

Even though the entire seating section is angled toward the presentation, each chair is not. With the exception of those lucky few whose chairs are facing the presentation directly, everyone else is still required to accommodate the "placed" direction of the seating by turning her neck to see the presentation.

A Source of Brand Pride
"Our director of convention operations has been here for 30 years. We are sure he knows everything there is to know about seating," proudly stated the marketing vice president of a four star hotel brand. The reason that entire hotel brands think they are so modern and up to date in seating is that they have failed to simply sit down in one of these chevron sections when chairs are filled. Those choosing the room sets don't have a bottoms-on, real life experience of the chair in that design, or they would be very cautious about suggesting it, offering it, recommending it, or considering it advantageous.

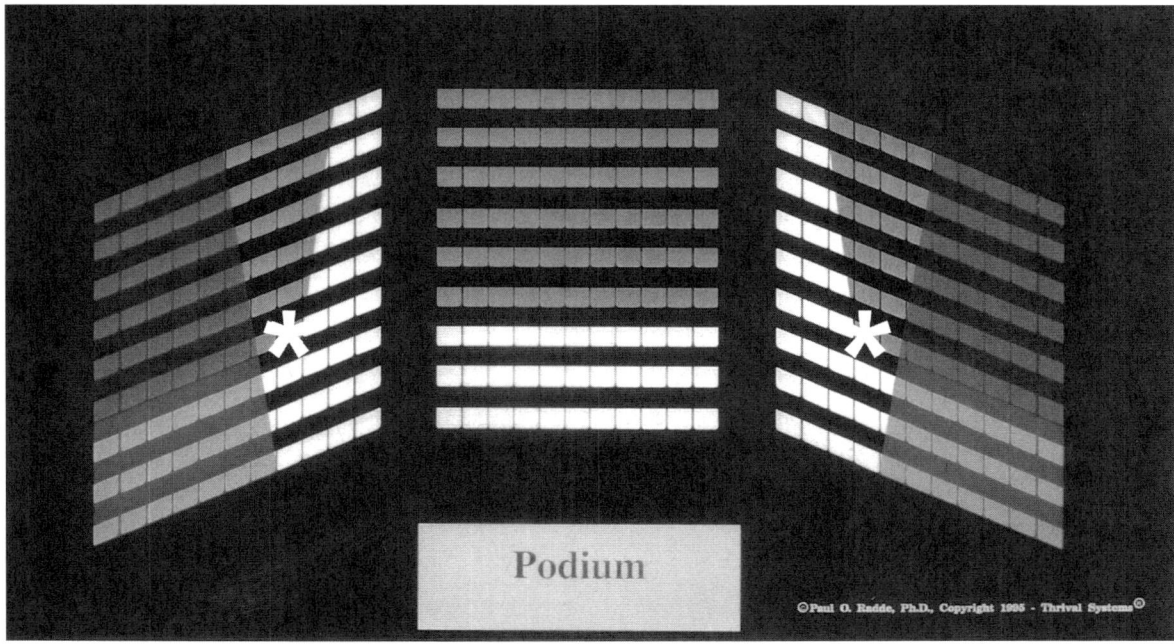

While the first diagram above points out the areas in which those seated feel pain inflicted by the room set, the diagram immediately above adds a second shading to illustrate those who cannot see the presentation. <u>Some feel pain and also cannot see.</u> That is certainly a dysfunctional set for them, not the modern little gem hotel brand administrators brag about.

Participation Suffers Due to an Inability to See the Presentation
Chevron works best for those in the front row. They can look relatively straight ahead or at a slight angle unhindered. Those in the second and third rows have to look either right

or left in order to see around the front and second row, respectively. And, unless the stage or presentation is sufficiently elevated, the fourth row back is challenged to see anything of the presentation as noted in asterisks inserted in the diagram above.

Networking Suffers Due to an Inability to See The Middle Section
Those who lose the most from the chevron set are those seated behind the third row from the front, and those inside the third seat from the inside aisle [see inserted asterisks above]. Not only can they not see the presentation easily, they have greater difficulty seeing anyone in the middle section.

The same fan of heads that blocks their view of the presentation to the front of the room can also block them from looking down the line in their row to see into the adjoining or central section. They can see even fewer participants, than if they were seated in traditional straight row theatre style seating in the outside sections.

So, when you have a less than favorable room set-up, you can frequently make it better by selectively applying one or more of the 5 principles you will learn in the following chapters, together with the 17 factors you will meet in the hints throughout for "fine tuning" the room. Simply angling chairs toward the presentation even in a chevron set, solves many of these straight row chevron problems. Angling the chair faces it more directly at the presentation. See the next illustration.

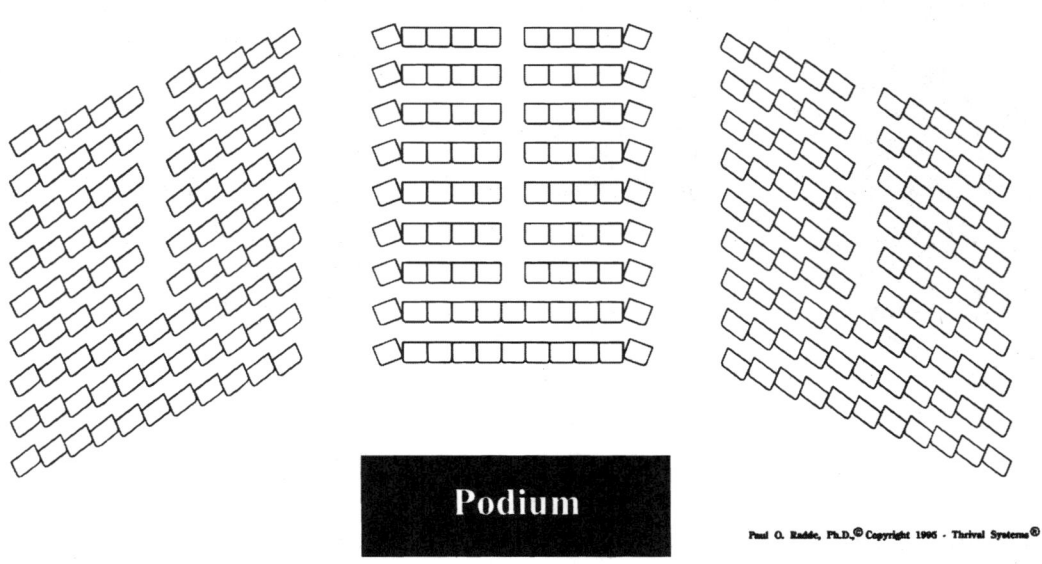

Additional Problems with Straight Row Seating

Presenter Challenges from Straight Row Seating
The presenter bears a greater burden for meeting success. Straight row seating sets up a 1:1 relationship between the presenter and each individual audience member. The presenter/speaker bears a greater responsibility for the meeting success. The presenter becomes the single source. If the presenter does not connect with the participants and hold their attention, there is little available to bail the presenter out. S/he is on her/his own, more vulnerable to bombing without recourse or resource.

A Challenge for the Speaker to Attend to Everyone
Whatever degree of neck turning is required of the audience, the speaker is required to turn the same number of degrees as the seated participant. One advantage is that the speaker is more mobile on foot than the seated audience member.

However, in order to see those on the extreme outside of the front rows, the speaker has to pivot a minimum of 160 degrees to cover the spectrum of seated audience members from the front of the room. Even more pivoting is required if the presenter walks down the aisle and into the seating section

At that point the presenter needs be aware of any personal preference in attention to one part of the audience over another. If you are the speaker, master of ceremonies, or presenter, one way to take in most of the audience at once is to continue to stand in front of the audience, while remaining quite relaxed, mindful, and present. If you are kinesthetic, you will be able to read the audience just by feel. You can sense what is going on with them. At the same time, relaxing your focus to soften it and widen it, you can take in a wider peripheral area – often upwards of 160-180 degrees. Now, that will not be direct eyeball-to-eyeball contact, but rather a general "corner of the eye" awareness. If you then detect movement, hands being raised, or other cues, you can pay closer attention. Begin with the mindful, relaxed, widened peripheral vision.

Know your natural tendencies to favor one side or section of the room to another, so that you can intentionally correct this tendency and attend to everyone more evenly. Speakers may have a bias for turning to the right or left, or may focus right on the front rows and then to the back of the room. So, those on the fringe of a seating section could feel marginalized or ignored.

Speaker Strain: The Need to Sweep the Crowd
The speaker can adapt to this strenuous straight row challenge by adopting a delivery style of sweeping the front of the stage from side to side and making sure to look at and address everyone within the sweep of that movement. Or, the speaker can swivel from right to left

to right in a circular motion to take in everyone in the audience. This can be an added burden, and the speaker finds herself concentrating focus on the more densely populated central seating sections. One additional approach is to engage individuals in the front area in conversation and in protracted or extended gazes so that the audience feels the connection to these representatives.

Summary

You have just had a review of how straight row seating undermines a meeting. Having stated the major problems in seating, we now move forward to explore remedies and improvements to the traditional straight row room set.

Prepare Yourself for a Glacial Pace of Change

Change does not come easily, especially in the meeting industry, whose predominant temperaments are based on tradition, what is secure, predictable. You, meanwhile, will do considerably better in effecting change if you know the criteria upon which future decisions can be based, and justified. Those begin in the next chapter.

Chapter 3

Criteria to Optimize Your Meeting

Focus on the Ultimate Customer!
One assumption underlying and pervasive throughout this book is that the meeting industry, whether buyer or supplier, has one major ultimate customer – the audience member. Call that person the participant, registrant, audience member, it is that person that the meeting facility, presenter, and meeting planner need to work for in partnership, to serve and please.

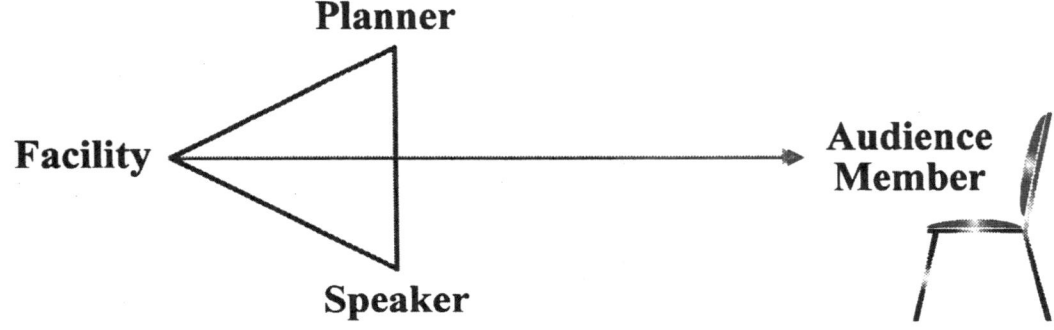

Criteria I: Audience Safety
Safety is the first and foremost criteria in selecting a seating arrangement that optimizes the learning experience.

Which Participants are Most in Peril?
The person most in peril in any seating arrangement is the one with the greatest number of chairs [read, potential obstacles] to get past, the greatest distance from the nearest exit. That person is frequently seated toward the front and middle of the front seating section. Degree of risk is determined largely by the room set-up.

Strictly speaking, the person most in peril might be he or she who is disabled and for whom there is no clear path to navigate without assistance to get out of the facility.

Choose your site with safety in mind.
The physically challenged want to have access to hotel rooms on all floors just like everyone else, so hotels have outfitted rooms on a variety of floors with special fixtures to meet ADA code. However, during one Vietnam Veterans of America Convention there was a fire alarm requiring quick evacuation. Less challenged Vets rose to the occasion to help their brothers from all floors, especially the top ones. In their hurry coming down the steps, however, more than one disabled evacuee was dropped.

SEATING MATTERS

Another association for the physically challenged met in a downtown Washington, D.C. hotel with its meeting facilities one floor below street level. There were more participants using special motorized apparatus to get around than there were participants who could possibly assist them in the event of a quick exit.

Safety appropriately begins with the meeting facility
At one point, a heavily used Washington, D.C., meeting facility exhibit area, located below street level, spans nearly 300 feet across. There is no safety problem when exits are clearly lighted and delineated. However, once the velvet backdrops for exhibiter's booths go up, one is hard pressed to find any indication of an exit sign or the exits.

While previewing the general session site for a national convention at another nearby DC hotel, someone posed the question, "We're sitting here during the keynote presentation and there is a fire alarm. How do we get out of here?" We were then in a meeting room below street level. "Interesting question. Well, let's see," said the sales manager.

He immediately checked a door to the left of the front stage. Our committee walked through the exit doors to a corridor aisle bordered by tables tipped up against the wall. Table legs protruded out into the aisle. Not the exit you would want for our 1600 participants, especially if in a panic in a smoke filled room. Brushing against those table legs would leave bleeding shins. A toppled table would create a major traffic jam. ...And beyond the tables were <u>some 180 steps</u> everyone would have to navigate in order to get to fresh air and the street.

There was a special elevator on the floor of that ballroom to raise those in wheel chairs up to a ramp they could then use to roll out to the elevators in the lobby if that way were clear and the elevators were operating. Otherwise they were dependent on the kindness of colleagues to lift them over 180 steps to the street.

Last in: First Out
The curved row seating arrangement for that 1,600 person audience in that ballroom proved safer than expected when initially set up. Not only did everyone completely clear the seating sections, they were also exiting the room at a normal walking pace within 90 seconds of the end of the session! Even when you can't control all the safety factors, at least create a design that optimizes safety.

Do your own due diligence. Ask questions and expect an answer. In no case assume that the facility is up to fire code or has recently looked with fresh eyes at the facility.

Room Evacuation: Legislating Safety
Prior to the November election of 1994, there was a bill before the Connecticut State Legislature proposing that all gatherings of over 300 participants require semi-circular seating set-up. The main reason was for safety, not learning environment, line of sight, comfort or networking. It has been found that semi-circular room sets can be evacuated in one-half the time that traditional theatre style sets can.

State of the Art Seating Arrangements

SEATING MATTERS

Put No One In Peril !
Of all the people who have attended my seating programs, the only one who most completely "got" the importance of room set in providing safety for the participants, was a fireman. Of course, his mission is making people safe. But isn't that everyone's mission as well? At least, put no person in peril.

Be Prepared! Don't Leave Them in the Dark
While many facilities have storm lights, especially on the East Coast, invest in a handheld, high lumen rechargeable portable light, available at boating, hunting, hardware, and outdoor stores. You can get 500,000 to 1,500,000 lumens for $20-$50, to illuminate inside your meeting general session or hallway in the event of a power failure.

Outfit your "safety patrol" of officers or a designated group with responsibility to pay special attention to where the exits are, outfitting them with visor lamps or blinking lights similar to diode lights a bicyclist might use at night, just in case.

Criteria II: Lines of Sight Obstructed Sight Lines
Straight ahead, unimpeded sight lines are preferred. Yet, straight row seating, and especially "ganged" seating, is a major culprit in creating sightline obstacles.

"Ganged" Seating
Locked, ganged, linked or coupled seating occurs when chairs are hooked or locked together, usually in straight rows. The chairs are manufactured with a coupling mechanism so that they can be bound together with a small hook or extension on both sides with which to fix or fasten the chairs together in a row.

The Trouble With Ganged Seating
Ganged straight row seating typically lines chairs up directly behind the row in front even more than does ganged chevron. That means that **only the front row has an unobstructed view**. The second row has to tip heads right or left. The third row has to tip heads left or right to adjust to the second row's choice of tilt. And the fourth row has a fan of heads left, right, and center to try to see over or around. This is true for regular theatre style ganged setup, as well as for chevron or herringbone design that is ganged together – People are lined up directly behind each other, obscuring the lines of sight.

NFPA Sets the Safety Standards
The National Fire Protection Association in Battery Park, Massachusetts, is one agency charged with developing the fire safety standards for hotels and meeting facilities. For example, new meeting rooms with 300 or more participants are supposed to have a detailed plaque near the entrance that provides clear directions to the nearest exit. Newer hotels are required to have lights along the floor similar to those in airplanes to lead occupants out exits. In many cases the facility or local fire marshal either does not know the ruling or is operating under a different ruling authority on seating safety standards. The rule from the National Fire Protection Agency on ganged seating states:

State of the Art Seating Arrangements

SEATING MATTERS

> *Thou shalt join together no more than 7, nor fewer than 3 chairs.*

Apparently the ruling grew out of a situation in which panicked participants tipped over chairs in their frenzied exit from a fire. Chairs tipped over randomly in a rush to get out of the room can form a phalanx of chair legs that blocks the exit for others.

One Midwestern convention center director was curiously unknowledgeable about the NFPA rule on ganged seating, and was in violation of the fire code, ganging rows of as many as 25 chairs. Another Midwestern convention center had asked for an exception to the fire code and was setting the ganging-prepared chairs separately, not linked.

Meanwhile, a major chair manufacturer informed me that they called a prominent hotel corporation to inquire why they were still ordering ganging type chairs. It seems no one else was ordering them, and the manufacturer was ready to move on. That hotel brand was now the major customer. The response of the hotel chain was that the safety officer for the corporation had made his reputation on his approach to safety. That included ganging the chairs. So, as long as he was employed there, they would continue to order gang-able chairs and set ganged seating.

Today, with some of the super-sized individuals attending meetings, more chairs are filled beyond capacity. Ganging the seating may unnecessarily crowd participants so that they have to leave a chair in between themselves in order to be comfortable. Now there is a lot of dead space. That cuts down on capacity, for no one would choose to be sandwiched in between two large individual.

Criteria III: Audience Comfort

Comfort is one of the top criteria considered in choosing an Audience Centered Seating™ design. Straight rows do not provide comfort to participants.

SEATING MATTERS

Evidence of Audience Discomfort
Nate Bailie, Assistant Director of the University Center at the University of Alabama, Huntsville, said he can determine the level of comfort for the audience by how much they tend to rearrange the furniture. He noted that over a period of three nights, with three different events hosted in the same room for 400 people, the re-setting of rows after the event was absolutely minimal. That room was initially set in a semi-circular arrangement.

When there is little to no rearranging, he maintains that audiences are relatively comfortable with the seating set the way it is. Nate noted that when he sets straight rows, compared with curved row seating for events, the straight rows are often upset into patterns reminding him of jagged sharks teeth, no longer straight and requiring considerable re-setting.

First, Cause No Pain
Susan Guay a facilities manager from Providence College reported upon returning from my ACCED-I training session, "The day we got back to campus we had a group of 50 auditors in a training program in (ugh!) straight rows. Fortunately it was a two day program. On the second day, we changed the set-up ourselves and think they looked much more comfortable. Surprisingly, our set-up guys were enthusiastic when we told them about it. No resistance from them."

Audience members should not have to hurt when they attend your meeting. Audience members bring their bodies to a meeting. How your seating arrangements affect the audience member physically is one major concern and focus here. Audience-centered seating reduces strain and constriction, which allows greater blood flow, an important factor considering that blood flow is going to the brain! It optimizes the learning experience for everyone in attendance.

More Participants Face the Wall Than Face the Presentation
Unless one is right in front of the podium or lined up directly behind a projection screen, straight row seating designs do not face you directly toward a presentation. More seats in a straight row are set facing a fake *ficus benjamina* ornamental tree, or the bland wallpaper of a ballroom. Few actually face the presenter, necessitating head turning and neck craning just in order to see.

Positioned for Pain
Try sitting straight in a chair and turning your head 15-20 degrees in either direction. After about 15 minutes, you will begin to experience tension in your neck or back. In the short run it is bearable. In the mid-term, within 17-20 minutes, you will seek relief.

Blood Flow Constriction
According to my Northern Virginia chiropractor, Dr. Joe Esposito, what happens when you are required to turn your neck for a period of time is that blood flow to the brain is restricted. Turning your neck blocks the vertibular arteries, especially when they arrive at the circle of Willis. At this point, there is little likelihood that your brain is operating better, due to restricted blood flow. You will also not be getting adequate oxygen to the brain. Plus there is the potential discomfort and imbalance of having your head turned on your neck, rather than balanced.

State of the Art Seating Arrangements

Others have maintained that those on the extreme outside and front of a standard straight row traditional theatre-style set experience the following: The blood flow into the frontal lobes of the brain exceeds the outflow. Pressure builds up in the frontal lobes, necessitating a straightening of the neck for relief. Since those on the outside of the front seating sections have the most extreme angle to the presentation – ranging from 65-85 degrees – they have the most potential for pain. And the pressure buildup and resulting release for relief may all be unconscious to the participant. But the discomfort is burned into his memory.

I have been unable to get a definitive response as to whether turning your head to the right or to the left creates the greater blockage. You may want to check that out for yourself. The mere awareness of what you have put yourself through in the past may help you to avoid extreme neck turning and distress.

The best way to look straight on is to find a chair facing the presentation, or to face your chair toward the presentation.

Autonomic Nervous System Effects
When you twist your neck or your lower back to compensate for a poor chair set, in order to see a presentation, you are likely to create nerve interference. A few of the health problems that could be caused by the vertebrae and the discs between them, producing pressure and irritation on nerves include:

1. **Neck Twist – C 4 and C 5 Vertebrae:** Neck pain and stiffness, nervousness, muscle tension, insomnia, throat & thyroid trouble.

2. **Lower Back Strain – L 2 & L 3:** Back ache, menstrual cramps, female disorders, impotency, sterility, bladder problems.

The chiropractic profession benefits directly from straight row room sets by gaining patients seeking relief.

Why The Reluctance to Sit in the Front Rows of Straight Sets?
In many training sessions or speeches, it takes major coaxing to get U.S. participants to sit toward the front. This is especially true with straight row seating, according to several meeting planners and speakers, who say that audiences naturally gravitate to the front when seating is curved. One exception in which the audience comes to the front in straight row seating might be if the speaker is a celebrity and people want to get up close and personal.

For the longest time I have heard the presenter try to make light of the back seats filling first by saying he "didn't bite," or "this looks just like church," but there is "no offering, so feel free to come up front." On occasion, audience members sit in back so that they can beat a quick retreat if they choose to leave, or avoid involvement.

State of the Art Seating Arrangements

Why Participants Sit in Back

But one good reason to sit in the back row is to avoid the pain of turning one's neck at a severe angle just to see the presentation. Certainly they turn necks back there less than they would have to turn in the front row, unless they are among the few facing the presentation directly. Back row seating is not necessarily a desire to remove themselves from involvement, but to observe easily,…and maybe not be called on.

Criteria IV: Access and Egress
Dealing with the Cumbersome and Slow

Irrespective of how closely rows of chairs are set to each other, getting to the chairs inside a seating section may be awkward, cumbersome, and slow. If you don't take into consideration access and egress with the length of rows you set, you may actually lose time in getting people out to refreshment breaks, out for lunch, and back in to keep the meeting running on time. Several recent industry ads show general session rows of 25 and more chairs across. The "access lane" alternative and the "notch" in the back central seating section is introduced in Chapter 8, Principle 4.

Back of the Room Sales Suffer

If none of these disadvantages so far have been sufficient to nudge you toward altering your seating arrangements, then consider the fact that back of the room sales increase when you curve the seating. This is the reported benefit noted by Orvel Ray Wilson, head of the Guerrilla Marketing group that runs seminars all over the world. And in a tight economy where speakers may negotiate a reduced fee based on the amount of product sales, the meeting planner benefits by promoting increased sales, thereby paying less of the amount agreed to as the minimum income from the event.

This may also translate to more interaction in the back of the room for meetings whose agenda includes enrolling audience members in a cause, getting signatures on a petition, getting new membership or membership renewals.

The next chapter explores several other current seating practices and issues. Chief among these is the sense that form, or "how it looks", precedes function, "how it works" in reality. This is fostered largely by current practice, as well as the room set-up photos of meeting rooms, all of which are beautifully symmetrical.

SEATING MATTERS

State of the Art Seating Arrangements

Chapter 4

Room Set Function Trumps Form

This chapter may seem like a Shakespearean aside, but it is appropriate to address form and function here. People expect to see certain traditional seating configurations when they enter a meeting, event, or learning environment. No matter how uncomfortable, inefficient, or unsafe, they will accept it as the "way it's supposed to be" because it has symmetry, it's familiar, or seemingly has good form. However, the room set may limit, even hinder the meeting function.

> *Curved rows look sloppy,*
> *So I don't use them.*
>
> **HOTEL GENERAL MANAGER**

To All Appearances: Form Rules

One of the deciding factors that perpetuates the current standard, is all about looks and form, not function. It looks like it "should." So, even though the design is dysfunctional, meeting facilities personnel and meeting participants are so accustomed to looking at a few limited straight row ways of doing things, that as long as it looks symmetrical, they think their job is done. Look at any meetings industry magazine, and some facility is proudly offering a big horseshoe or U-set with table cloths in place, or a large general session with rows 15-25 chairs in length. But it looks neat! How can it be wrong? Keep reading and you will find out how to do it right.

Promoting "Safe Sets"

Many who plan meetings are part-time or one time meeting planners. They don't want any surprises; will take no chances with anything different. Most of them do not want to be wrong. They want the room to be set up in a way that will not upset their boss, the board of directors, founders. That means it has to pass a "first glance" test. It has to look like any and every other meeting they have been in. So, they don't even consider optimizing the environment. Rather they do it the way they've seen it done…the safe way.

SEATING MATTERS

Function Precedes Form
In the current meeting industry, in case of a tie between form and function, function loses.

While training the set-up crew at the Philadelphia Airport Marriott, we set one-half the ballroom to determine curved row capacity, and to demonstrate how to fine tune that room. There was no need to set the whole room. About the time we had finished, the higher ranking convention operations manager appeared and cautiously looked over the set. He commented that for 30 years his standard for setting the room "right" was whether he could fire a rifle through the eyelet or hand hold loop at the very top of the back of each chair without hitting anything. He was looking at the space between the back cushion and the top of the frame. Of course they didn't shoot any rifles, but you get the idea.

As you can see from the photo of half of that ballroom (below), this more functional setup with a range of sight lines broke with the tradition of firing a rifle through the eyelets at the top of the back cushion. It also introduced a new approach to comfort, safety, ease of access, and networking. No fan of heads blocking your view below.

Forget Symmetry
Symmetry is not the standard for whether a room set is useful. You have to sit in it, and do so for a period of time to determine the viability of a set. Sit in various chairs around the room. Assume nothing. Rather, check it out. Prove it out.

State of the Art Seating Arrangements

SEATING MATTERS

One Dysfunctional Form—Overlapping Tablecloths Look Nice, But
While there are many examples where what looks good does not work, one example of a dysfunctional – form eclipsing function – is when rectangular tables are joined end to end to form straight rows, with no gaps except for aisles and ends of rows. As a result, table draping has taken on specific practices.

One practice is to overlap the tablecloths between tables, making this a method of joining or coupling the tables, keeping them from being pulled apart. To emphasize and secure this juncture point, a water pitcher if often placed on top of the overlapped table cloths. Frequently in that set, the bottom of the pitcher straddles both tables. The tacit message is "don't move the table or dire consequences will befall you." Many a wet carpet has resulted from shifting the tables.

Facilitating a Classroom Set-up: Individually Pre-draping Tables
Full-sized ballrooms are frequently subdivided into 3-6 smaller slices for breakout or concurrent sessions. When you are pressed for time to reset the rooms from straight-row set to classroom set, you can do so quickly if an adjoining room is unoccupied prior to the turnover. Drape each table separately in the vacant room in advance. Then, when the session ends, merely pull the air wall to pull out extra chairs and fill in the set with tables. Whether you are setting a straight row set or curved with the tables, this approach saves major time.

Curiously, the hotel setup crew commented on this time saving feature of draping the tables individually in advance. They were open to learning. That is why it is so important to continually learn from your own experience and to demonstrate to others the advantages and disadvantages of different features for the participants, speaker, learning experience, even for the set-up crew.

Several other time saving maneuvers will be provided in later chapters, such as directions on how to go from a general session in one large space, to two breakout sessions in under 3 minutes, using one set-up person.

Elevating *Function* to Job One
Function is primary – especially how the room setup serves the meeting, audience and presentation. You have to design everything toward attaining the purpose and intended outcomes of the meeting. How can you serve your customer best?

When you provide room sets that really work, remember to point out the features to your participants who have just experienced that set-up. Sometimes they need to have their learning underlined. That is how you start a minor revolution in meeting facilitation, effectiveness, and comfort nationwide – one audience and one person at a time.

Pay attention to the rationales provided all the way through the book, the benefits and advantages, and to your own experience.

State of the Art Seating Arrangements

SEATING MATTERS

Howie Mandel did a skit in which he posed as a ticket seller to productions playing in Los Angeles. He told ticket buyers that they would have to be resilient in viewing the animal acts by not looking directly at the animals. Supposedly it made the animals nervous. So, Howie warmed them up for the act by having them face directly away from him, and then look back over their shoulders. His suggestion was a total joke.

The most that anyone can be angled away from a presentation is 180 degrees. Many straight row sets face 30 to 85 degrees away from the presentation. The following room set, meanwhile, puts each audience member in chairs facing within 0 to 10 degrees of the presentation. That should be the function of facing a chair, so one's neck need not turn.

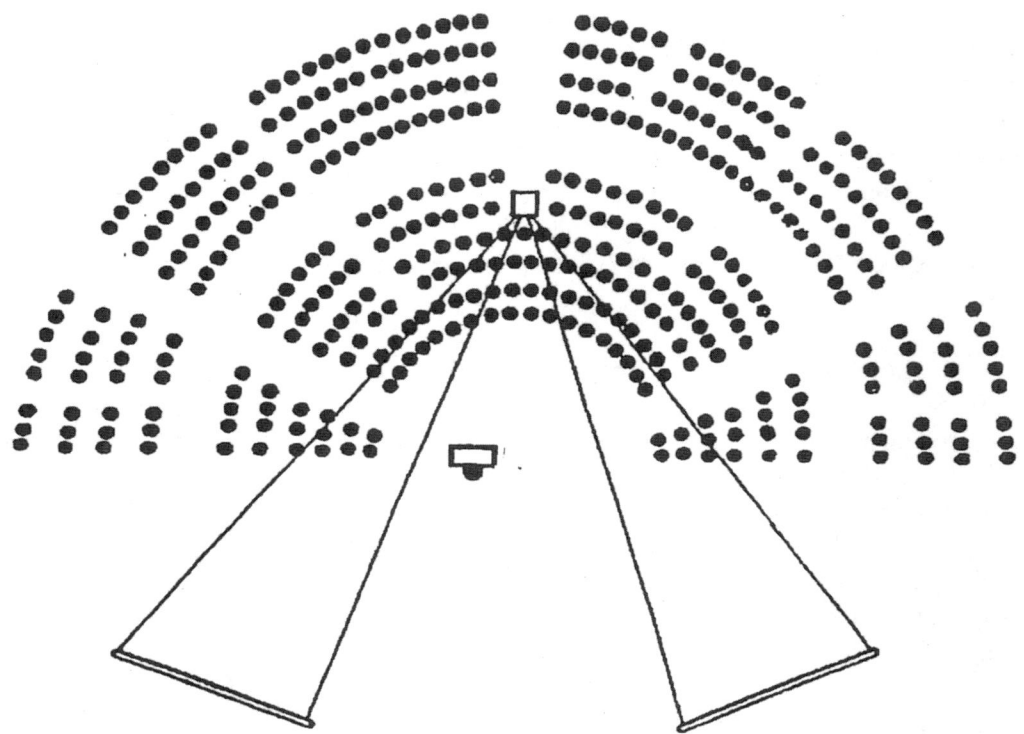

The seating arrangements set for most audiences are not supposed to be a joke, nor are they supposed to ultimately be debilitating. But many are. Our work here is to give greater consideration and deliberation to what we offer our audiences, so that everyone benefits. Hence, you are about to be introduced to five principles that can be used as criteria of judgment in setting and troubleshooting various meeting spaces in chapters 5 through 9.

Look forward to correcting even more of the deficiencies of straight row sets, as well as opening up innovative room sets that optimize the learning experience. Alternatives and improvements to these straight row sets will be provided in Part II. You can also assert your own creativity by experimenting with and applying these five principles to your current and future room sets.

State of the Art Seating Arrangements

Part II.

Five Principles To Set or Troubleshoot Any Room

Combining Principles to Optimize the Room Setup
This part deals with creating and optimizing the environment for the event, learning, or meeting room based upon 5 room set principles. Applications include the use of space within a residential or non-residential meeting facility where a majority of time is spent in the educational enterprise or meeting.

In order to optimize the learning environment, each one of the five principles which follow, is intended and designed to be used together with as many of the other principles as possible. They are presented one by one in order to fully develop and demonstrate the benefits and rationale for each principle.

There may be times when the set-up you are confronted with is problematic and you cannot readily revise it due to time, space, or circumstance…or due to resistance or downright intransigence on the part of meeting facilities management, city code, the meeting professional, the meeting schedule, or even people in the organization for whom you are presenting. It is under limitations especially, that you need to know what options are available to improve the room set and learning environment, even slightly.

Applying as many of the first four principles as possible, will improve the environment. Examples of optimizing the situation are given for each of the principles when applicable. On rare occasion, the use of only one principle by itself might actually worsen conditions for the audience members. Those downsides will be red flagged.

Part II.
Chapter 4. Principle 1. Set to the Long Side. No Bowling Alleys.
Chapter 5. Principle 2. Face Each Chair Toward the Presentation. Curve the Rows.
Chapter 6. Principle 3. No Middle Aisle. Flare Aisles Off Podium 45 Degrees.
Chapter 7. Principle 4. Cut Single Chair Access Lanes in Seating Sections.
Chapter 8. Principle 5. Place the Last Row on the Back Wall.
Chapter 9. Applying Principles in the Small and Board Meeting

State of the Art Seating Arrangements

SEATING MATTERS

Audience Centered Seating™ Principles

Set Room to the Long Side

No Middle Aisle. Set 10:30 & 1:30 Aisles.

Curve the Seating

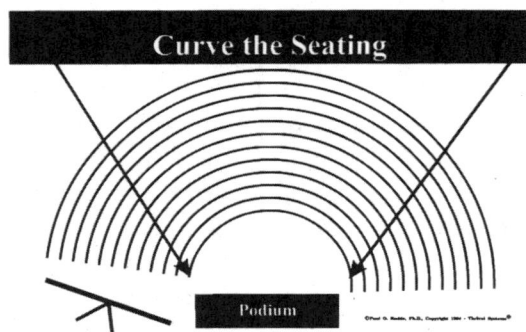

Face Each Chair Toward Presentation

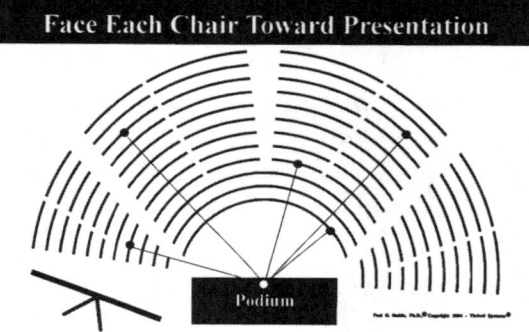

Cut Single Chair Access Lanes

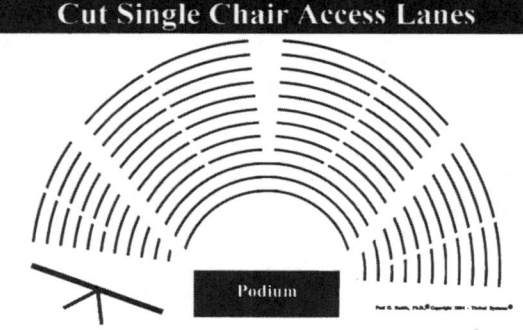

Set Last Row on the Back Wall

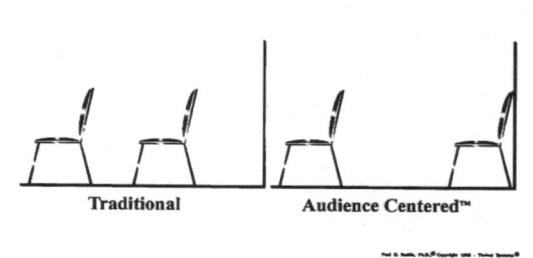

Traditional   Audience Centered™

State of the Art Seating Arrangements

SEATING MATTERS

Chapter 5

Principle 1. Set to the Long Side.

No Bowling Alleys

"Whenever possible, we place the stage against the long wall of the room. The effect has been to focus all of the energy of the group on the presentation. I also noticed right away that people are less reluctant to sit in the front rows. I never would have guessed that such minor adjustments in the setup architecture could have such profound affect on the audience, but our experience is undeniable." So says Orvel Ray Wilson, President of the Guerrilla Group, that was producing over 400 public and corporate seminars all over the country, ranging from 50 up to several hundred. Orvel reported a marked increase in audience participation, reduced audience fatigues, and an upturn in back of the room product sales.

This illustration compares the distance from the last row of the narrow side room set, to the increased intimacy of setting the seats to the long side of the room, one major benefit of principle #1.

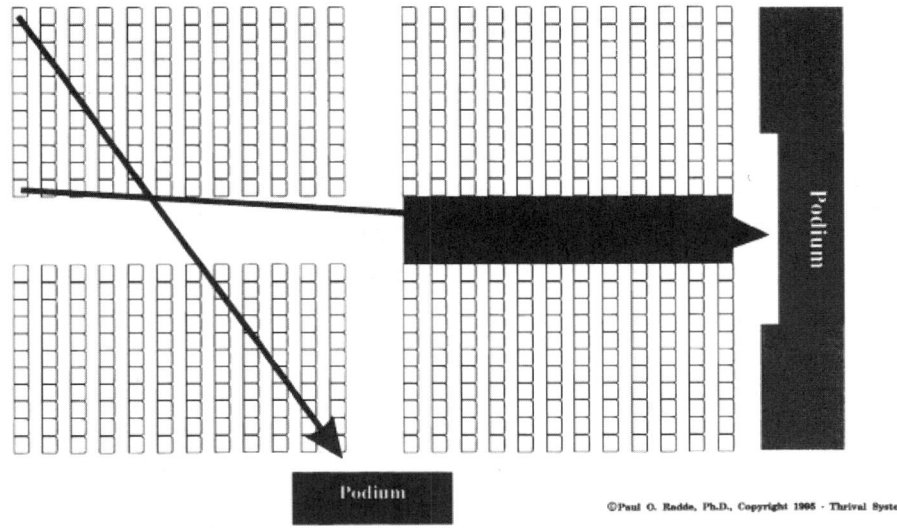

State of the Art Seating Arrangements

SEATING MATTERS

Set What? Why?

Setting to the long side means that you are to set the chairs toward the wide side or the long wall of the room. In the absence of a square shaped room, and unless there is a major entrance in the middle of that wall, set to the wide side away from the entrance. Major reasons for doing so include the problems with the bowling alley set for sight lines especially, but also for sheer closeness to the presentation. Simply doing the geometry will inform you that setting the presentation on the middle of the long rectangular room gets everyone significantly closer in.

Distancing the Participant from the Presentation

The preceding straight row room set illustrates how setting to the narrow side of the room <u>distances at least one-third of the participants</u> from the presentation. When they may have been drawn to the event in order to see a celebrity presenter, they are denied any degree of close contact. They find themselves resorting to watching the projection screen in order to see at all and come away disappointed. This separation and distance could have been remedied by setting to the long side.

The Conference on World Affairs, CWA, is conducted for five days every April at the University of Colorado. One of the rooms in the Memorial Student Union demonstrates the problems with a bowling alley set. The room is 80 feet long and 16 feet wide as you can see below.

When set to the short side, you can set seven chairs across the room with aisles on the wall (right) and windows (left). The chairs are lined up one right behind the other for the typical panel discussion consisting of 4 panelists who sit at the end of the room. Each panelist has come from around the country or around the world to make a 10-15 minute presentation

State of the Art Seating Arrangements

for CWA followed by discussion among the panel members, then a Q & A with the audience.

So far no platform has been provided so panelists can be seen beyond the fourth row without standing. So unless the panel stands up while speaking, or participants stand along the walls or in the back of the room for the entire program, one has little chance of seeing the presenters from beyond the third row. Unless you want to pose a question, you may as well buy the recording since the dignitaries who come from all over the world at their own expenses, are not visible.

One quick intervention does work to make the panel more visible. We asked the panelists to stand during their presentations. When they do, they can be seen by everyone in the room. The value of attending the session increased measurably. Meanwhile, an initial setup to the long side and/or 18 inch riser for the panel, would make the presentation visible to the entire audience.

What Principles Can I Apply in this Situation?
That college union room is pictured above in a classroom set to the long side. At most, that room can only accommodate eight chairs and a single chair width aisle for the bowling alley set. So, when set to the short side, it is even more limiting than it first seemed. The pictured room set would also exact a toll from participants with severe neck turning in this "mess hall" set with a panel at the end of the room. But even then, the room set in the photo is an improvement over the bowling alley with the tables set to the long side of the room.

The diagram that follows is one best case solution for setting the narrow room to the long side. This "J Set" allows for ease of entry, sight lines, and closeness to the presentation.

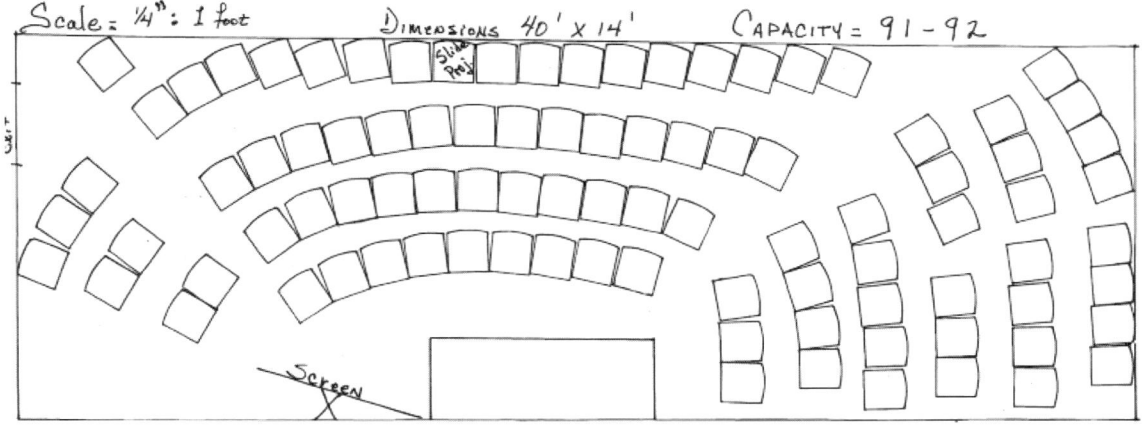

State of the Art Seating Arrangements

SEATING MATTERS

The set-up crew at the Indianapolis hotel located just off the approach to the airport could not be bothered to reset the seating for my session the next morning. We were scheduled for one sliver of the larger ballroom. I paced off the back row at 96 feet from the projection screen I would be using at the front of the room. The room was set bowling alley style for 238 participants. The count came from the meeting planner.

The crew was content, they had done all that could be done. So, when I began to move chairs at midnight, they only looked on from adjoining sections of the ballroom, occasionally sneering just a little. I completed transforming the room, setting to the long side, and curving the seating so that every chair was facing the presentation directly. The final set placed even the farthest chair no more than 55 feet from the screen. Now 2:20 am, the crew chief came over and commented, "Well now, I never thought you could get 238 chairs in by setting it this way."

If that set requires tables, participants can at least angle or turn their chairs behind the tables toward the presentation. But the tables themselves are best bowed out in an arch to face the presentation directly, as in the illustration below, and as you will read in Chapter 7. If you were to arrange the tables in the photo above, you would curve toward the presentation, which would be placed at the middle of the long side, as done in this diagram.

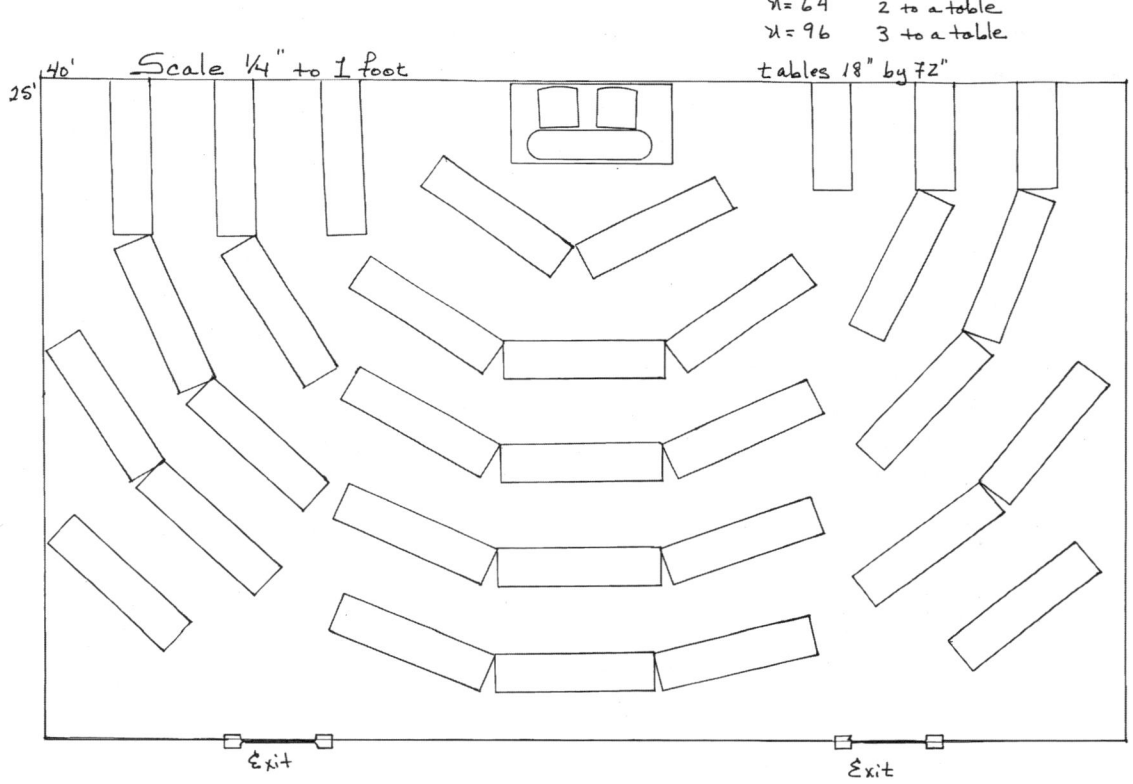

State of the Art Seating Arrangements

SEATING MATTERS

Discernment Is Always Your Responsibility

Your discernment is always required. On a few occasion the use of only one principle by itself may actually worsen conditions for the audience members. This principle of setting to the long side of the room when it is the lone improvement, may be the single principle whose application can worsen the learning environment, especially if you cannot curve or angle the seating toward the presentation, such as the following illustration, which has been angled in the outside sections.

When you can utilize only this principle by itself, there are several things you will want to consider, especially the actual width of the room. If it is very long, then those seated in straight rows on the outer reaches of the front rows will have a severe angle from which to view the presentation. Set in straight rows only, it is better set to the narrow side

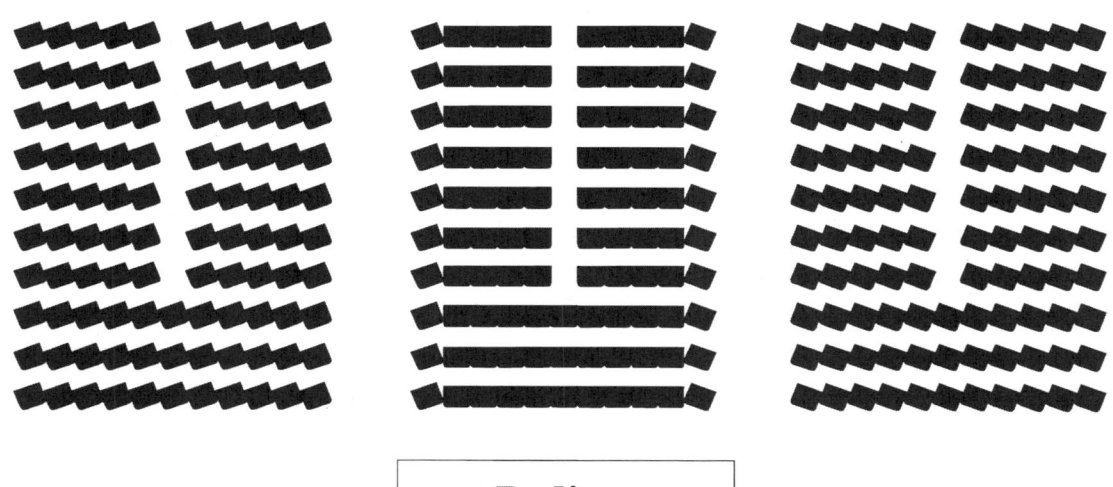

©Paul O. Radde, Ph.D., Copyright 1994 - Thrival Systems®

The main benefit of setting to the long side is to assure that the maximum number of participants have the greatest proximity to the presentation. When that benefit is offset by placing a portion of the participants in extreme discomfort and struggling to view the entire presentation, then you may be better off going with the bowling alley set to the short side of the room.

Room obstructions, especially columns, can complicate setting to the long side. The illustration that follows shows how to open the area behind the column, using it as aisle space to bring in participants since there is no clear line of sight behind the columns.

State of the Art Seating Arrangements

SEATING MATTERS

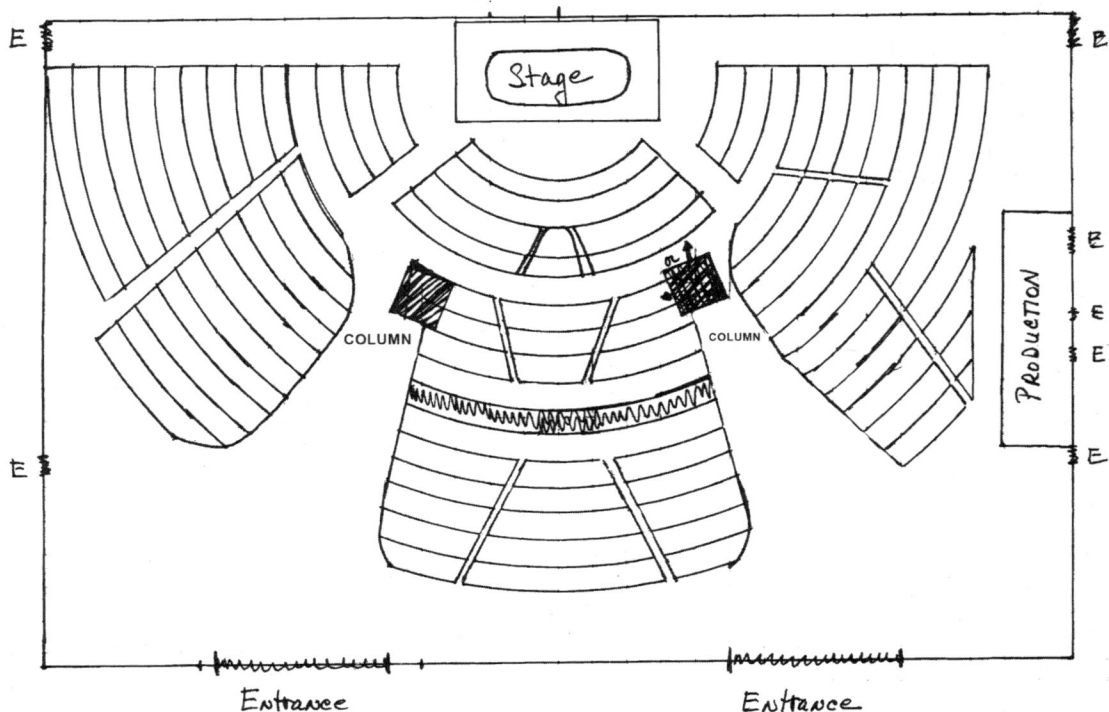

In the Absence of Time or Assistance: Provide Your Own Set-Up

Learning Point: Put your energy where your conviction is.
You have to be ready to physically make the changes that you require to optimize the learning experience for your group. That means re-setting the room, sometimes with the assistance of a benevolent convention operations supervisor or employee. [A tip may be appropriate.] Or you may end up doing it alone. But you will know that this is part of your professionalism in ensuring the platform mechanics that optimize the learning environment.

Be sure to check in advance whether moving chairs might prove problematic in a union serviced facility. Those in charge of the meeting might be treading lightly with the union or the facilities staff over other matters, and your moving the chairs could provide the last straw that ignites their conflict.

In most cases, it would seem that your moving furniture should pose no problem if you replace it. Or, your moving it should not be problematic if this is the last session of the day in that room and they are going to break it down anyway. However, you may have to consider returning the room to its original, condition at the end of your session. At the end of the presentation, you can ask your participants to assist you in re-setting the room.

State of the Art Seating Arrangements

Chapter 6

Principle #2: Face Each Chair Directly Toward the Presentation. Curve the Rows.

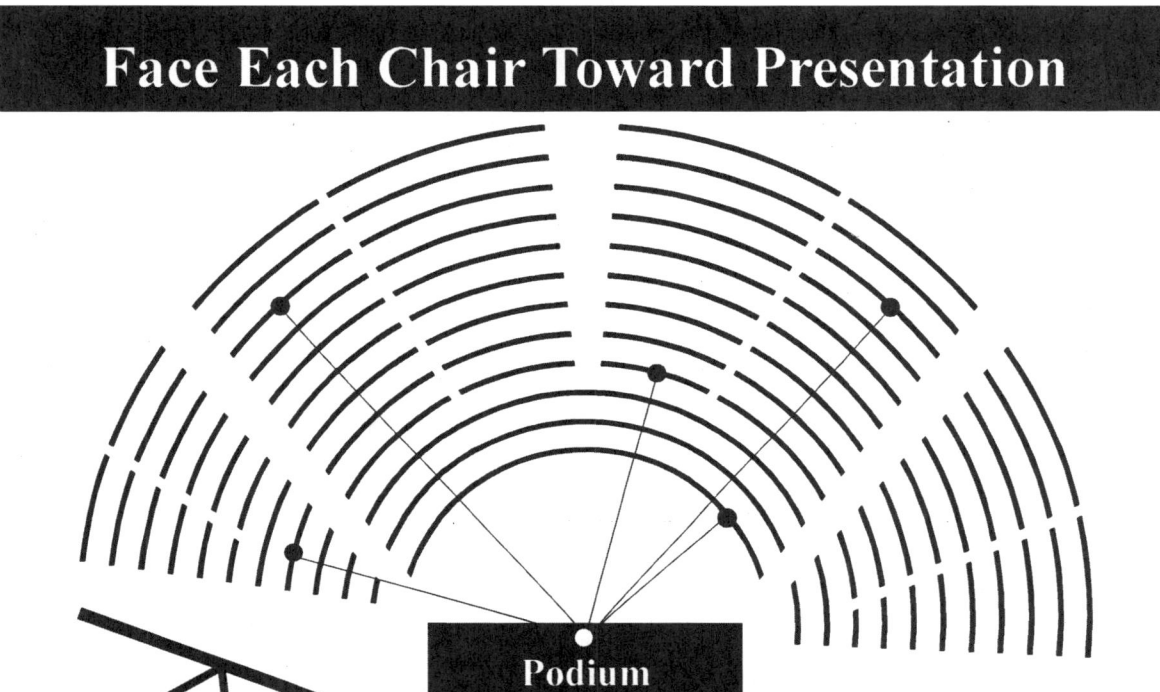

The Second Seating Principle
If there were simply one principle that is most comprehensive, that includes the overall intention of all the principles, it is this one. Essentially, the audience member should have his/her chair facing the presentation as directly as possible.

Initially there were 6 principles. However, facing each chair toward the presentation requires curving the rows. To avoid redundancy and overlap, those two principles have been blended into this one principle. You will find separate reference to the initial principles in the illustrations in Part IV.

SEATING MATTERS

The Historical Case for Curved Row Seating

Early Amphitheatres Were Curved Toward the Stage
Nature provided the original impetus to curved row seating. The Greeks and Romans only followed nature's lead. Original amphitheatres were often hewn out of hill sides or utilized natural overlooks as in Cuzco, Peru, where the annual celebration of Inti Rymi on June 24th, was staged where the natural configuration of hills allowed for seating in the round and elevation.

The Greeks and Romans both utilized curved seating, either a semi-circle facing a stage, or a circular arena like the *Circus Maximus*, or an oblong arena for chariot races. So, straight row seating is rather a new comer to festivities and meetings, not "the" long established way to go. The curved row seating of theatres provided an acoustic advantage of hearing the principals on stage, long before electronic sound amplification.

Curve the Rows: The More Elegant Facing
Curving the rows, rounding in at the edges, allows for two basic things to occur even better than angled seating:
1.) **The participant faces the presentation more directly, no neck strain.**
2.) **The participant can see other audience members.**

These two benefits alone are sufficient reason to instigate the change to curved row seating from the traditional straight row theatre style or angled seating.

The Dynamic Rationale for Curved Rows: Why "Three's a Crowd"

Pairs Have One Bond Maximum
When any two people are together, talking, the most bonds that are possible between them is one. And that bond can vary greatly in degree of connection based on what exists between the two individuals.

Pairs Have Two Strands of Communication
There are two strands of communication for each two persons. Basically there is an exchange from A to B; a return or initial transmission from B to A. If there is a flow of communication, the relationship could be seen as reciprocal.

Basic One-To-One Relationship

One Bond Two Strands

Why Three's a Crowd: And Baby Makes Three

Many couples do not know what hit them when they have their first child. Life was so simple and then you experience an exponential increase in bonds. This makes a "triangle affair" so complicated, usually one of the three is left out. Here the third party is added.

State of the Art Seating Arrangements

SEATING MATTERS

Strands Increase Mathematically

The increase in strands of communication continues to be a simple multiplier effect of two strands between each pair…over and back. So when you go from 2 to three individuals, you merely increase the number of strands from 2 to 6. If you go to four persons, the number of strands would be 12.

Bonds Increase Exponentially

Bonds increase from one to seven. See the illustration above. The mother to father bond is intact. Now add mother to baby, father to baby and you have three. But trios frequently leave someone out. So now we see the case of baby observing what is going on between mother and father, father observing how mother and baby are relating, and mother seeing how father is doing with the baby. And there are those rare occasions when there is a synthesis of all three having a laugh at something funny, or having a startle together due to a sudden earthquake, sound of thunder, or flicker of electric lights. Given the 3 1:1 bonds, 3 2:1 bonds and the synergy of experience for all three, you get a total of 7 bonds.

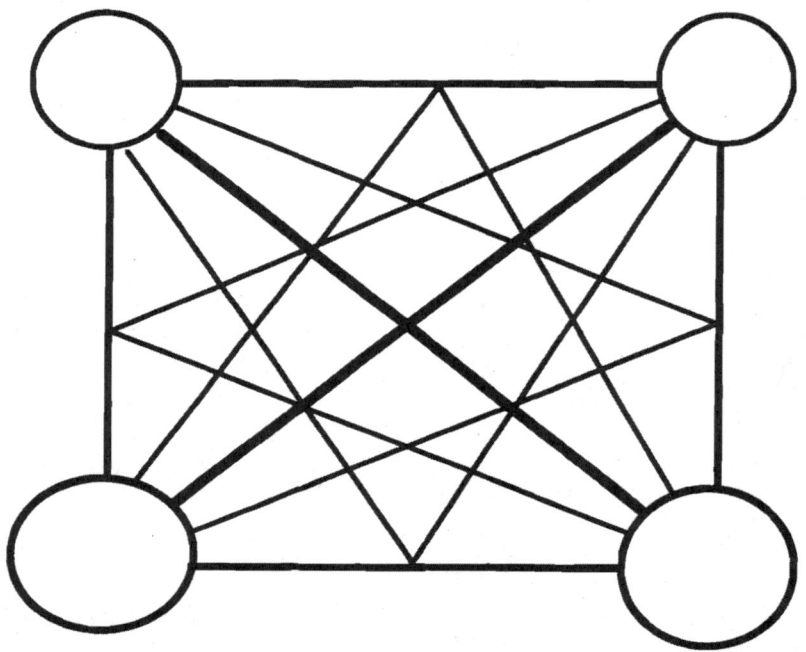

With Each New Visible Individual Comes An Exponential

Increase in the Bonds Possible
4 Participants: Strands = 12   Bonds = 19

One of the big differences between standard straight row, and angled straight row or curved row seating is the number of bonds promoted by angled; prohibited, eliminated by the straight row. That is the difference made simply by curving the seating so that one participant can see more than one person on each side of him – massive increases in connection, bonding, contact, networking.

State of the Art Seating Arrangements

SEATING MATTERS

Facing the Presentation: Three Major Approaches
There are varying degrees of facing the presentation. Here we see three variations:

I. Limited, Incidental Facing: One result of straight row seating is that it makes the degree to which you are facing the presentation one of luck, choice, range or spectrum of the presentation. Not everyone is assured an equal opportunity at facing the presentation. Varying degrees of effort are required. Straight rows require the most adaptation from the audience member.
1. Select one of the few chairs already facing the presentation
2. Turn your chair to face the presentation, if practicable.
3. Turn your head/body to face the presentation
4. Do nothing and hope the presentation positions in front of you.

Only 1. is a truly acceptable solution. The other three are partial measures at best. So, consider the advantages of angling the chairs, then curving the rows. Each of these is portrayed in the following illustration. First we will consider angling the chairs, then move to curving the rows.

II. Angle the Chairs
One of the simplest adjustments you can make, even as a meeting participant, is to angle or slightly rotate your straight row chair toward the presentation. So, rather than facing the front wall or edge of the stage, you are facing toward the presentation.

Of all the resistance to these adjustments, anticipated and real, this one should meet with the least resistance. For one thing, it continues to preserve the straight row, so it is in perfect alignment with the industry mythology that you are maximizing the body count for that room by keeping straight rows.

Here is how you make the adjustment from straight row to angled chair straight row:

1. Uncouple or un-gang any chairs linked or locked together.

2. Begin with the chairs nearest the central aisle.

3. For each succeeding inside chair, beginning with the chair on the left aisle, facing the front of the room, keep the back inside leg exactly where it is, using it as a pivot. For chairs to the left of the middle aisle, keep the right back leg planted and use it to pivot the front leg some 2-4 inches to the right, at the angle most directly facing the presentation. The chairs to the right of the middle aisle keep the left back leg exactly where it is, using it as a compass point to pivot the left front leg 2-4 inches toward the presentation.

4. Once the middle aisle chair is adjusted, adjust each succeeding chair in the same manner proceeding out and away from the middle aisle. Those chairs on the extreme outside may require being turned more than 4 inches. But even if limited in

State of the Art Seating Arrangements

movement by the spacing in between the chair, 2-3 inches rotation toward the presentation is a vast improvement over facing the front wall.

5. The chairs should remain in a straight row for the purists who insist on having straight rows and to maintain clear access and exit.

The Origin of Angled Seating
I discovered this adjustment one-half hour into a government contracting session seated in the 30th plus row of a straight row set. Even though at that distance, some 75+ feet back, the degrees I had to turn my neck to face the presenter were fewer than had I been seated in front, my neck was fatigued from turning my head toward the presenter. So, I said to myself, "Come on Paul, you're the seating guy, so figure this out." I looked down to see how much space I had between chairs. There were 2 inches. So, I simply angled my chair to face the presenter more directly, leaving it perfectly in line with the row. It worked. No more neck pain. I have used angled seating ever since as a quick adaptation, one simple and immediate, yet elegant approach and solution to improving a room set.

You will soon see that this is only a half-way measure at improving the learning environment and reducing wear and tear on the participants. It gets even better when you use can use all the principles. Angled seating faces the audience member more directly toward the presentation, and yet we can do still better.

Explore the Benefits of Angled Seating
Experiment with this variation in seating. All you need is 3 chairs lined up in a row. Angle them and see what a difference it makes. There is no increase whatsoever in the square footage of floor space required when those chairs are angled toward the presentation.

Comfort: More Room. No More Rubbing Shoulders
If people are going to be wide, it is at the hips and shoulders, not at the knees. Angled seating provides an elegant solution to being crowded, crimped, and cramped in the squeeze of straight row seating. The angling of the backs of chairs offsets participants hips and shoulders so that they no longer bump up against each other.

Accommodating the Super-Sized Participant
Especially in this era of working out with weights and with two-thirds of Americans overweight, and one-third clearly obese, seating needs to take into account body size and body overflow from regular sized chairs. The super-sized individual who requires a larger casket and can't fit into a single airline seat, clearly poses a problem. Seating has to accommodate these expanded sizes. Certain organizations require special seating allotments, but now require extra space. The spatial estimates no longer work. You have to make adjustments to accommodate.

Decipher your audience's needs based on spatial requirements. If they are males and work out, they will need more shoulder room. If they are older, weight shifts downward. If they are heavy set or obese, you need to provide a more expansive arrangements.

State of the Art Seating Arrangements

SEATING MATTERS

The typical individual is usually 16-18 inches wide, yet a six foot tall man who lifts weights might measure 22 inches across. Any more girth and breadth than usual, and you are rubbing up against your neighbor. That is not comfortable in popular US culture where touching a stranger is avoided at best. Most are not comfortable and do not welcome that level of intimacy.

When the National Automobile Dealers Association met at the New Orleans Convention Center, the set up of ganged straight rows, 10 seats across, posed a distinct problem. Many of the automobile service department directors were very large, broad shouldered men. When one reached for a handkerchief, the entire row had to move to give him access to his pocket.

It Is Easier to See the Presentation: Reduced Neck Strain
You are facing the presenter more directly, reducing neck and back strain, especially for those on the outside of the rows.

Expanded Span of View: You Can See More Participants
When you are set up facing the wall, your span of view takes in only part of the room. You have to make a special effort to turn you neck to see the presenter. And with straight rows, you typically can only see the person on either side of you.

When you angle your chair, you can follow the presenter on any approach or entry into the audience. Plus, you can see many more of your fellow participants. That promotes humor, bonding, and networking. You feel more a part of the presentation and organization when you are actively participating with more people. It costs you less muscle strain to see others. Now you have a real meeting.

A Bonding Experience
The more people you can see, the more likelihood of networking with them, sharing a laugh, creating a bond. Bonds between the audience and the presenter form the infrastructure of the event. Take out one person or remove her from view, and you lose all those interconnected linkages. And that is just with one person…who could be one of the more important contacts you would have made during this meeting.

What about the time required to do this set-up?
After a few runs, you save set-up time. Each new set-up is going to require a few runs in order to make it second nature. I'm only talking 2-3 times, not weeks and weeks. The crew from the Grand Traverse Resort in Traverse City, Michigan, reported shortly after being trained in Audience Centered™ Seating that they could set an angled straight row set *even faster* than they could line up the traditional straight row set.

SEATING MATTERS

Application of Principle 3

Angling Improves the Chevron Set

You already know the difficulties with the chevron design, with its use of straight rows. Below are some illustrations of ways to improve it. The traditional chevron design is quite restrictive when it is ganged in a straight row format. But simply by angling the chairs in the chevron sections, and angling the seating on the outside of the center straight row facing section, immediately improves the set-up. You may angle more of the chairs in the middle section, depending upon the breadth of the presentation. When you angle the outside seating section of the chevron room set, you will be about equal in sight lines and networking with the regular straight row theatre set when angled, only more comfortable.

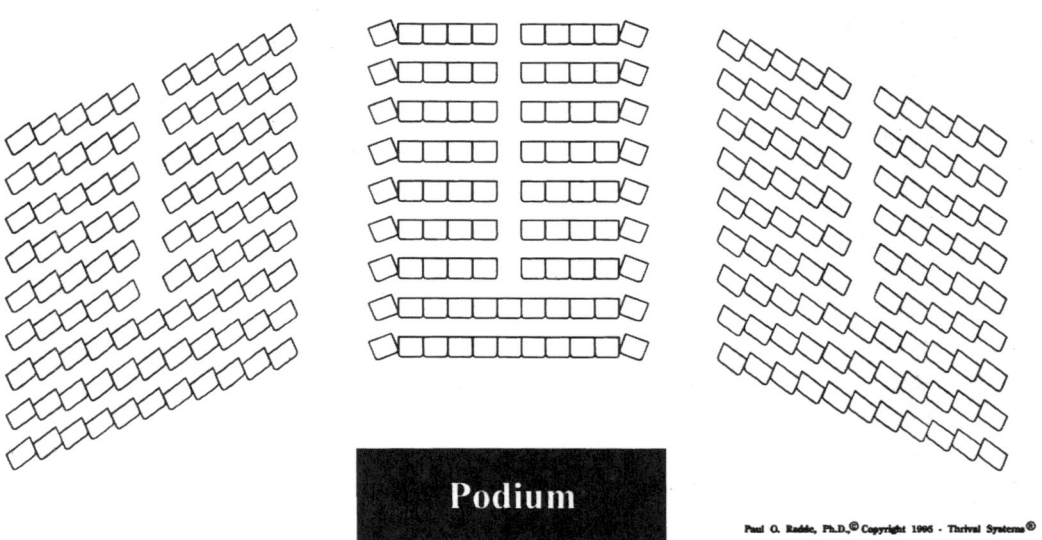

Neck Strain Required to See Presentation

Several straight row sets are part of the standard seating capacity sheets in meeting facilities. These include: theatre, chevron, box-shape, and the so-called U-shape tables utilizing rectangular tables and 90 degree corners. Each one provides designs of "seating which requires neck strain" simply to watch and see the presentation. Angling the seating can alleviate some of that strain.

State of the Art Seating Arrangements

SEATING MATTERS

Face Each Chair Toward the Presentation

There are <u>three basic ways</u> of optimally facing each chair toward the presentation, especially when moving from straight row sets to curved. We are mid-way in moving from the least to the more precise. We begin at curving the seating.

     I.   **Angle the Seating in a Straight Row**
     II.   **Semi-Circle the Seating**
     III.   **Curve the Seating in an Elliptical format.**

This is the basic synthesis of the message and progression of this book.

1. We began with straight row seating, which probably has more participants facing away from the presentation, than facing it. This is our point of reference for improvements.

2. Then we moved to angled seating, keeping the row straight, but increasing the number of participants who are facing toward the presentation.

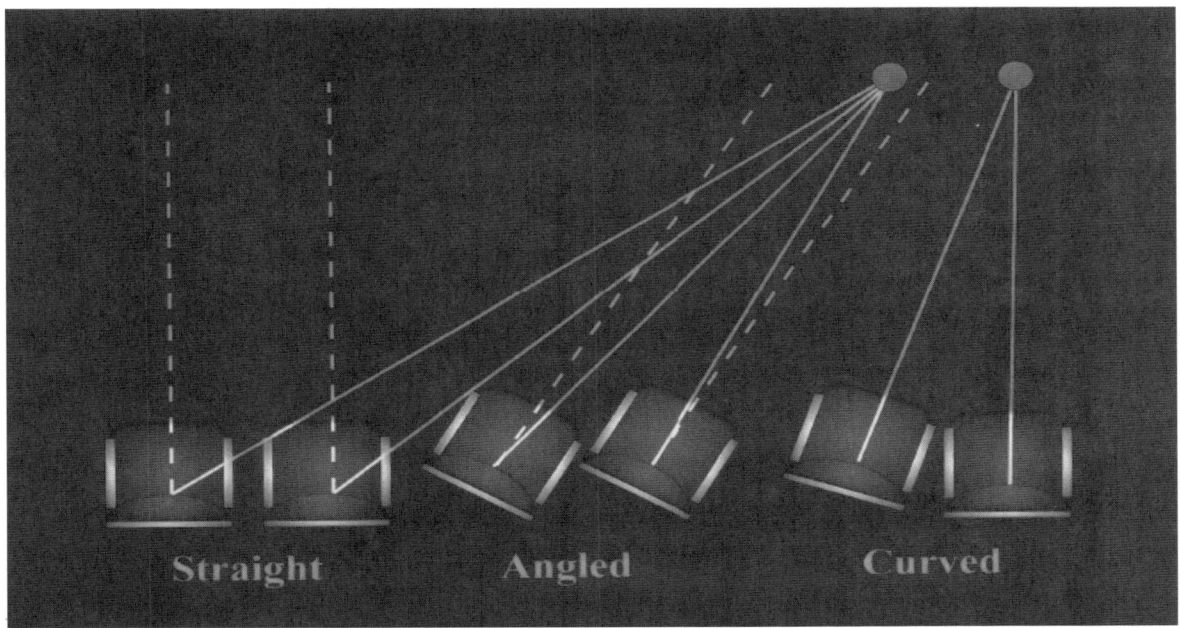

3. Now we come to the practical part of the principle for this chapter, curving the chairs to face the presentation directly.

Semi-circular and Elliptical sets Facilitate Interaction with the Audience.

If you wish to have close interaction among your audience members on their level, curved rows and flared aisles provide even more intimate access than is afforded by the gaping middle aisle. Straight row seating makes it very difficult on those in the front rows when the presenter goes up the aisle or into the audience. They have to crane their necks and twist their bodies to follow the action, sometimes over 160 degrees to the right or left. Curving the seating allows the audience to be able to follow the action with little twisting, straining or craning.

State of the Art Seating Arrangements

SEATING MATTERS

You can make cuts into the middle section without draining energy e.g. with an access lane. Susan Roane is a petite presenter who speaks on networking. She likes to get down and face to face with her audience. She used the **U**-shaped bridge [immediately below] into the front of the middle section. This way she can use the U-shaped aisle and the flared aisles with corded or wireless mike, or even walk into the single chair access lanes cut into the very front sections, so that she can take 3-5 steps into any section in many different locations. Wireless microphones afford the most options for roaming into the audience without limitation.

Even when you plan on the flexibility afforded by using a wireless microphone, you still need a fall back position should there be an equipment malfunction. Know how much free cord is attached to the wired mike stuck in the introducer's lectern on stage or at the front of the room. Frequently that cord is curled under the platform or knotted. Check out the "lengths to which you can go," before the presentation, rather than scrambling when you suddenly are forced to revert to the wired mike midway through the program.

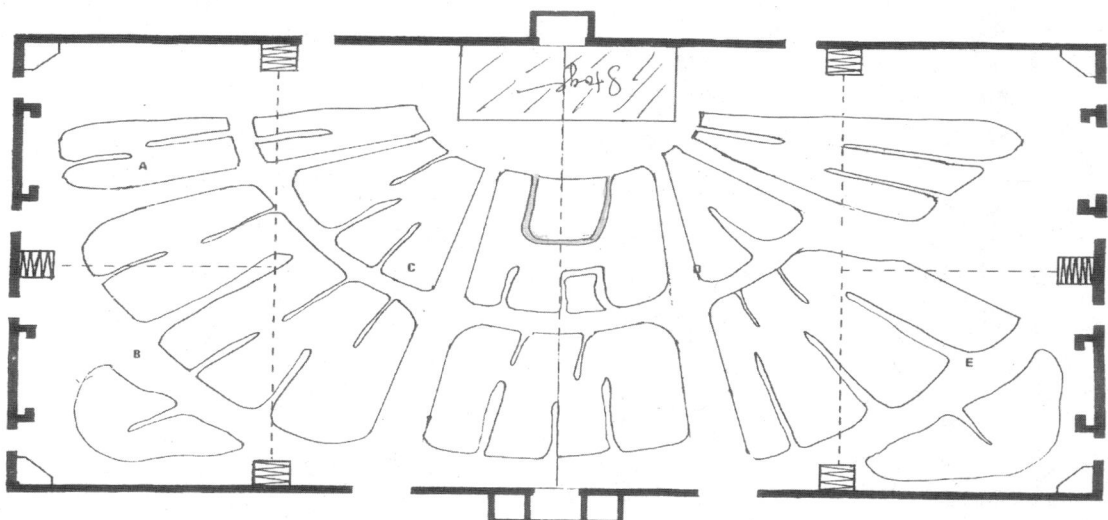

The dotted lines in this illustration are the slivers or subdivisions of the ballroom referred to throughout the book.

Semi-Circle the Seating
We have already addressed specific presentation-determined criteria for semi-circling the seating. Most often it is done when the presentation is fixed in place with a limited or stationary focal point, such as behind a lectern, a panel seated at a table on stage, or a speaker whose movement defines a restricted or tight orbit, or a W.

Designing the Curved Room
This seating design can be imposed on meeting facility diagrams set at ¼ inch per foot. The Berol RapiDesign R-2127 Metric Civil Engineers' Radius Guide is particularly suited to designing the semi-circular room set. This plastic stencil has a central point from which

State of the Art Seating Arrangements

SEATING MATTERS

the radii extend. Place this central or focal point over the point on the diagram to which you wish to direct the audience. On the diagram above, that pivot point would be at about the "e" in "stage" written on the podium. Then draw out the design in pencil. Mark off aisles from drawing off the corners of the stage toward the exit doors. Create aisles and access lanes using white out tape. Or use darker lines to draw them in as was done below.

A Compass Will Serve Nicely
Since the Radius Guide described above may not be available, due to a merger of companies, you can always use a basic compass to draw out the semi-circular set. Begin with the point of the compass at the determined focal point for the presentation on stage. Then, opening the compass to 1.5 centimeters, draw out the first row around the stage. Then increase the opening of the compass one-half centimeter for each succeeding row.

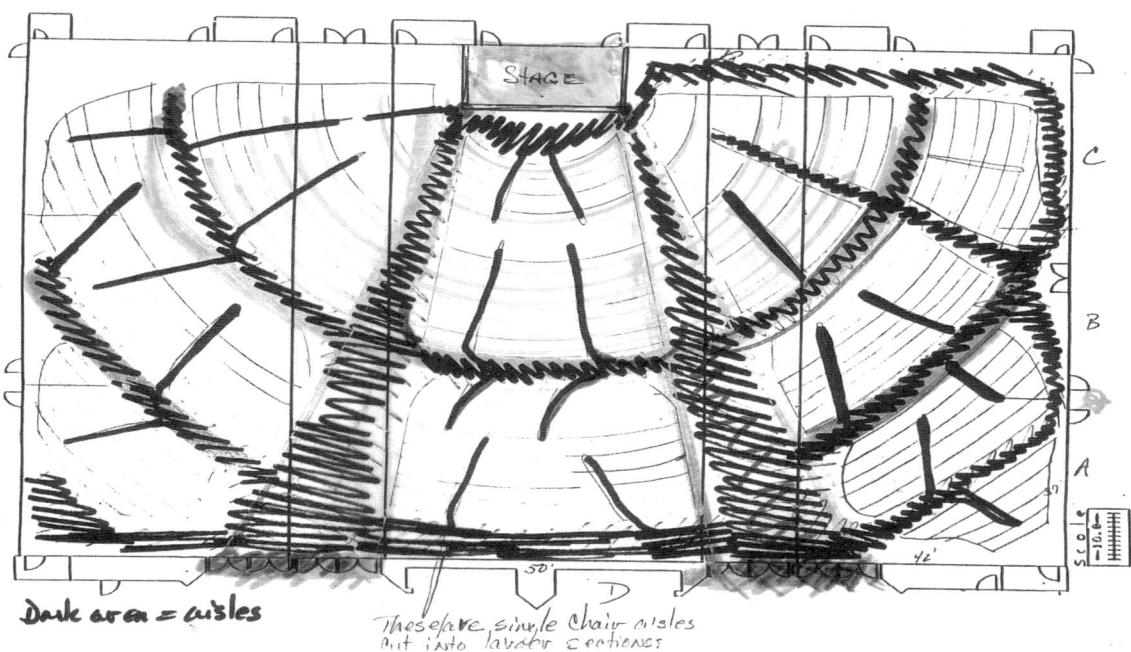

Note that you will not necessarily be drawing precisely what the room set will look like when set, e.g. the number of rows, but you will be providing a clear illustration of what you want. If you want more precision, then calculate what constitutes 34" at ¼ inch to the foot, and set the compass to increments equal to 34 inches, or about .94 inches each increment. Draw in pencil or lead so that you can erase the curved lines that run beyond the rows and through aisles and access lanes. Find out and adhere to the fire codes for that room.

Advantages of Curving the Rows
The usual advantages occur with Audience Centered Seating™ classroom style with participants facing the presentation directly, participants being able to see each other with few impediments, and the actual improvement of seating capacity in the room.

State of the Art Seating Arrangements

SEATING MATTERS

n. b. Facing the Chair Directly Takes Priority Over Curving The Row
In most cases, facing a chair directly toward the presentation will result in curving the row. However, just because you have seen symmetrical semi-circled rows offered in this book, and they look good, you are still to <u>face each chair directly</u>. That is the basic core rule. The resulting row will not necessarily look circular, but it will probably be curved to some degree.

III. Elliptical Design
The elliptical design provides the most audience comfort in the event that you have active movement on stage. The following illustration provides the type of set-up you would require for a Tom Peters-type, lion-stalking-across-the-savannah presentation where the speaker ranges back and forth across the full breadth of the stage. He operates within a self-styled orbit or track.

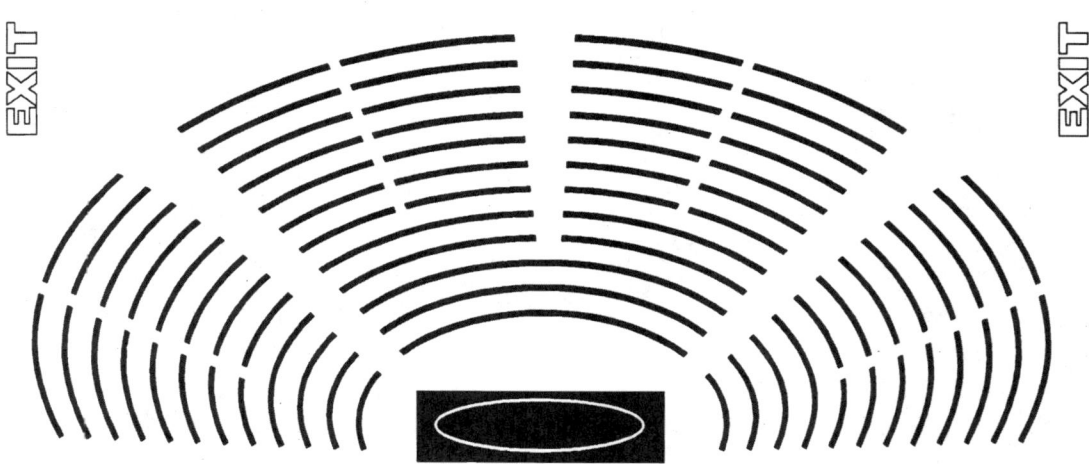

You will continue to face each chair toward the presentation. However, you have to figure out what will constitute the focal point. Those in the front row would be up close and personal. Those seated in the mid-stage area would have to pivot their necks to follow the action, but those toward the outside would be able to take in the span of movement without constant neck rotation.

You have already seen aisles, such as in the elliptical set above, that are angled off toward the exits from the corner of the stage. The next chapter provides the principle for setting your aisles.

State of the Art Seating Arrangements

SEATING MATTERS

Chapter 7

Principle 3: No Middle Aisle.

Flare the Aisles Off At Forty-Five Degrees

Two Main Problems Created by a Center Aisle:
   I.   **It eliminates the best orchestra seats.**
   II. **It drains energy from the presentation.**

No Middle Aisles.

I. Middle Aisles Eliminate the Best Straight Row Orchestra Seats
In the traditional theater style straight row set-up, the main aisle is typically smack dab in the middle of the audience. If the crowd size is large, that aisle is large as well. And most often, the space right directly in front of the presenter or presentation is left open to serve as a center aisle. Some of the potentially highest priced orchestra seats are pre-empted by aisle and foot traffic, the poorest utilization of that space.

The Best Seats in the House Aren't There
This particular configuration means that the best seats in the house are not there. The aisle space right in front of the stage affords the best view, the prime viewing of the presentation. Yet, that space is not set up. This aisle space is the only place in the room with that straight row setup in which people can see the presentation without having to turn, hence, bend their necks.

II. Middle Aisles Drain Energy
If you consider the room set in a manner that can either leak or contain the energy of the presentation, the middle aisle tends to drain energy. The presenter broadcasts energy straight out from the stage and there is nothing in the aisle to contain or absorb it.

Michael Doyle and Richard Strauss, co-authors of Making Meetings Work and experts on the New Interaction Method of meeting facilitation state that there is a loss of energy containment in presentations that occurs due to the middle aisle.

State of the Art Seating Arrangements

SEATING MATTERS

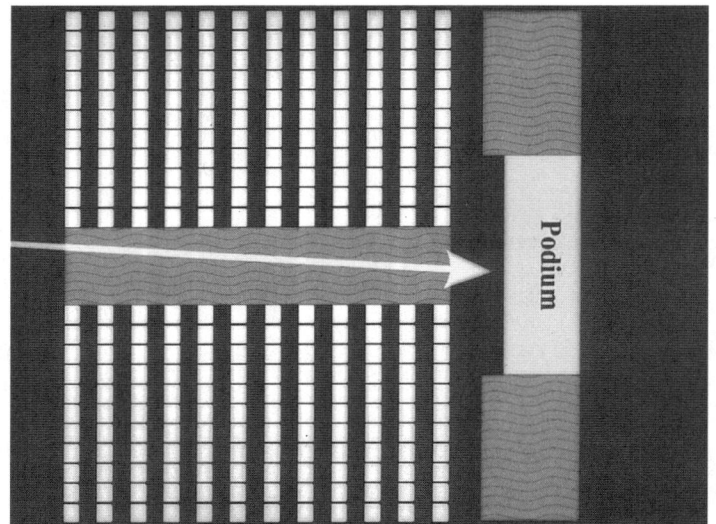 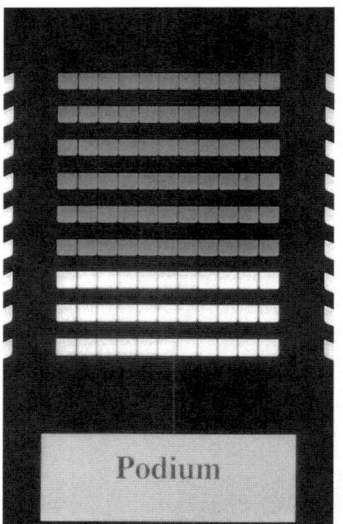

Quick Solution

One quick, though minimal, solution to correct a traditional straight row theatre style set with a center aisle, is to close up the middle aisle and place two side aisles running down the sides of the middle section. This also provides the people in the new middle seats with a dead-on view of the presentation, and it seals up or contains leakage of energy up that middle aisle. However, the straight rows abound.

In the illustration above right, there is an obvious problem with ganged seating that requires an elevated podium so that everyone can see. It would be better to stagger the chair sets, even when set in straight rows, so that everyone can see without physical gyrations, pain and suffering.

Platform Elevation

Bruce Harris stated that in these straight row sets, unless you are in one or more of those rows lined up directly facing the presenter, so that others in your row do block your view, you are likely to be able to capture a well elevated presentation at even a slight angle. Hence, the farther back, the more range of the stage that opens up to one with minimal neck movement.

Once you begin to curve the rows, you have additional options with the aisles. Cut notches, little pie sliver shaped aisles out of the curved seating section. Begin at the front corners of the central stage or platform and extend directly out toward the exit.

In some cases you will be setting up in an auditorium in which there are multiple doors at the back and side of the room. And, while it is preferable to have a seamless straight shot

SEATING MATTERS

from each corner of the front stage to the exits, in larger auditoriums, you can generally provide an open flow by setting the row at a 45 degree angle off the end of the stage.

If you need another point of reference, consider yourself standing in the middle of a circular clock face (podium position below). To determine 45 degrees, you would extend your arms as if they were two hour hands, toward where they would be at 10:30 and 1:30 on a clock face as illustrated below. Now adjust the angle toward the entrance at the back or side closest to the aisle that is 45 degrees off center stage.

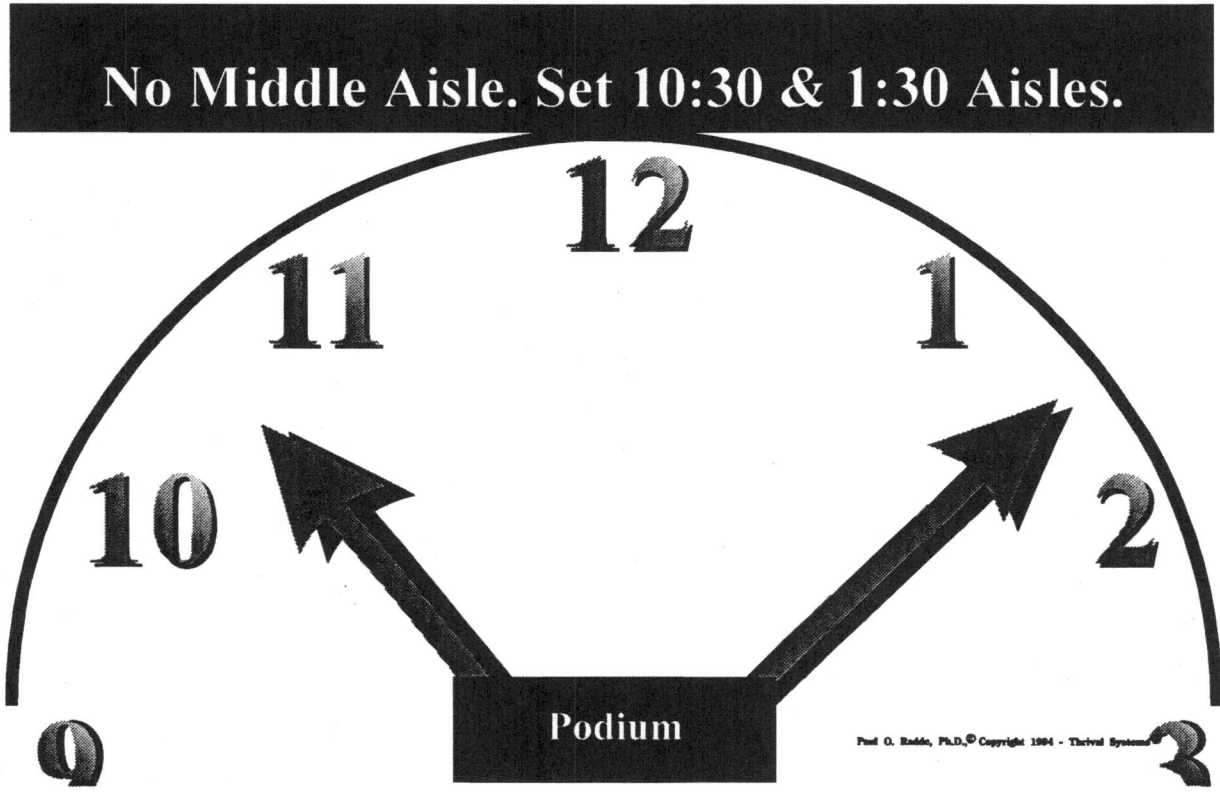

Another way to remember this way of setting up the aisles is to stand toward the middle front of the stage, called the "podium" below. The view over the top of your head is the positioning of the platform. Now sidle over to the right front corner of the stage. Once there, and directly facing the back of the room, extend your right arm directly toward the major back or side exit. Point toward it, and you will be designating the location of the aisle. Then walk over to the left front corner of the podium and point with your left hand directly toward the most accessible and largest side or back exit. That becomes your major left aisle. The illustration immediately below is an example of these aisles.

State of the Art Seating Arrangements

SEATING MATTERS

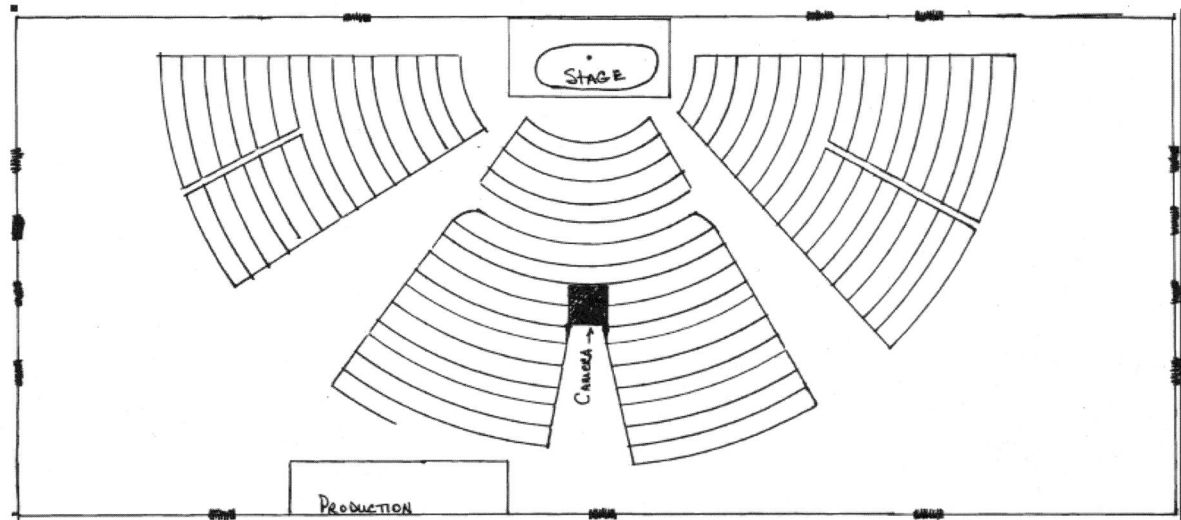

Aisle Width

Make sure the aisle is a minimum of 4 feet wide at the front of the room, the width required by ADA standards. Then widen out or expand the aisle all the way to the back or side door in order to handle the increased traffic that comes with emptying an auditorium. Just as the Mississippi River is but a few steps across in Itasca State Park at its source in northern Minnesota, the volume of water at its mouth near New Orleans, is sufficient to carry an oceangoing vessel. You need to anticipate and accommodate the surge of foot traffic toward the exits.

Widen out the aisle. The aisle should be about 8 feet wide for traffic up to 500, larger commensurately for more foot traffic. You want to easily accommodate two wheel chairs and allow room for them to maneuver in the aisle as well as for others to walk on either side of the wheel chair.

Remember it's a meeting. People will spot each other and want to stop on the spot to talk.

SEATING MATTERS

Leave Space For <u>When, Not If</u>, People Stop to Schmooze

When people come to a meeting, they do just that – meet. And often they will congregate near the exit doors, often impeding traffic. Leave an open space at the exits on both sides of the doors in order to allow for people to meet and greet while others exit. Even with refreshments being served in the hall, people surprised to run into their friends tend to stop dead in their tracks and start conversations when they have not seen each other in a while.

Since you already know that happens and tends to block traffic, anticipate and plan for "when" it happens in your initial set-up, not "if" it happens. Leave a little alcove of space near the back doors so that participants running into each other can pull out of the main stream and chat with each other.

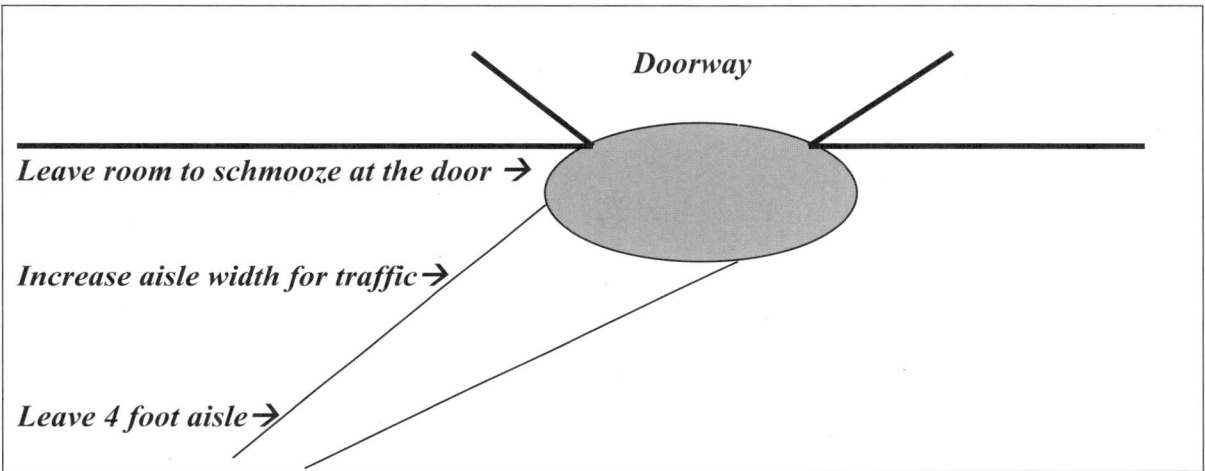

Consider how a river flows and the banks widen as it gathers volume. You want the river bank/aisles smoothed off to facilitate ease of flow. When chairs jut out into the aisle, you have to remove these potential obstacles. Remember the aisle is to be gradually widened outward toward the exit and the "banks" of the aisle smoothed on both sides, but especially rounding any curves where participants are more likely to catch a foot or tip over a chair. Remember you are also facilitating break time in and out of the room as well as safety and traffic flow.

Major Advantages of Flared Aisles

Of course, you can flare aisles even through a straight row setup. It can be done, even though the aisle will be a bit jagged. However, the greater advantages to flaring aisles, come from when you flare aisles through a semi-circular or elliptical room set. Now the aisles are flared like radii or spokes on a bicycle wheel. See second illustration above.

SEATING MATTERS

Entering and exiting presenters, performers, ceremonial contingents, and audience members alike can walk right up to their row and not block anyone's view. This is something that simply cannot be accomplished with straight rows. This is especially useful for:

- latecomers,
- additional participants in the program
- people who have to get out in the middle of a performance,
- anyone taking photos or video who wants to vary his perspective during the performance, and
- anyone entering or exiting the stage or the room during the presentation.

The unobstructed view and access afforded by flared aisles and curved rows is a major selling point of semi-circular seating. And it extends to aisle access. You may approach the stage from right or left all the way to the front row of the room and not be in anyone's way or be distracting to anyone.

We have covered the first three seating principles. We will explore the fourth principle, "Cut single chair access lanes" follows in the next chapter.

State of the Art Seating Arrangements

Chapter 8

Principle 4. Cut Single Chair Access Lanes

This chapter emphasizes "access" to seating as well as getting the chairs filled so that they become seats. We also address accommodating "grazers," late registrants who stress spatial limits, and convening a small group in a large room.

> *A Chair is not a Seat,*
>
> *Until*
>
> *Someone Sits In It*

You have already paid for the room set-up. The chairs are in place. There is plenty of seating for everyone registered and expected. However, until participants are actually seated in the chairs, the chairs are not serving their purpose as seats. A chair still stacked at the back does not become a seat unless someone sits in it. So, your set-up should serve the purpose of getting people seated before and during the presentation.

Getting to a chair easily, as well as getting out of the room rapidly for breaks and in the event of an emergency, is very important in making participants comfortable and keeping the meeting on time. This solves a safety issue, helps to keep the meeting on schedule, and provides seating access and comfort.

Accommodating the Late Comer
In most large meetings you are going to have latecomers to the meeting, or to that particular session. Whether someone sleeps late, arrives late, or time zone changes bring

confusion, you have people coming in when everyone else is already seated and the presentation has begun. How can you best accommodate them?

The flared aisles in a curved row set, allow each late arrival to approach the front rows without blocking anyone's line of sight. So, the latecomers are less likely to stand in the back of the room. And they are more likely to look for and take a seat. All empty chairs are still in play.

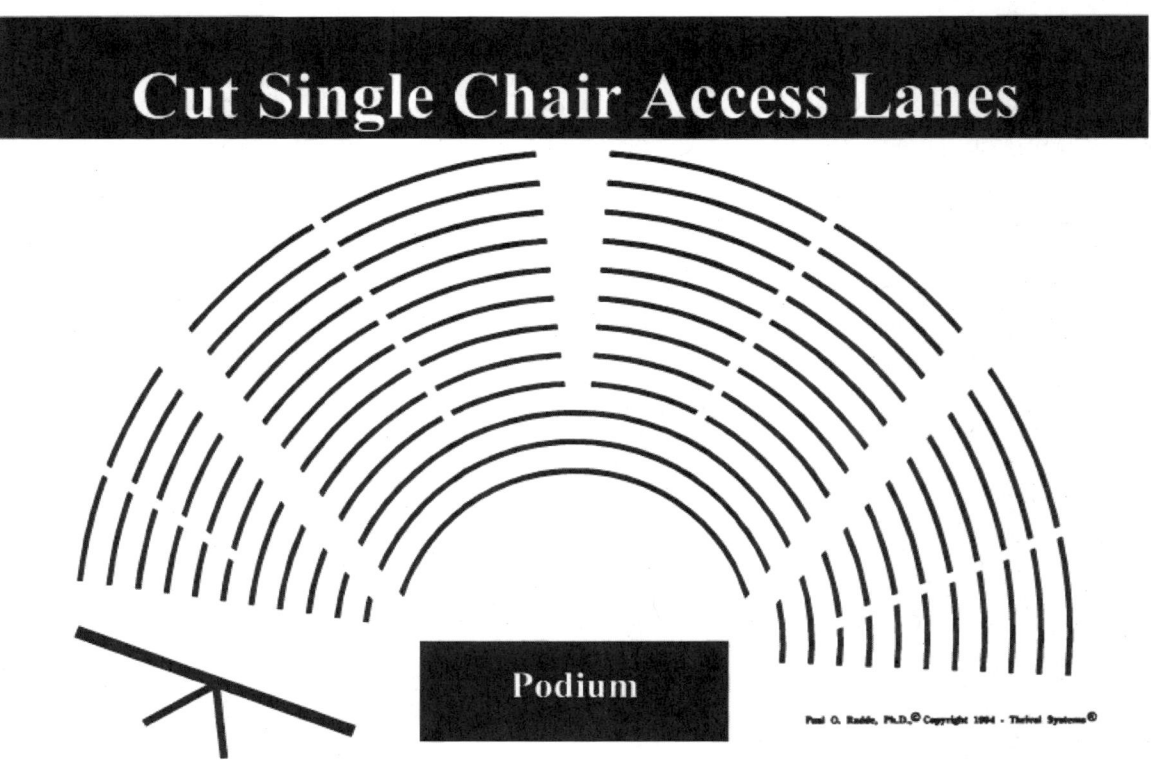

However, most late arrivals are squeamish about taking a seat more than two chairs in from the end of a row. That would be two "excuse me's" to get in. That is why so many chairs go unoccupied during a session while people stand in the back and the side of the room.

That unoccupied middle of the seating section looks inaccessible from the back of the room. Not only would one be disrupting folks who have already settled in, but while entering a row during a session that has started, one might also block the view of those seated behind your chosen row. So, rather than being a nuisance, they don't try for a seat.

SEATING MATTERS

Cutting a Notch
One way to accommodate the late arrival is to cut single chair access lanes into the middle of larger seating sections. That means that in order to cut into a seating section with 15 rows of 15 chairs each, you would consistently pull out the 8th, or the middle chair. That creates an access lane most central to that row and seating section as in the diagram above.

In larger seating sections you might even widen the access lane by pulling out two or more chairs per row toward the back of the section in order to provide even faster traffic flow. So, in a 15 row section, you might take out two chairs per row as far in as the 9th row from the back, and then take only one chair per row as far forward as the fourth row from the front.

This indented area, immediately under the "air" of Chair above, can also be used for video cameras, physically challenged in wheel chairs, spot lights and other items that can benefit from the easy access afforded by the rather larger notch. You can see a good example of the notch in the diagram above, in the middle top of the central seating section. There is also a notch shown in the diagram below.

Distinguish "Access Lane" from "Aisle"
You want to make a clear distinction between an <u>access lane</u>, which only provides access to specific rows within a seating section, and an <u>aisle</u>, which provides not only access to, but also passage past a seating section. An aisle is space dedicated to traffic flow. The access lane, meanwhile, can quickly provide ease of access to chairs by doubling the number of easy to reach outside chairs which facilitate getting to a readily accessible chair.

Audience members new to the use of an access lane, will often start moving chairs around. Many think a mistake has been made, and plow through the row where the access lane stops, to get to the front of the seating section. That is why you leave at least three rows in a seating section complete as is. The access lane stops 3-4 rows from the front.

> **Caution: <u>Do not</u> take out chairs from any closer than the fourth row from the front. Participants will still cut an aisle all the way through the seating section if there are only a few chairs to move. They are less likely if it stops 4 rows short.**

If you wish to make access to the front of the seating section as easy as access on the back side, you may also cut access lanes into the front of a section. Once again, if you do cut in a second access lane into a seating section, make sure you have 3-4 chairs of separation from any other access lane.

The Fire Marshall Role
When people encounter the single chair access lane the first time, they may also interpret that space as an invitation to slide their own chair over and fill in the open lane. That is

State of the Art Seating Arrangements

SEATING MATTERS

where you or someone needs be vigilant in maintaining the access lane, requesting that they leave the lane open.

To make sure everyone has sufficient room to sit comfortably in the first place, leave 1 to 2 inches space between chairs in the same row. However, if this is a group of particularly large sized people, you may have to separate chairs by 2-3 inches. But, none of our innovations here exact extra square footage from a setup. Participant size requires more square footage to accommodate the larger sized.

The Access Lane Advantage: Expands the 45 Degree Aisle Benefits
All of the advantages gained from cutting 45 degree aisles into curved row room sets, are continued and expanded by introducing the "access lane." In addition to doubling the easiest accessible seats, you have doubled the number of chairs within one "excuse me" of an access lane within a seating section. Twice to four times the number of individuals can now easily come in and sit down in what amounts to an aisle seat, even with tables.

Classroom Sets Can Maximize Aisle Seats and Access
Orvel Ray Wilson reports, "It's an ongoing battle with the hotel setup crews (who want to put everything in straight rows) but we're now placing our tables in a semicircle arc, with the arc relaxing as you move toward the rear of the room, so that all chairs are pointing naturally at stage center. Every table is separated from every other table by an aisle, maximizing the number of aisle seats, and we always maintain an aisle between the ends of the rows and the walls."

Murky Research
In training workshops on seating, I cut one access lane into the seating section on one side of the room at the back, and, all things being equal, leave the other side with full, uninterrupted rows. Then, at the beginning of the session, I draw attention to the fact that the section with the access lane has more chairs occupied. Interviewing those who sat there, discloses that "it looked like an easy choice."

Caveats

Earthquake Provisions Require Aisles
1. In San Francisco, the fire code has no terminology for an "access lane," nor does any current code in any city. Your access lane would be termed an "aisle" with all attendant requirements under regulations. They have no way to differentiate it. And due to earthquake requirements, you could not have an access lane, but rather would have to extend it all the way through a seating section, thereby making it an aisle.

   This might change when the concept of the access lane – not meant to function as a flow through aisle – catches on. In fact, the access lane may very well disperse the audience more quickly and evenly. People make use of their own access lanes to go

State of the Art Seating Arrangements

straight to the back of the room and the exit, rather than moving laterally to the aisle, and only then exiting by way of the aisle to the back of the room. That aisle, meanwhile, is filled with other participants exiting from numerous rows.

The Charge: You Are Losing Seating Capacity
2. Critics state that in the event of a capacity crowd, you would be reducing capacity by using the access lanes. You would be denying participants the opportunity to occupy those seats you removed or never set in order to create the access lane. To the contrary, those removed chairs can be stacked in the back of the room at the ready. And, if seating capacity truly becomes an issue, then simply pull a chair behind you through the access lane and place it and yourself in the row nearest the front, thereby filling in a one-chair gap for the access lane in that seating section.

No Less Safe Than the Original Set-up
3. Then some would complain that you are not meeting your safety obligation when you fill in the access lanes with the chairs you had removed. Well, if that is the issue, remember that prior to the introduction of the access lane, many of those chairs would have gone unoccupied as inaccessible. Now that the chairs are fully filled in, the section would constitute no more of a hazard to the seated participants now than the very same seating section without the access lane taken out in the first place. If a filled seating section suddenly constitutes a hazard, then perhaps we need to rethink what constitutes adequate safety standards in seating in the first place and require access lanes as standard fare.

Accommodating the "Grazers"
Numerous conferences and meetings schedule as many as 20 concurrent sessions for their participants. It is hard to differentiate from the descriptions on the program just which session to choose. So, numerous participants will find their interest waning in the session which was their first choice and elect to look in on another. They go grazing.

Grazers Love It
Many of us enter a new session with the intention of determining if we have any interest. We could be hooked by an excellent handout, the energy level, a connection with the presenter, the content, or the rapt attention of the participants. You get a pretty instant sense of whether "anything is happening in there" that attracts you and makes you want to stay. If it does, then you want to be seated.

Some graze quickly in order to make decisions about purchasing a CD or DVD's of a session. They determine if they can capture the essence of the experience of that session by buying a recording or if they have to be present to benefit. If the participation level is high or the visuals are an essential part of the presentation, they may opt to stay in that session because it cannot be fully experienced any other way. Those not committed to staying for the entire session will only commit to an aisle or access lane seat, from which they can easily exit. They will not sit inside the row.

State of the Art Seating Arrangements

SEATING MATTERS

As an inveterate grazer myself, I check for fit between the description of the session and the actual presentation. What is the session really about? Often the initial description has been written months before. It may have been shaped, even bent out of shape, in order to accommodate the theme of the event. If the presentation is not just a predictable "off the shelf" and if the presenter is a continuing learner, then a lot has happened since the writing of that description. You may witness a totally different presentation than the one described. Or the title is more hyperbole than descriptor. And you may have to be there to determine if what is going on is worth your time and attention. The presenter's presence or energy alone may be enough to shape content and the presentation itself.

Your job in setting the room is to make it easy and comfortable to get in and out for the grazers, whether they decide to stay or not.

Accommodating Overflow Registration
Occasionally there is a last minute rush of registrants for your meeting. How do you then accommodate the added numbers when you planned for fewer? The facility itself might have been at capacity with your earlier numbers. One way to accommodate overflow is to leave more room in the back of the room for participants to stand. They take up less square footage standing rather than seated anyway.

Tell Them What You Have Done to Accommodate Them
To gain appreciation and allay criticism for what you are doing for your now oversubscribed meeting, explain in the opening session that you have provided standing room for their ease of access to each concurrent session. There are few things as frustrating as being locked out of the one concurrent you came to the meeting to attend. Give them your rationale for that "standing room" and the real space limitations. Help them to understand so that you don't have to deal with the disgruntled over lack of seats.

Let the disgruntled know that this is a judgment call. Had they been excluded from a session once the seats were filled, it reduces their flexibility in attending that session and any others that are initially filled. Often a session will empty slightly of grazers and leave room for those who have been excluded.

However, anxious staff sometimes will overplay their original order to seal the room, and not let anyone else in, even though there are seats or standing room. At times staff don't even know that seats are available inside.

Being turned away from a session that you really want to attend can be disheartening, especially when you know there are seats open and you should have gotten in. Now there is serious cause for complaint. This is especially true of sessions of special interest to you. Come to the meeting and miss those, and you may not care to come next year. Standing room in the back accommodates many more than the "chairs only" approach.

In some venues, the fire marshal is especially active. So, if you are going to leave standing space in a room for which the fire code specifies a limit, find out what applies to seated only, or total bodies under any condition. For example, what is the "banquet" limit on the room?

Gain Additional Space: Scale Down the Water/Refreshment Table
In a breakout room, the refreshment table is often 3 x 6 feet, or 18 square feet. Most participants will not dehydrate during a 90 minute session. In fact many people carry their own water bottle anyway. And if they were in danger of dehydration, they could easily step out in the hall, where the water table would not restrict 18 square feet of standees from benefiting from the presentation.

As a half-way concession to those standing, scale down the water table to 6' x 1.5', or place it in the corner to save space, or the water in an urn on a 3 x 3 table. You can also provide a free standing ice tub with water bottles, though that solution is not "green." The AT&T Training Center at the University of Texas at Austin has standup water towers recessed into the walls in the hallways with cup dispenser on the side – total space occupied, about one square foot.

Take Time to Fill the Chairs
At the beginning of the program, usher people to the open chairs, especially those in the middle of rows. Ask that they sit there. Be flexible with those who really do want to keep their options open by standing. There are many reasons people would prefer to stand rather than sit. However, the concerted effort to seat people will help to fill the interior chairs.

In your plan to get people into the room and seated, include:
- Move Furniture, Plants, Stanchions and obstacle from potential standing room.
- Designate session hosts to keep aisles and fire exits clear.
- Provide maps of the facility and visible traffic signs.
- Develop a contingency plan for assisting the wheel chair mobile.

What Do We Do With Sparse Numbers in a Large Room?
The dynamics of the meeting may depend heavily on whether the group is compacted, tightened up, or not. Regarding group dynamics, Harvey MacKay said, "It's the room size." Getting people to rub shoulders and concentrate in a more targeted section of an auditorium can provide higher energy and a more uniform dynamic for the speech or meeting. Participants scattered throughout a large room feel little cohesiveness or sense of being a group. Group energy fragments and disperses rather than building up. So, one way to deal with this and contain the energy is to "tighten the room." Bring the people together.

In large auditoria, when the participants are dwarfed by the volume of seats, cordon off the section used for seating, or bring in screens or portable dividers to section off that portion of the seating. Clearly directing people, for example, to sit only in the bottom left corner of the seating section will provide definition as well.

State of the Art Seating Arrangements

SEATING MATTERS

Tightening the Room
Typical groups will seat themselves in straight rows, somewhere from the third row back from the front. Pastors say this is typical church seating as well. However, a widely dispersed group, spread among the full breadth of seats, can provide a definite challenge for the presenter to keep rotating around from right to left in order to pay attention to each participant. If you are that speaker, then know whether you have a tendency to look more at one side of the room or the other. Then concentrate on sharing your eye contact with everyone.

Short Set The Room
Bob Chesney, speaker and video producer, contends that sales people especially know the value in "packing in" participants in a compact space. That improves the dynamic markedly. In fact he short set a room, providing fewer chairs than the anticipated number of participants. That way every chair gets occupied before additional chairs are added. This ensures there is no need to wrestle, cajole, block out, or muscle people out of back rows to fill up the front.

Other assists to getting people to move to the front include:
- Meet them at the door and request they move forward.
- Place signage in each aisle that requests they "fill the front seats."
- Put up a power point slide that requests they sit in the front.
- Turn off the overhead lights in the back.
- Open with an exercise that requires them to sit with new people in a pre-designated area.
- Cordon off the back section with duct tape, rope or string.
- Prominently place handouts on the chairs in the front of the room.
- Assure them that there will be breaks during the program during which they can exit the session if they choose.
- Let them know you will start once they move up and fill in chairs in front.

Meet them Half Way
Another way to tighten the room is to recognize that the front rows will not be filled. So, the presenter simply walks back on the floor to the row where participants are seated, and makes that the front row for the presentation. Removing the front row then becomes one option. If there are no impediments between the presenter and the first row of audience, the presenter can stand as close as 6-8 feet, or on a riser of adequate elevation to be seen by the entire group. However, the proximity to the audience is still 6-8 feet.

Establishing Proprietary Interest in "Your Seat"
U.S. audiences are very proprietary about their seating. If they sat in one seat in an auditorium for a full day workshop or meeting, they tend to think they have taken possession of that seat, and will return to it as if it were assigned. When that seat is then restricted, or changed, the norm is broken and they may respond with some resistance, even hostility.

SEATING MATTERS

Rope Off the Back Section
Professional speaker, Michael P. McKinley, CSP, CPAE, restricts the seating area in the back rows right from the beginning, expanding the area as it fills in. He will cordon off seats at the back of the room with stanchions, a string, or tape. He may then observe how audience members react and notes their comments. Since Mike McKinley does sessions on managing change, his changing their seating evokes telling attitudes and fresh material for how the group members actually deal with change. He makes it part of the act and utilizes the environment in the learning exercises.

Safety tape of the type used by police at crime scene investigations carries an implicit sense of authority. Use it to close off the sections that dissipate your audience.

Air Wall Off the Back
If an air wall can be drawn midway across the room, or toward the back one-third of the room, you have increased control over seating. Set the area behind the air wall. Then, only when the front of the room is filled, you can open the air wall to reveal additional seating in the back.

The Outsider: The Energy Drain
We have already addressed the need to have everyone seated within a certain definable circumference in the room, lest they be disruptive by taking a position outside the circle. Those who sit outside the inner circle not only can leech the energy of the group, but draw attention outside to themselves, becoming a distraction. That breaks up the coherent dynamics of the inner group.

Every time an outsider interacts, he drains energy from the meeting. On occasion this person is registering his protest at having to attend the meeting at all, is expressing his noncommittal stance, or is passively resistant. He enjoys an attention getting or power position. And you may just have to put up with him. In the best of all worlds, he would move within the circle and contribute from that position.

Nudging Them to the Front
Audience members are more likely to occupy the front row of the room without prompting when the room is set in a curved row setup. They are, as stated, also more likely and more able to both approach and to fill in chairs in the front of the room even after the presentation has started without being disruptive. A major advantage of curved row seating with flared aisles is that you can enter the room and walk to the front row or stage without blocking anyone's view.

Chapters 5 through 8 have addressed mainly the larger keynote or general session. Chapter 9 deals more specifically with the smaller meeting, under 350 participants. The principles up to this point have been applicable to both small and large meetings. The next principle applies to the small meeting only.

State of the Art Seating Arrangements

SEATING MATTERS

Chapter 9

Principle 5:

Place the Last Row on the Back Wall

This chapter deals with ensuring small audience safety and access, and traffic flow in crowded concurrent sessions by placing the back row on the back wall. It all has to do with safety.

Principle #5: Set The Back Row on the Back Wall
Of all the seating principles, this one is the most narrowly applied specifically for safety purposes. It is meant to be applied in the smaller meeting room where aisle space may be limited for quick exit.

In a small meeting room filled to capacity, there is often a premium on space utilization. By moving the last row back to the back wall, you improve and secure the use of the space in front of that row to remain as aisle space in the event of an emergency. The only downside, and it is very slight, is that the row on the back wall is a few feet farther from the presentation.

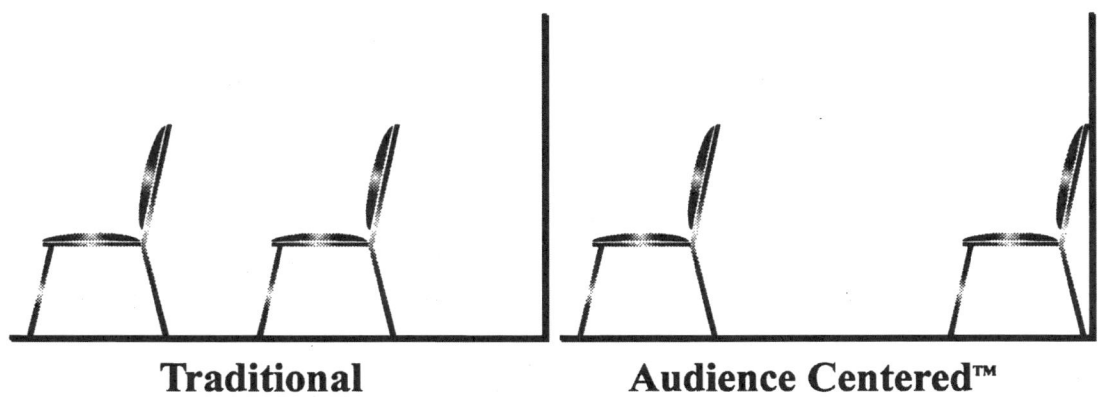

State of the Art Seating Arrangements

SEATING MATTERS

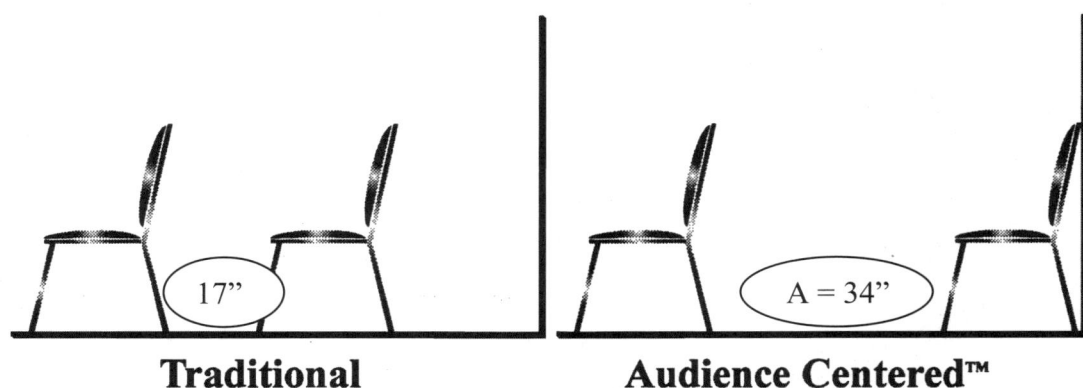

Traditional   **Audience Centered™**

The space in front of the back row provides an aisle walkway [designated with space A=34 on the right above]. The space separating the last row and the next row toward the front of the room is now some 34 inches, the width of 2 regular rows. That last row acquires extra aisle space for access and egress, or stretching out legs during the session as you would on the bulkhead seats or emergency row on an airplane.

With the last row set on the back wall, those chairs are quite likely to stay put in case of any rapid or emergency exit from the room. They are less likely to be tipped over, to be pulled out, or migrate out into the aisle.

Let us look for a moment at what space would be likely to be left were we to leave the usual 17 inches between the last and second to last row. There would then be one 17 inch passageway available between the back row and the back wall. In the event of rapid or emergency exit, chairs would likely be in disarray, blocking up some of that 17 inch passageway.

However, with the back row on the back wall, and a 34 inch aisle in front of the very last row, even with the second to last row in disarray, there should be some aisle space available for exiting the room. With 34 inches between the second to last and the back row, even when the front chair is shoved back, there is still room to negotiate the aisle.

Space Utilization: Devoted Space vs. Dedicated Space
There are two kinds of space utilization within a meeting room, Flexible and Inflexible.

    I.   Flexible Space: Adaptable
        Devoted space is generally more flexible, for the space itself is set aside for specific functions. For example, there are two active devoted functions of an open space between rows in a meeting room.

SEATING MATTERS

1. One function of an open space is an aisle four feet or wider that provides mobility in access and egress for a large number of the audience to get to and from a portion of the room and to specific seating sections. That space is essential and devoted. Use beyond serving as an aisle, access and egress, is limited by fire code.

2. The second function of open space is solely for access to the chairs within a row in that seating section…space dedicated to ease of access and egress for a limited number of people between rows is essential and devoted. This space is also used as leg room before and during a presentation.

The foot space used to allow access to one chair in a row may also provide the clearance essential for stretching out legs during a presentation. However, the initial and basic function of that space is to get people in and out of the 3rd to 6th chairs within a row. So, unless that space can be better utilized in another way, you do not want to devote more than 16-17 inches clearance in between rows. Super-sized, XXL [not simply Large] participants might require more given space.

Enough clearance always needs be available for someone seated to be able to allow someone accessing or leaving a chair to pass in front of her or him without everyone vacating the row. The fewer the people that have to be passed in front of, the less space that needs be allowed between rows, for the inconvenience is less when there are fewer people passing in front of those already seated.

II. Inflexible Space: By Prior Decision, a Fixture
Dedicated space means that there is a certain fixedness of function or inflexible permanence of use designated for that space. For example, the room might be tiered on several levels as in a lecture hall. The chairs and tables might be permanently bolted to the floor. That space is definitely dedicated. The remainder of factors, for example, type and shape of table might be negotiable. But the chairs and tables become fixtures when fixed in place.

The trick then becomes how to optimize and safeguard the use of space that is already devoted to one function.

Many set-up men gauge the distance between rows by tipping forward a chair from the newly set back row. The top of the chair is leaned forward until it touches the top of the chair directly in front of it. That is how the spacing is typically determined. The tipped chair is then placed exactly where it rocks back on the front legs. However, the distance between rows using this method of spacing comes to 22 inches for the standard sized stackable chairs like those illustrated above.

SEATING MATTERS

> *The amount of space required between rows to accommodate long legs and still allow people to pass through to get to their seats, is generally 17 inches from the back of the front row chair at top of chair height to the front of the seat cushion in the row behind.*
>
> *The footprint of the chair varies by chair design, often extending in front of the cushion by 1-2 inches. So use the chair seat as the point of reference, i.e., the 17" gap. The difference between 22 (tipped distance) and 17 inches (measured distance) is a cost in space of 5 inches of space per row. Over a seating section of 10 rows, that is a 50 inch loss of space, almost two additional rows of audience who are now 50 inches or 4'2" farther removed from the presentation…and adding 5 inches or more for every row.*

One website explains that 20 inches between rows is not enough; 24 inches would be better. This amounts to even more waste. And wasteful spacing diminishes seating capacity. And the added/wasted space in between rows increases the distance from the presentation for those in the increasingly distant back rows. So, to improve closeness to the presentation and seating capacity for that room, <u>close up the distance allotted between rows to 17 inches each and save space</u>. Of course you would allocate more for a National Basketball Association meeting.

As you see, the 17 inches is between the top-back of the chair in the front row to a perpendicular line rising up from the front of the chair seat in the back row.

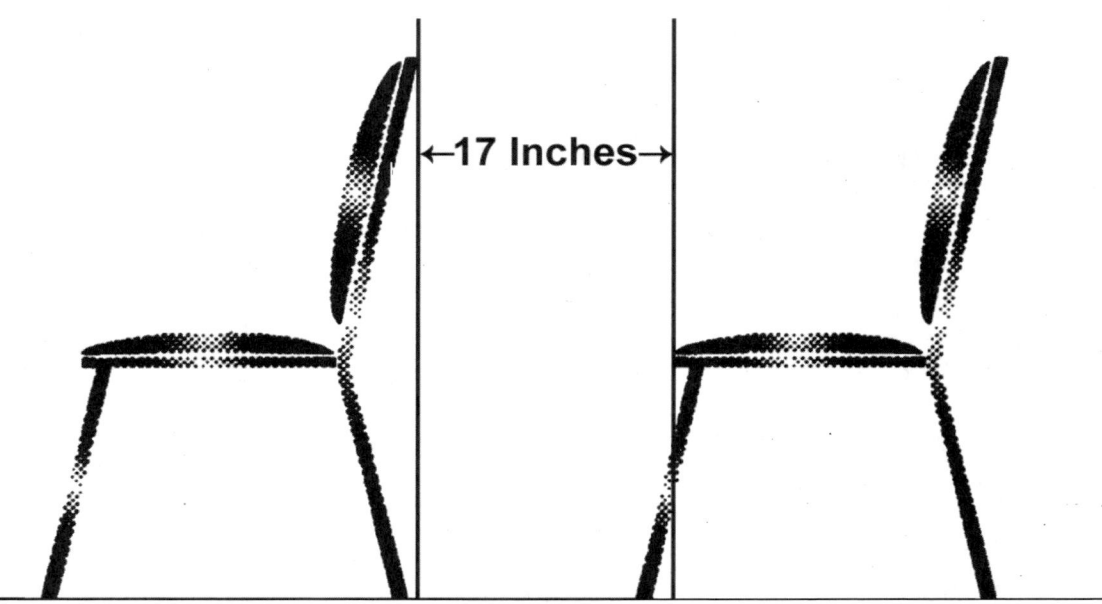

This completes our individual consideration of the five principles that optimize your meeting room set up. The remainder of the book is devoted to applications of these principles as well as to arming you with influence skills and rationales to overcome the resistance that is sure to crop up among those with whom you deal to get your requested and desired state of the art seating arrangements.

State of the Art Seating Arrangements

Part III.

Application of Principles and Refinements

Now that you are familiar with the five principles and how they can be applied, we can turn our attention to optimizing the meeting environment. For, there are other elements that go into state of the art seating arrangements and room sets that rock.

The Malleable Space
Throughout, we have been addressing the non-dedicated room, those spaces in which the seating is not bolted to the floor. And while there are many dedicated rooms that incorporate and utilize the ACS™ principles perfectly, others could have benefited by applying these principles in their initial design. They could do so now by making revisions ranging from minor to a total makeover.

Part I dealt with setting the stage in general for recognizing problems with current seating arrangements from traditional straight row to chevron.

Part II introduced the 5 principles together with applications that would remedy problems created by straight rows, as well as adjustments that would optimize opening general sessions of conventions, and larger breakout sessions, including the sliver of a ballroom.

Part III will deal with smaller meetings 350 and under, as well as board meetings. But in a more inclusive sense, smaller events may also include classroom settings, community meetings, weddings, funerals, worship services, wherever these numbers gather and sit down.

In many cases tables are part of the design. Many room sets are for working sessions that require horizontal surface for binders, workbooks, laptops and other instruments of learning. However, you find that the five seating principles apply here with the addition of tables as well. And in doing so, the principles necessitate improved coordination in the arrangement of tables as well as of chairs.

SEATING MATTERS

Meeting Room Checklist
For each item below, check to see if there is an added cost:

What is scheduled next door during the time your meeting room will be in use?
  All you need is one band rehearsal to know why this is important.

Unknowns: What follow up do you require from sales and marketing to update you?

What lighting fixtures are available and programmed from within the room?

Can lighting be controlled from within the room? Differentiated by section?

What track lights or spot lights are available for highlighting the presentation?

Where are the electrical outlets?

From where and by whom is the sound system controlled?

Can engineering program the light switches to optimize lighting?
  Who is your contact and how much lead time is required?
  Can you lay out in advance the precise focus for the spots? Use masking tape…

What is the preferred placement of the presentation?
Consider the room set next door in terms of noise carrying through the air walls.

What AV do you require? Is there a screen in place? Where would you place it? Angle?

Platforms? Height and width. Ceiling height? Screen height and width?

Staircase placement to get on platform?

What room set optimizes the learning environment for each planned event in this room during the course of one day? By when can you obtain the presenter's AV, movement, and specific requirements for AV, e.g. number of minutes utilized?

What time will the room be set? Who is the foreman for that shift? Number?

Chapter 10
Accommodating Participants in the Smaller Meeting

What Constitutes a Smaller Meeting?
We have been focusing on the keynote or general session for larger meetings, generally consisting of 350 or more participants. This chapter focuses on the smaller meeting, the breakout session, board of directors or business session set around a table, and committee meeting. Generally these meetings number 6 to 350 participants, although more could probably be accommodated under the designation of "small" meeting.

Usually one thinks of a breakout room, the subdivision of one-third, one-fourth, or one-sixth section of a full ballroom, a boardroom, even a session held in a hotel suite or conference center as constituting the smaller meeting. Whatever constitutes a smaller meeting for your facility, feel free to utilize the principles and rationale related throughout the book. They all apply.

These meetings may call for participation, audience involvement, or be established more for passive observation rather than for interaction. However, that does not mean that participants will not benefit from safety, comfort, line of sight improvements and networking opportunities. Each smaller meeting can utilize the principles already introduced for use in larger sessions, whether that meeting is set around tables, in a classroom setting, in rounds, in a theatre set or a fishbowl design.

All Five Principles Apply In the Smaller Meeting

In no way are the seating principles diminished when applied in a smaller meeting. The fifth principle alone only applies to the smaller meeting setting – "set the last row on the back wall in the smaller meeting room" to assure adequate aisle space for people to exit.

The other four principles apply as well:
1. **Set to the long side of the room. No bowling alleys.**
    You still want all participants to be close to the facilitator or chairperson.
2. **Face each chair toward the presentation. Curve all rows.**
    This can be more of a challenge when adding in tables. There is less flexibility. However, the tables are faced toward the presentation or focal point of the meeting as are the chairs.

State of the Art Seating Arrangements

SEATING MATTERS

3. **No middle aisle. Flare aisles off at 45 degrees toward the exit doors.**
   This is every bit as important with small groups as with large.
4. **Cut single chair access lanes into seating sections.**
   This practice is done slightly differently, especially with a classroom set. It involves leaving adequate space in between adjoining tables for passage between tables for access to front rows of tables and chairs. Spacing is important both length wise as well as width wise. Access to seating still requires aisles sufficient to carry the main burden of traffic in and out. But you still provide exit lanes in between tables in the same row, so that participants from the back can walk in between them to access and exit their seats up front.

You will find additional information on the application of these principles throughout the text, as well as in *the folio of large and small room seating arrangements* in Appendix A, which provides criteria for implementation. Several of those applications follow directly below.

Single Table Sets

What do we do with the $50,000 Boardroom Rectangular Table?
I have been in a number of corporate boardrooms in which the central table represents a major purchase of $50,000 to over $100,000. And usually that purchase has company history, someone's historical or emotional investment. It could be a work of art all by itself. It may be tailored to the established board room and destined to stay. No matter how many long straight sides that table has, there are some fairly economical solutions for these problematic business furniture purchases.

Mobil Oil Corporation had a circular table of exotic wood cut from a single tree and breathtakingly beautiful. No problem with that design. However, a long rectangular table in the Marriott Corporation headquarters, together with the large gray leather executive chairs limited communication in that room, made worse by bad acoustics.

One quick solution, even in that narrow room, would be to place a boat shaped or oval piece of glass over the wooden rectangular table. That reshapes and improves the seating arrangement without sacrificing the beauty of the wood grain. It would actually enhance and protect the wood. That glass cover would ensure no spilling, staining or gouging, essentially preserving the table, while improving the meeting function of the table.

Prior to dismissing your furniture as unworkable or beyond accommodation, look for the simple solution first. Let's take a look at the smaller meeting room sets with an eye to optimizing each meeting environment efficiently and economically.

SEATING MATTERS

Better Diagrams

The following shaped tables are more commonly recommended for small to medium sized boardroom meetings. Remember that rectangular tables can be topped with a glass top, smoked glass or clear glass, to attain this very shape to reconfigure the meeting. Some of these tables will comfortably accommodate 4-6, while the boat shape in the photo below is set up for 14. The multiple table sets can accommodate many more simply by adding tables, or setting extra rows.

Boat Shape

Shaped somewhat like a skiff, rounded on the long sides and flat at each end. The rounded long sides bow out in the middle so that everyone along each side can see each other. There is seldom room for more than 2 at either flat end. So, sight lines are open.

Oblong

This shaped table has no straight sides, and therefore accommodates all those seated around it to clear sight lines to each other.

State of the Art Seating Arrangements

SEATING MATTERS

Choose on Principle and for Setup Variations

When previewing a facility or purchasing tables for your own facility, contract for tables that promote interpersonal contact, reduce strain, have a basic curve that promotes interaction, support adequate horizontal work space, and which may be able to be configured into multiple table sets in which they will also promote or be adaptable to the seating principles.

Multiple Table Sets

Standard Board Room

In most facilities, you will be given a standard board room rectangular table set. In the one in the illustration below, you will note that those on the long sides of the table are limited in the number of other participants blocked from view in their own row. Anyone seated on the long side would not be able to see 6-7 persons in their own row. In a meeting of 22 total, someone in the long row would be missing visual contact with at least one third of those in attendance!

With a simple bowing out of the middle of the three tables in the rectangular set and pulling each adjoining table out to connect with the bowed-out tables, you would reconfigure the set from rectangular to an oval board room set. Now, everyone can see everyone. Now you have a meeting.

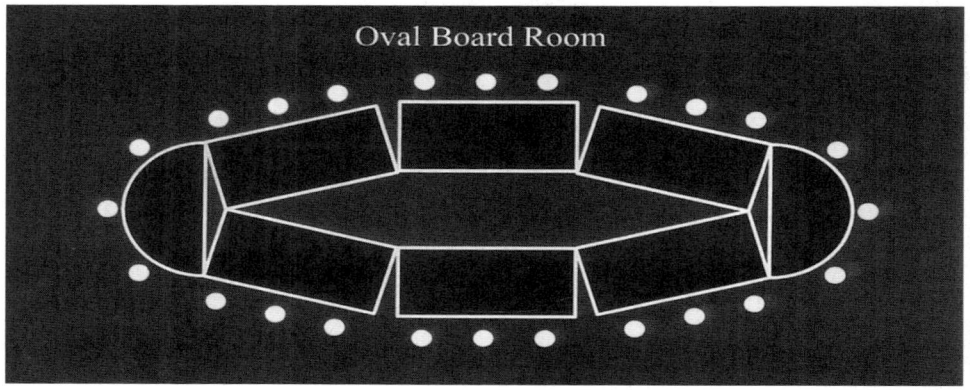

State of the Art Seating Arrangements

SEATING MATTERS

The half rounds are one way to "round" off the formerly rectangular set. However, lacking the half-rounds, or hemispherical tables, you can as easily seat one or two individuals at the ends of the rectangular tables in the design above. Another way is to find a short rectangular table at each end in place of the hemi-spherical table. Use it to block off the end, and place 1-2 persons at each table.

The Hollow Square Set

As a reminder, the problem with straight row sets is that unless you endure some strain, you cannot see people beyond those next to you in the same row. This problem is spelled out by the shaded participants on the left side of the hollow square. Here four participants at the meeting cannot be seen while one is seated.

So, in a larger meeting set around a hollow square box set with 14 persons to a side, you would be able to see only 1 to 2 people in your own row. Counting yourself in the total number present, you would be out of touch with a minimum of 11 people in your own row. That is 79-86% of the people in your row, and 19% to 21% of the total meeting participants missing from view! So, if it is important that people see each other, this set has to be revised.

SEATING MATTERS

You will find two alternatives to the hollow square in the following illustration:
1. The diamond for narrower rooms
2. The hexagon for more squared off rooms

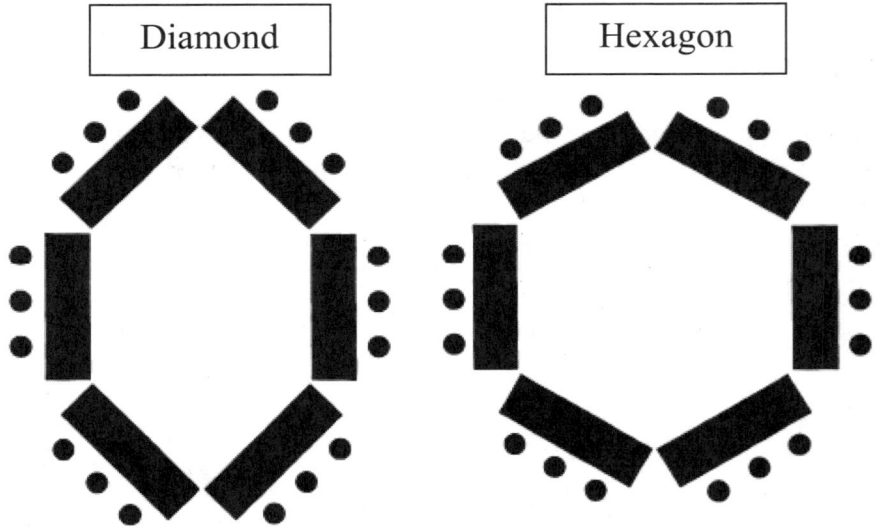

The Hollow U Set

By simply removing one of the narrower ends of the Hollow Square, you have set a Hollow U, which brings all the same problems as the Hollow Square. And these are the same problems that exist anytime you have a straight row set. You simply cannot see everyone in your row unless some are unduly tall, they stand up when they speak, or pull their chairs out and away from the table. But you will still have a problem seeing each one of them at any given time.

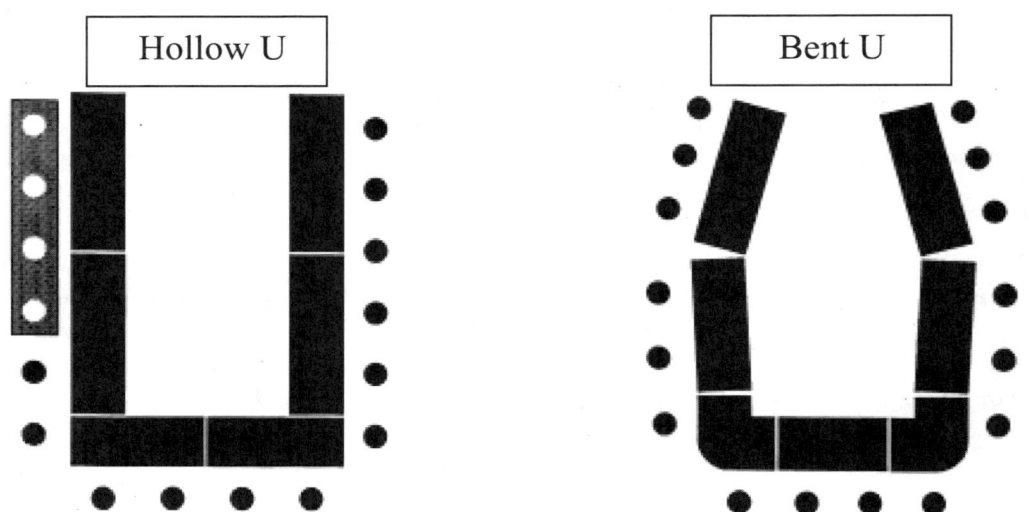

State of the Art Seating Arrangements

SEATING MATTERS

You can revise the Hollow U to a Bent U, even when made up of rectangular tables, i.e., a Hollow Square with one side taken out or not filled in. Simply bow out the table on the long sides of the U. This set is not going to look as nice upon entering the room, but it functions better. For, each person seated at the Bent U will be able to see everyone else. Form gives in to functionality. And the Bent U would fit under the general title of a Hollow U set. Only, you know the difference it makes.

Even better for the U-shape setup is to set it in a real U shape or horseshoe. That involves simply bowing the tables in that shape, even if they do not line up directly with the next tables. You could place a curved table, usually used only for standing receptions, at each corner of the horseshoe. You could also approximate the shape of the horseshoe by buying various 30, 45, and 60 degree table extenders for a continuous curved surface. And another possibility includes the trapezoidal shaped table, that can be linked together with regular 6 x 1.5 foot tables, shown below.

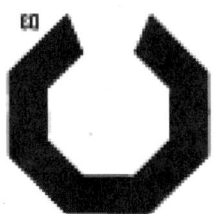

Trapezoidal U Works Well
The U made up of trapezoidal tables – actually an octagon with one side taken out – shows the versatility of that table, and the neatness of design when matched up with other trapezoidal tables.

The best basic table for classroom is a trapezoid, because it allow for joining the tables together, even while curling toward the presentation. Rectangular tables would leave little pie slices of empty spaces between them. And while you can purchase pieces to add to the ends of the rectangular tables, these two methods of smoothing out the design are both considerably more expensive. If I were in charge of purchasing, I would make sure that I had a percentage of my tables as trapezoids.

A Most Versatile Table: Trapezoidal
Shiela Guay of Bryant College reported, "Our conference rooms are going to be refurbished soon and we will most likely buy trapezoid tables. They were what our architect suggested all along. I kept laughing at him and thought they were weird. Now I see that they make sense."

Trapezoidal Tables Work Best
For sheer versatility and flexibility in design, the trapezoidal table can provide you a number of sets that remain elegant (form) and efficient (function). While generally more expensive than rectangular tables, the multiple uses justify the purchase of several to accommodate designs such as the circular effect of the figure below in which rectangular and trapezoidal tables are alternated, far superior to an all rectangular classroom set that follows several pages below.

State of the Art Seating Arrangements

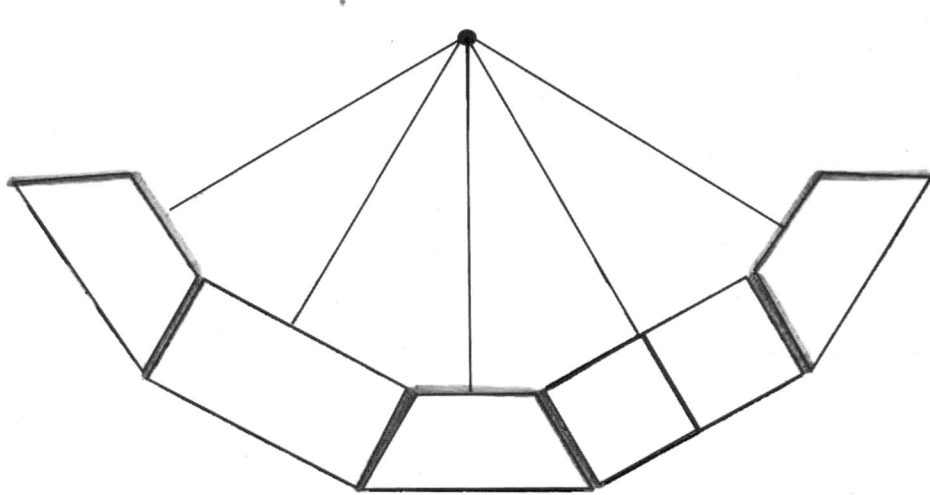

Simple, Economical Improvements of Current Sets

Often a working meeting of 15-50 individuals will be placed in a horseshoe or U-shape in a large room, or hollow square set with straight tables and 2-3 persons per table. These sets involve extended straight row sets on several or all sides. So they fall short of what we could truly recommend.

Even when the set seems limited by and dependent upon the equipment provided by the facility, it can be adapted as is. No additional purchases are necessary. For example, in an elongated U-Shape, really a box with one side out, one can simply ask participants toward the middle of each side to slide back their chairs and round out the long straight row, even without moving the table. Now everyone can see each other.

To make the set-up more workable, you can simply pull and round the tables out as well. This usually involves unlinking the tablecloths and letting them drape over each single table rather than overlapping with the next table(s).

The True Horseshoe Set

Taking the Hollow U a step further would involve moving to a true Horseshoe set. This involves angling the tables initially, or setting the "shoulders" of the U with the crescent shaped tables that are most often reserved only for receptions.

Generally, and most economical spatially, the 6 x 1.5 foot table is a staple item in the inventory and daily usage of most facilities. If you can tolerate the minor gaps in form that result from shaping rectangular tables into a horseshoe, you have already accomplished a major improvement at no additional cost with function over form.

SEATING MATTERS

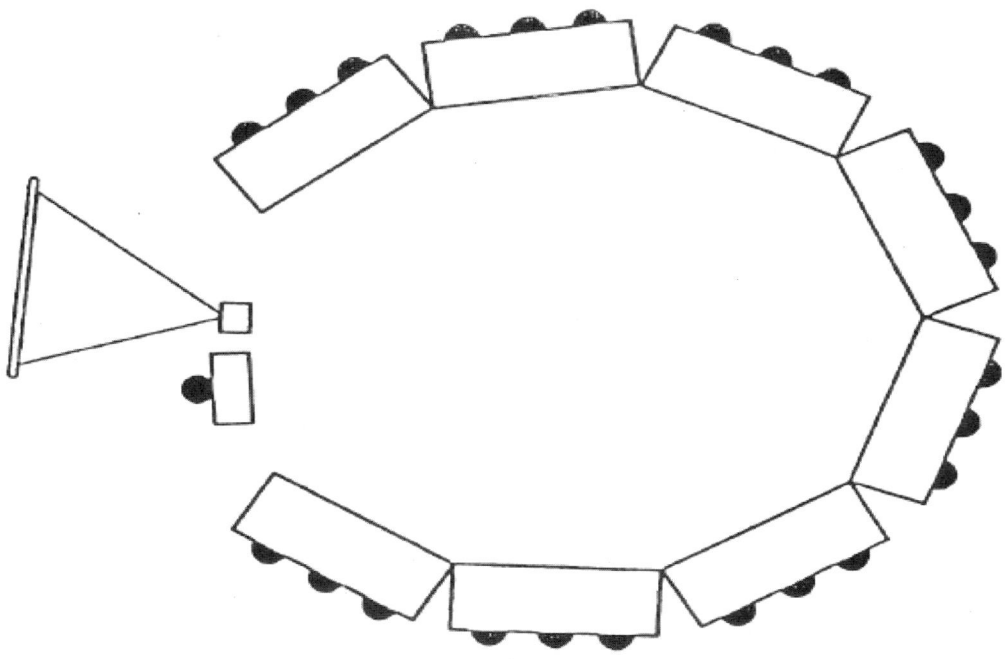

n.b. *One word of warning to the presenter in a True Horseshoe set is the following: The energy that can come off the ends of the set may be very high. Think horseshoe magnet. Some have experienced a flow of energy that made them giddy. If the presenter is not well grounded, the energy output might be destabilizing. On the plus side, the presenter can step inside the horseshoe and be in much closer and more intimate contact with each participant. The presenter can stay away from the ends of the tables and walk inside the circumference of the horseshoe.*

The Usual Classroom Set Up Table

The most common set-up table measures 1.5 feet by 6 feet. It is easy to move, and accommodates 3 participants easily; 2 when notebooks are in use. You have a photo of the classroom setup below, similar to the diagram of a classroom setup for a slightly larger room, also below. In each case, the table (like a bow) is aimed directly at the determined focal point for the presentation.

State of the Art Seating Arrangements

SEATING MATTERS

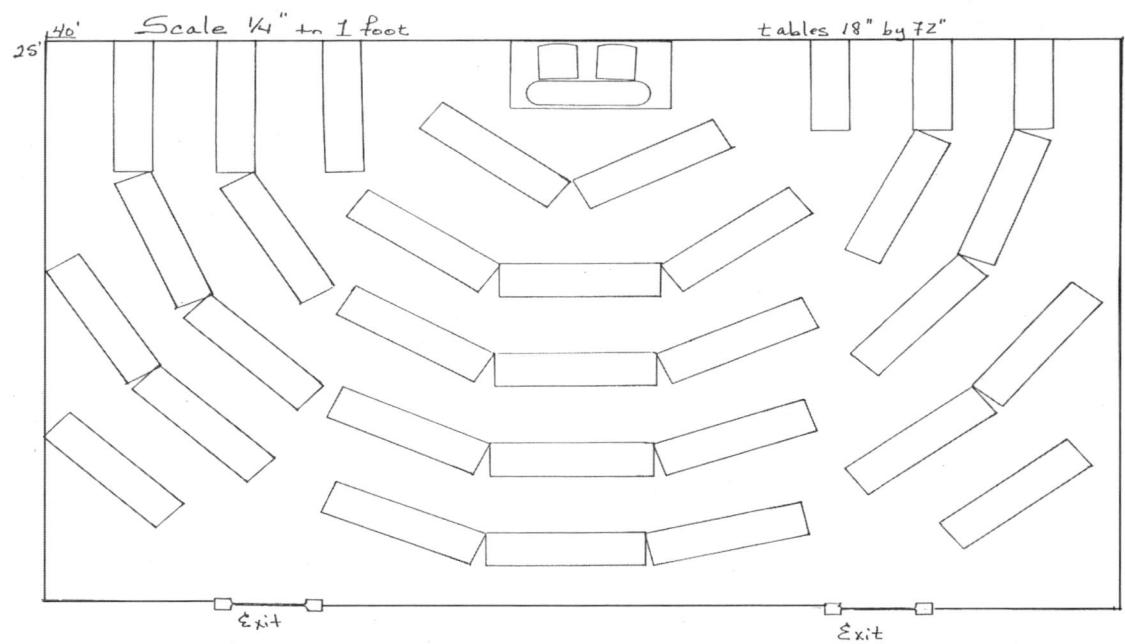

The Classroom Set

State of the Art Seating Arrangements

SEATING MATTERS

"The Coffin" Board Room Set

The coffin Board Meeting set-up by the Pennsylvania Credit Union Association illustrated below accommodates 29 participants. This set utilizes both 8 foot and 6 foot tables to accomplish this unique design. And it works for them.

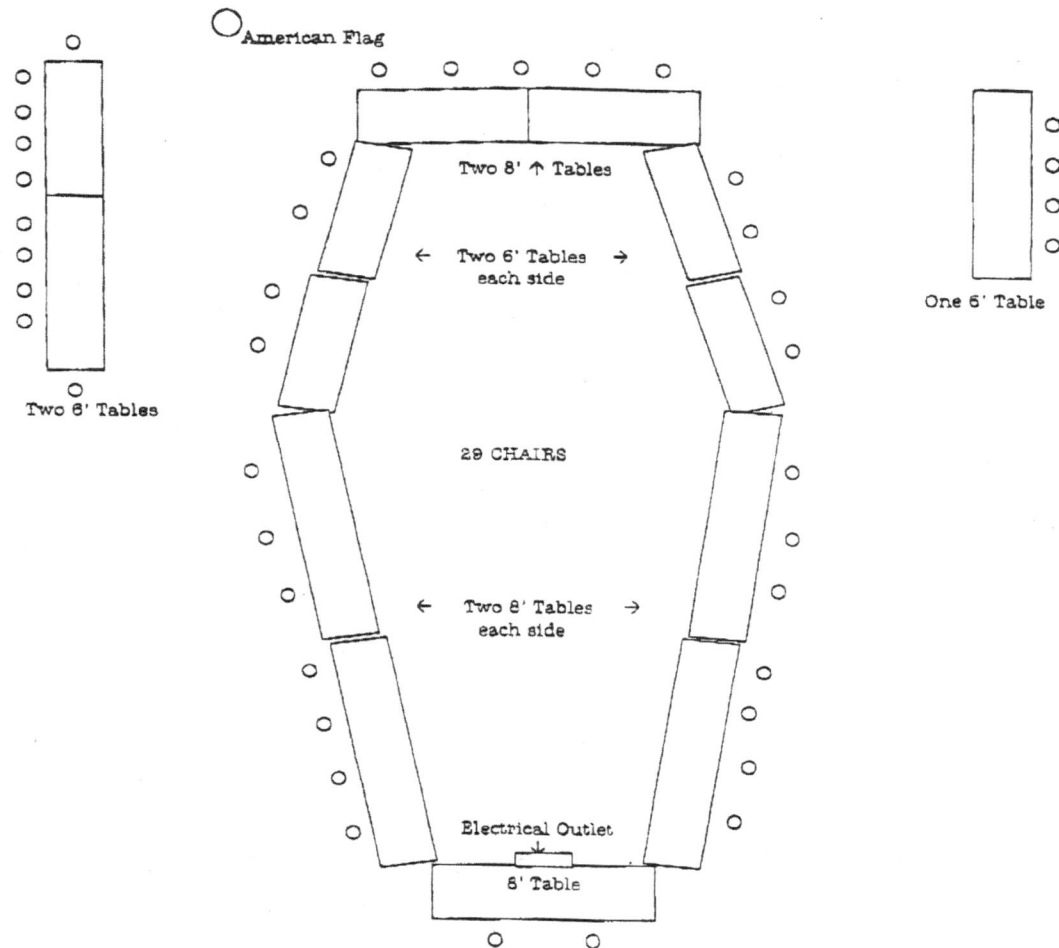

Rounds

Seating in rounds is now a popular set. It generally works especially well when the same space is used for meals and for presentations. It may require a bit more space to accommodate the round tables, but that is made up for in convenience. There is room for group exercises, space to lay out workbooks, to confer over designs, and sufficient room to accommodate an entire flip chart sheet to write on. The ten person round is a good set for 7-8, so that those 2-3 whose backs would be to the presentation do not have to turn around to see. It also provides a sight line opening toward the presentation for those at the back of the table, unless the presentation will be elevated on a platform or screen.

State of the Art Seating Arrangements

SEATING MATTERS

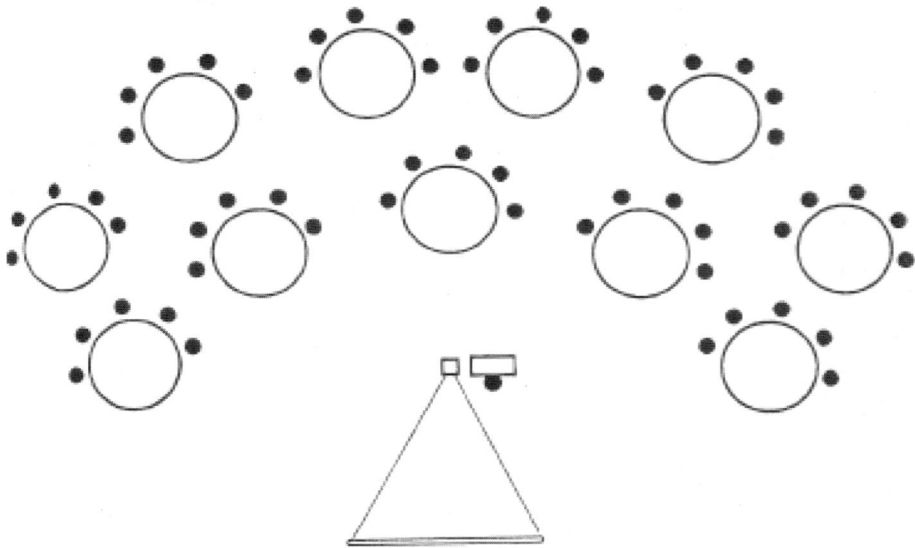

Setting in Rounds – Not All It's Cracked Up To Be!
In pointing out the following problem with rounds, we will also show how to overcome those limitations. But first the situation.

Picture a large convention center ballroom set in row upon straight row of rounds, with a center aisle up the middle. There is at least one microphone in the middle of that aisle for Q & A. Each table is set 2-3 chairs under capacity so that each table member can basically face the presentation while it is going on, then easily shift her chair back for table conversation. However, there are several problems with this rounds set that requires elaboration.

The first of two glaring problems is that the aisle up the middle drains energy and makes it very difficult to present from floor level without turning totally from side to side, and turning one's back on the other half of the room. The second major problem is the distance between presentation/presenter and audience members.

The larger the round table, the more dead space it takes up that adds nothing to the event. The middle of that table does several things:
1. It makes it more likely that people at the table will break off into smaller discussion groupings at the table unless there is a pre-designated facilitator. The larger the round table, the more likely this is to happen.

2. Rounds also require more overall distance in between tables in order for other participants to be able to access their seats and leave the room during an event when everyone is seated. Participants tend to move their chairs out somewhat more from the periphery of a circular table than they do with a rectangular table.

3. A 10 foot round may accommodate 8 or more people easily. However, each succeeding table, also allowing room for traffic flow, and granting this repetitious dead space in the middle of the table, is that much farther back from the presentation. Much of that additional distancing is an accommodation required by the table shape, not to the function it adds to the event.

Limitations of Rounds

A Room Set Straight Across in Rounds Hinders Contact with Participants
One slight improvement to this situation places the rounds in an arc or circular arrangement around the presentation as diagrammed above. Setting the tables in an arc allows the occupants of each table to see others in the room more easily. However, rounds lined up in straight rows present the same obstacles as any other straight row, even if somewhat less restrictive than traditional theatre style, or classroom set in straight across the room lines.

One improvement with the arc or curving the rows of rounds is to leave sufficient room between the rows toward the back to accommodate traffic going to the restroom during meetings and meals, with easy passage all the way directly toward the back doors for a full group exodus.

When set in a straight row of rounds, microphones for Q & A are set in the middle aisle mid-room and the mid-point of the back seating section. This puts those posing questions out there in the middle of the aisle all by themselves. And they place themselves in a potentially unsupported, vulnerable and confrontational center aisle exchange with the presenter. Placing the microphones on what would be flared aisles with at least 4 feet between chairs, makes one less estranged from the group, less out there all alone, by themselves while asking questions. Questioners get a sense of being more supported by those on either side of the aisle, as well as less confrontational toward the presenter.

Starburst Superiority
The "sunburst" rectangular table seating design that follows is superior in several ways to rounds – and here we are talking about a 3 x 6 or 3 x 8 foot rectangular table:
1. Less room is required for traffic between tables, so space is more efficiently used and more participants can be accommodated. Less dead space.
2. There are no edges jutting out between tables. And you could add 2-3 more people to the six foot tables pictured in the starburst design below.

True, there is the issue of straight rows when putting 3 or more on a rectangular table side. However, with a suggestion from the presenter, the person or persons in the middle of the long side can slide their chairs back slightly so that everyone can see each other. The more intimate distance facilitates exchange. And the person on the end of the table may or may not occupy a status position.

SEATING MATTERS

The Starburst

Given strictly rectangular tables, the starburst design provides a ready set-up for small group discussion and also clear viewing of the presentation. Each table is "aimed" directly at the presentation, narrow side forward. This provides easy viewing by those in each side of the table as well as the person at the "head" of the table. If there is someone seated at the "foot" of the table, s/he will have to turn around to view the presentation.

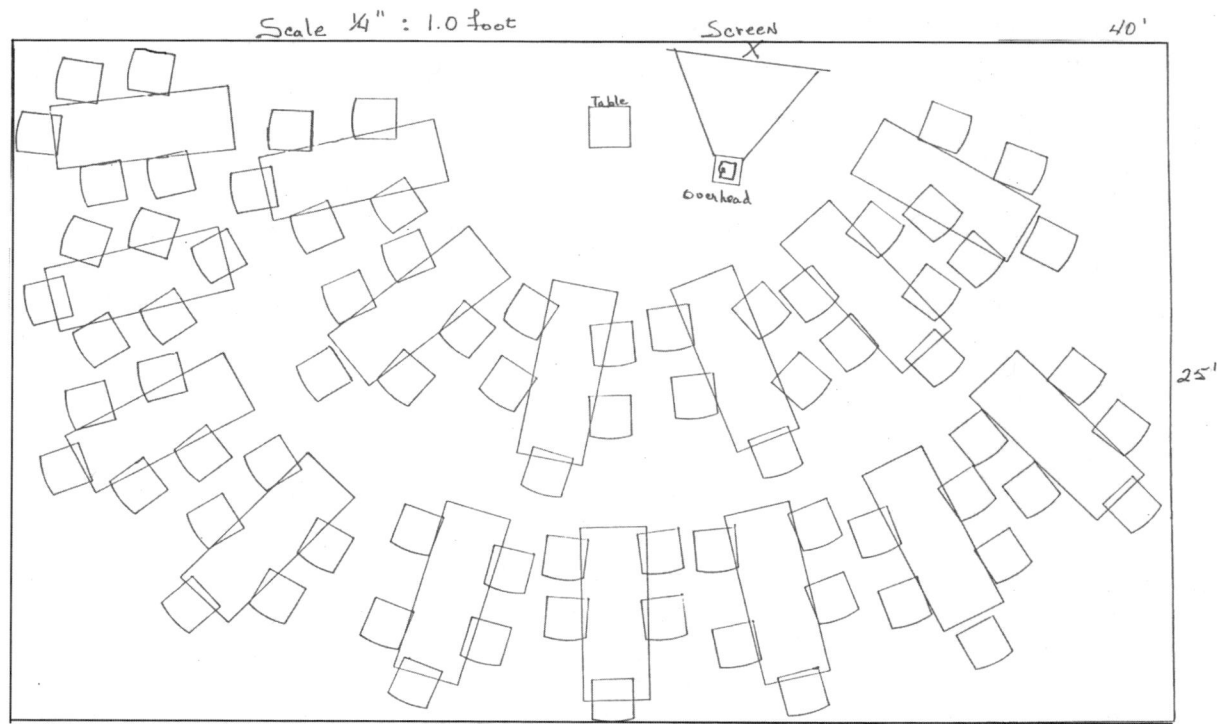

This set was used effectively at HSMAI Affordable Meetings in Washington, D.C. for a presentation in which the presenter walked around among the tables and interacted very effectively with the participants. There was an ease about his moving around, and participants seemed to be fully engaged throughout without suffering the typical school kid reticence. The movement also prevented the typical neck fatigue from screwing your head around for a long period of time. Line of sight was not a problem from any table. You would leave about an additional foot between tables as set above, to accommodate presenter mobility.

Fish Bowl Set: Community Meetings

Occasionally you will have a small group holding a highly participatory session with those in attendance being represented and participating actively. Note that there is room for AV equipment in the front of the room. Those represented may sit right behind their representative, who holds the primary role of spokesperson for the group. If there is need for the rep. to consult with the group, or someone wants to provide input to the representative, the meeting can call a brief pause for consultation, and the group is strategically positioned right behind the rep. for immediate contact.

State of the Art Seating Arrangements

SEATING MATTERS

On other occasions, there will be no interaction with the represented group, or the entire group may be watching a presentation or a demonstration or role play. When those outside the fishbowl are simply observing the proceedings, they are not only privy to the fishbowl deliberations, but also to the dynamics of the entire group. This maintains a common information base for the entire group.

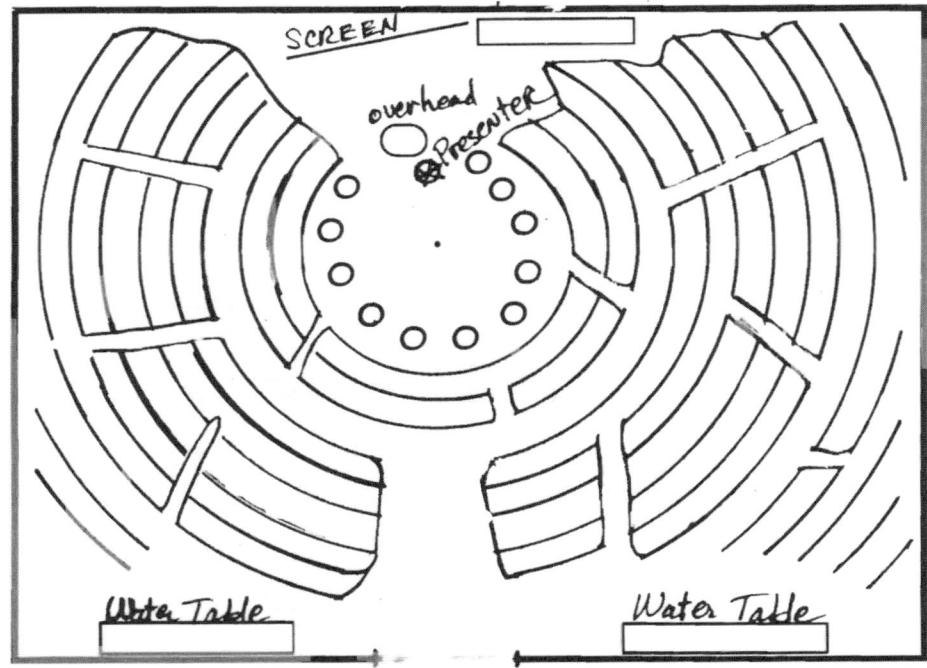

The design immediately above is slightly elliptical, providing a little separation between what can be "fishbowl" deliberants in the middle, and those on the outsides. This will also serve well for observation and not interaction. Drawing the audience into the interaction by a closer setting, they will feel more a part of it. They are breathing the same air, bringing intimacy to the exchange.

Summary and Conclusion
You can see that considerations for single and multiple table designs face some of the same issues as a regular chair set up, especially regarding the dynamics or lack thereof from straight row seating. That seems to be a major concern in improving multiple table set ups.

Even when you have a less than favorable room set-up, you can frequently make it better by selectively applying one or more of the 5 principles with the factors you will meet in the hints throughout for "fine tuning" the room.

What follows is a chapter on fine tuning the room, considering the points that make a big difference. Bear in mind that we have been providing tips that could have been saved for this chapter throughout the book. However, we are only now including those items that did not easily fit into the flow of other chapters.

State of the Art Seating Arrangements

SEATING MATTERS

State of the Art Seating Arrangements

SEATING MATTERS

Chapter 11

Fine Tune the Room

Determining the Focal Point

What Constitutes the Presentation?
Before you can determine how to face your set-ups toward a presentation, there are several criteria you will want to consider in determining the span or focal point of the presentation. The questions you will want to ask in choosing room arrangements include:
- **What are we looking at?**
- **What part of the stage will the presenter(s) occupy?**
- **How will the presenter move on stage? Over what portion of the stage?**
- **Will there be power point or other audio visuals?**
- **Where can the screen be placed? Is it recessed in the ceiling?**
- **For what amount of time will the screen be in use at any one time?**

Add in a Screen
We will work with the example of a screen to the right of the speaker, as you are viewing the presentation from the audience. Without a screen, the seating would be focused totally on the speaker. However, when you add in the screen support, such as for a power point presentation, you want to know for how much of the presentation the power point will be on. If it is a matter of 5-10 minutes at a time, you might choose the room set as if there were only the speaker to consider as the focal point. Most people can turn their heads for that time, or stand up against the wall.

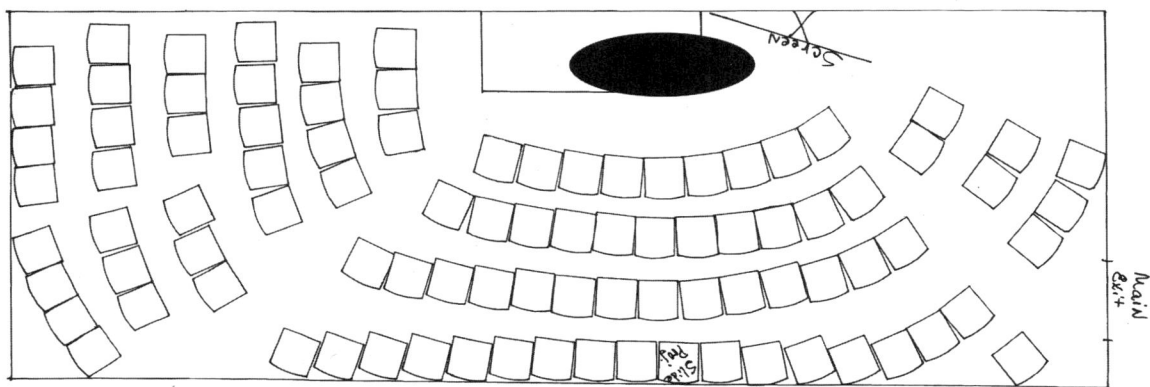

However, if the power point runs for the entire presentation, then you would consider the focal point for the room set to be a soft focus [vs. tight focus] somewhere between <u>the speaker and the screen</u> as defined by the oval above. The size of the room is also a factor.

State of the Art Seating Arrangements

In the narrow sliver of a ballroom shown above, the seating set-up soft focuses close to where the oval is drawn. Clearly, you would angle the seating more directly to face the oval. You can place the chairs on the extreme right to within 22 degrees of the screen to afford ease of viewing and reading the entire screen. If that seems too tight an angle, set it up and check it out for yourself. You will be surprised how close you can come to it.

Calculating Presenter Range of Motion & Viewing Time by the Audience
When setting up the seating, keep in mind several variables to benefit the audience members:
> Place the chair in order to keep them facing directly at the overall presentation for as much of the event as possible.
>
> Place the chairs in a direction, taking into consideration the amount of time visuals will occupy the screen. With a brief 5-12 minute visual presentation, audience members can tolerate a much greater neck turn than they could if the visual will continue beyond that period of time.
>
> Consider the size of the audience and how many of the members will requires some degree of amplification of image as well as sound. For a venue the size of the New Orleans Convention Center main ballroom, that site requires two additional projection screens to sufficiently enlarge the featured speaker to be seen by everyone in the audience.

Presenter Range of Motion
We have already devoted considerable attention to this factor, when addressing the issue of how to focus the audience, split the distance between presenter and visual screen. Then you would average out the focal point between live presenter and visual complements.

Screen Height
Bruce Harris set many large general sessions with straight rows. Bruce states that in order for participants to see the screens, they should begin at a minimum height of 4 feet off the ground, level with the front row. Then, for every additional 15 feet a participant is seated back and farther away from the screen, you elevate the screen 4 inches. So, for a room in which the back row is set 45 feet from the screen, the screen should be set at least 4 feet 8 inches off the floor.

Sight Lines

Columns, Cameras, and Other Obstructions
Sight lines can be blocked by predictable elements in the presentation. So, how do you set the room to provide everyone with lines of sight? First you need to know the range of movement of the presenter or presentations. If there is a large panel, or a choir on stage, then you have to align the seating to include the full range of presenters. Draw a line from

SEATING MATTERS

the edge of the presentation, e.g. stage left side of the choir back to the right front of the column (when seen from the stage). Then draw a straight line from the stage right extreme of the choir back to the left front of the column and straight back. These two lines form an "X" on the diagram. The inner portion of the X behind the column will have at least partially obstructed sight lines to the choir for anyone placed behind that column. So, use that space behind the column as an aisle. At least, do not place any chairs behind the X portion behind the column.

The "V" space set, below, shows how the tables have been placed in order to stay within the sight lines. The crossed lines to the stage clear the area behind the column (small black mark behind the table, to clarify sight lines for the back tables.

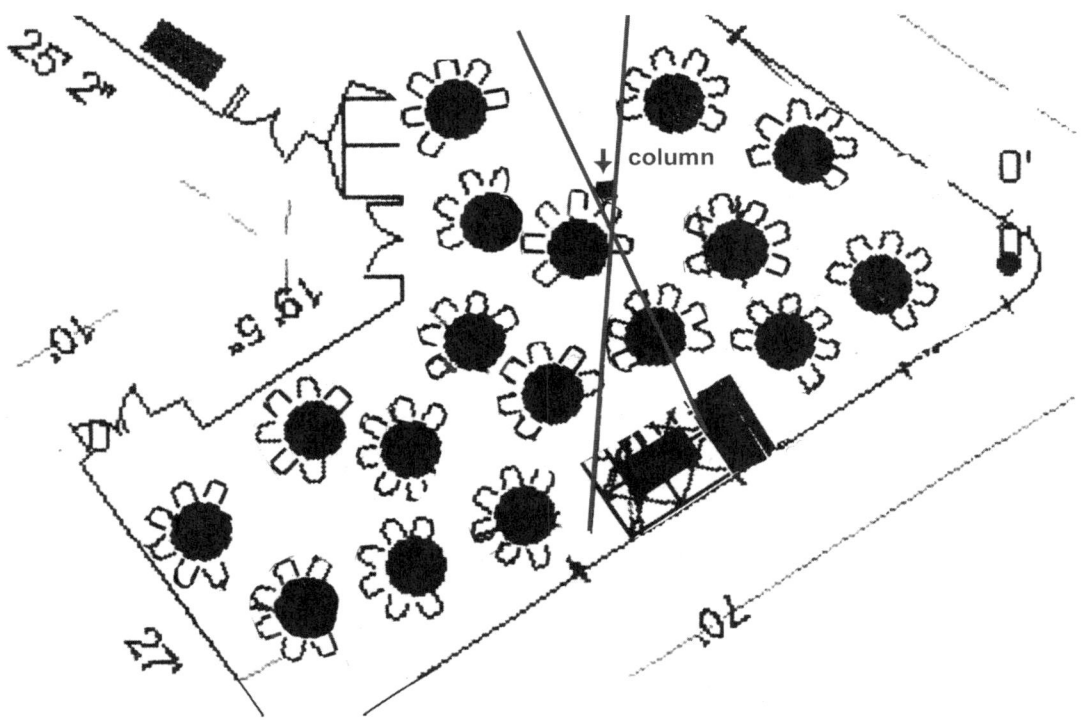

Determine the Optimal Room Set With the Presenter
There can be nothing more disconcerting as a presenter than to have someone else choose how you are going to deliver to the audience, your delivery system. The meeting planner may think you will really enjoy the raised platform with a monitoring screen on the floor directly in front of you to track the power point presentation on the two screens behind you. However, your preferred style of presentation is walking down and among your audience. At that point the monitor becomes useless, unless you can turn it perpendicular to the stage so that you can approach the audience and still see it by glancing over rather than back. With enough cord, you can move the monitor farther out from the stage. Make that request early enough to make it part of the original setup.

State of the Art Seating Arrangements

SEATING MATTERS

So, meeting planners, even when you think you are providing the most benign, optimal room set, check with the presenter in advance. Provide a diagram so that she is forewarned to adjust her positioning. And be ready to adapt the setting more to the needs, requirements and specifications of the presenter.

Setting for One Sole Presenter or Panel Based on Placement/Movement
If the presenter is the <u>sole visual medium</u> for the entire presentation, that simplifies focusing down to two criteria: (1.) presenter location and (2.) range of movement. You can arrange the seating by fixing on the lectern, or on a mark or a spot on stage. You can mark that spot with masking tape and focus lighting on it and face the seating toward it.

Fixed Place Speaker
If the presenter is choosing not to stay "fixed" on a spot on stage, not hitting a specific mark, or standing behind a lectern, you will want to select seating and lighting to minimize the head movement required by participants to follow the presenter. You have moving sight lines that require neck rotation.

If you have a 3-5 person panel without visuals, you would have a relaxed, soft focus toward the central three persons of a five person panel, as opposed to a tight focus on the middle panelist. That would mean choosing an elliptical curved arrangement, rather than a perfectly rounded semi-circle as a seating design for the front row on the back row.

Up and Back Speaker
Some presenters move in a "W", moving at center stage with little variation in distance, but addressing the entire audience and emphasizing points by getting into the face of the audience at the top of the W, and then making poignant commentary deeper back in the stage. You can light the presenter with a fixed spotlight, as long as her range of motion is marked off on the stage and the spotlight is sufficiently powerful. The configuration for this movement could be semi-circular curved rows. It would not require much neck rotation, because the speaker occupies a limited part of the center stage.

Lighting

Let the Sun Shine In
A presentation with all the natural lighting of a wine cellar is shutting out natural sunlight, a major contributor to the meeting environment. So many meetings use their location as a drawing card, then keep the participants so confined during daylight hours to windowless rooms, that they may as well be in a mushroom cellar.

If the concern is air conditioning bills due to direct sunlight, you can remedy that by double or triple pane all weather windows, the placement of the windows, and window treatments such as insulating, translucent blinds.

State of the Art Seating Arrangements

SEATING MATTERS

Is the Outside View Distracting From or Reinforcing Learning?
Over a period of days, being shut off from natural lighting can affect an individual's bio rhythms and distort their reality. Your meeting room should have more ambiance than a Las Vegas casino. Let the sun shine in. And give them a view.

Left brained school children were found to have better reading scores under fluorescent lighting, in the absence of full spectrum sun light. Meanwhile, right brained school children were found to have lower scores under fluorescent lighting, preferring incandescent or soft lighting – in the absence of full spectrum sun light.

Skylights can bring in natural sunlight, as can roof mounted fiber optics. The latter do not bring in heat, only light. And since indoor lighting is perhaps the major contributor to indoor heat, we might take a lesson from these new sunlight conveyors. Major facility construction completed in this era would do well to utilize natural views and the beauty of nature as well as natural sunlight

Nature Enhances the Event
Southwestern Bell built a training center that placed the corridors around the meeting area, cutting off any access to natural sunlight, save a room door that might let in distracting light and shadows during a presentation. If this is based on some pedagogical practice of keeping the children from seeing outside, therefore being distracted from their studies, it falls flat for both children and adults.

One of the best views I have had from a training room was at the YMCA Camp at Estes Park, Colorado. Beautiful, snow capped peaks as a backdrop to the presentation made it most memorable. The shrimp boats going out to the Gulf of Mexico from the Best Western in Corpus Christi, Texas, was a beautiful backdrop to the day and the meeting site.

Turn Off Sconces Behind the Presentation
Sconces are those candelabra-like lighting fixtures as well as other more modern lighting fixtures that are placed midway up on the wall of meeting facilities for light as well as for décor. For banquets, the sconces provide a kind of formal lighting for the event. But, when these sconces are located behind presenters and left on, they create tremendous eye fatigue for those for whom they backlight the presenter.

The pupil of the eye will continually contract in order to protect it from looking directly into the light, then expand to once again see the presenter. So, if you cannot control the background wall sconces at the light switch, then unscrew each bulb individually. In some rare cases where you cannot unscrew the bulb, you may have to cover the fixture with aluminum foil or block the light in some other way. It's best to consult engineering way in advance of the presentation. However, many times you have to deal with these issues immediately. That is when your solutions may be best. Just remember to use your handkerchief to keep from burning your fingers on hot bulbs.

State of the Art Seating Arrangements

SEATING MATTERS

Let Your Audience Choose the Room Lighting Level
Your audience may choose to have the lights on their seats or tables at a level different than full on or bright. You can offer them a more preferred setting by taking the lights down, and then bringing them up slowly and awaiting their okay on the level. This will be helpful especially for power point presentations. They only need to be able to refer to their handouts, if any, and they know the lighting required for that.

Overhead Incandescence
Most facility lighting comes from above, leaving mid to deep shadows under the eyes of the presenter(s). So many meeting rooms have overhead incandescent lighting built into the ceiling, and these become the sole source of lighting on the presenter. Unfortunately, these overheads really cast a ghoulish appearance to the face of the presenter. Short of renting a spot light or utilizing the track lights installed on the ceiling, bring your own portable extensions. Swivelier ("google" for your nearby dealer) Lighting provides a variety of fixtures that screw into the lighting fixture and drop down the light so that it can be trained directly on the face of the presenter. Home Depot also carries such a drop down fixture.

The "No Ghoul" Policy
To counter this effect, either focus a spot light from eye level on the presenter's face or get stage lighting that sits on the floor and casts light upwards. That will eliminate the "eye shadow." The long shot spot light can be a big assist as well. It all depends on the room, what is already in place, and the basic cost of engaging them. Become informed about that as soon as possible.

Pin Point Spots
One Alexandria, Virginia, hotel has small pinpoint spotlights in the ceiling. Rather than track lights that generally favor setting up to the short side of the room, these were placed evenly throughout the room – six sets per room—two on either side front, middle, and back.

These pinpoint spot lights were not utilized until it was pointed out that they were there and would light the face of the presenter. The room set-up staff did not seem to be aware of the spots, surprisingly, since it was a major upgrade for their brand. When requested, they attempted to punch up the spots through the wall switch.

In one room you could not call up the spots without shutting off all the other lights. The darkened room did not work for workshop participants with handouts. And the banquet manager indicated that you could not have it any other way. However, with advance request, the same engineer who set up that room switch in an on-off mode, could reprogram it to specifications for that session, or at least to be more useful. In another room, the spots were turned on for the speaker, but the speaker was on a platform, and the spots lighted her only from the waist down.

Know the Location and Working of Light Controls
Be aware that when you pull the air wall on a ballroom, the light switch in one section or sliver often controls more than that section. So, when the lights were being turned on and off, they were doing so in more than one room. This is where engineering needs to anticipate, or the set-up staff have to know where the master controls are and how to work them.

Sound

Consult an Audiologist to Literally Fine Tune Your Room
For the young who have already blown out their hearing registers, as well as the over 50 crowd, who experience hearing loss as part of aging, each will have to see the presenter in order to "hear" the presenter. Even if those with hearing loss do not read lips, seeing the speaker's lips assists the process of hearing what is being said.

Gender Based Sound Range
Dr. Ben Rodriguez, Jr., AuD., of Dallas, Texas, notes that diminished hearing starts around age 35 to 40 for those who have abused their hearing with high decibel count in their activities – shooting, drumming, rock concerts, high volume iPod listening, motorcycle riding – mostly pertaining, but not limited to males.

Age Based Range of Sound
At age 50, females tend to lose facility in both the higher and lower registers, while males lose in the higher register. So, it is possible that a couple will attend a concert or presentation, or even go to dinner with friends, and miss distinct and different parts of the presentation or conversation.

Those who plan events in the future will have to consider this more and more with an aging population, and an increase in ear-drum blowing instrumentation. You might check with an audiologist before your determine the best sound system for your group. Find out what range of sound will reach the preponderance of your audience, in spite of their own hearing loss.

Check the average, or the median age of your audience in order to supplement the gain in that area of loss. And make sure the audio person on the sound board is proficient in all registers, as well as appreciating the hearing loss for which he must compensate in his audience.

After attending Les Miserables three times at the Kennedy Center in Washington, D.C., the third time was the charm for hearing both the spoken and the sung words. During the first two presentations it was difficult to make out the sung words especially. The sound system, and/or the person tuning it, was right on for the entire third performance. Sung and spoken word came across

SEATING MATTERS

with equal clarity. I sought out the sound technician at the end of the performance to thank him for enhancing my experience of the musical. Without having two tune-ups for this performance, I would not have had the experiential basis from which to compare and enjoy the improvement that technician made.

Buyer beware when it come to securing a production company together with the audio component. Check to be assured that those handling the sound portion can distinguish the nuances of sound sufficiently to transmit them through to the audience. Many of those who love sound, love it too much and blow out their hearing at an early age.

Air Walls
Should you encounter an air wall that does not close completely, you may get a lot of noise leakage. Set your chairs as far from that opening in the air wall as possible.

Set Presentations Back to Back
Work with whomever is setting up the room next door to place the back of their stage to the air wall, or at least direct the presenter away from that corner of the room. You then do the same, placing your platform on the adjoining wall, and presenting out and away from that presentation.

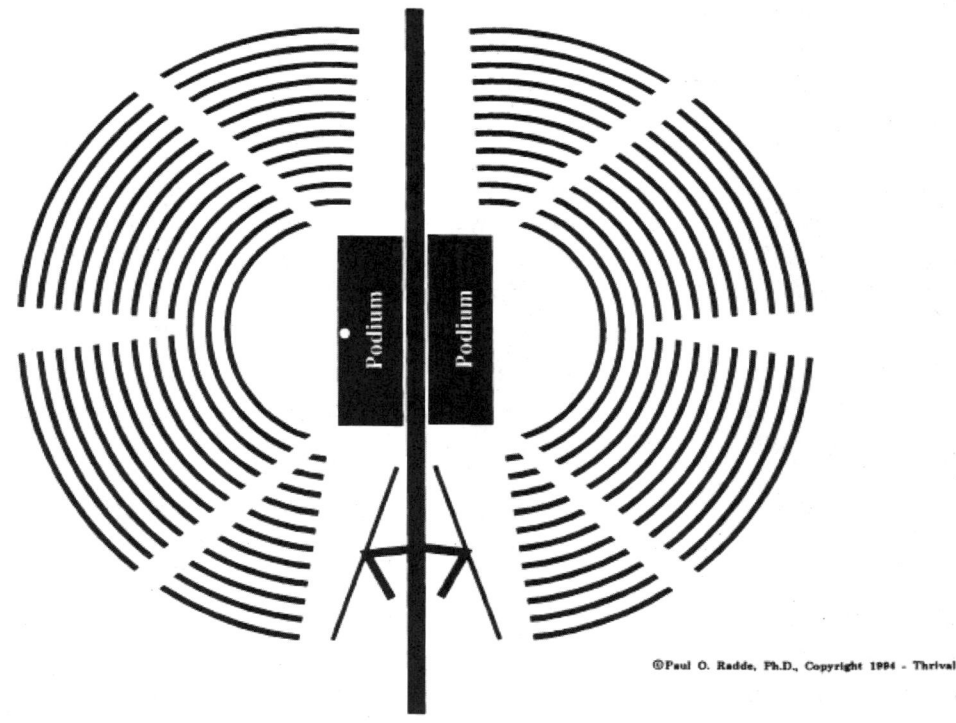

State of the Art Seating Arrangements

SEATING MATTERS

To avoid interruptions or the next door presentation talking over your session, set the presentations back to back, even off setting the speakers so that all the broadcast is directly away from the next room, and fully directed out at the appropriate audience.

Quieting Late Arrivals and Departures
Have you ever been distracted by the clicking of a door opener or the slamming of a closing door? When this happens during a meeting it diminishes the experience. So, there are several ways to reduce these disruptions.

    1.) Use a wrench or screw driver to secure the door opener so that the door latch is in a permanent "open" position. This takes care of the latch clicking.
    2.) Tape the door opener bar in the open/depressed position to secure it and the latch in open position.
    3.) Directly tape the latch into the open position to eliminate clicking.
    4.) Place some material into the door frame so that it buffers the door from slamming shut. This material can be taped to the frame to hold it in place, and needs to have sufficient bulk and durability to withstand repeated compression.
    5.) Oil the door hinges using WD-40 to lubricate squeaking door hardware.

Reducing Corridor Traffic Noise
Those opening the doors are not the only offenders. An open door can channel or deflect corridor noise into the meeting room – another distraction, potentially major. So, once you find out the direction of the traffic flow in the corridor outside, direct anyone entering or exiting to open the door on the side of the approaching traffic. For example, if approaching corridor traffic is coming from the left, then open the left door; if traffic from the right, then open the right door to deflect their noise.

One simple way to remember which door to open and close is this: Consider that the approaching traffic is like a high wind. The last thing you want to do is allow that high wind to fling the door open and be scooped into the meeting room. Place a sign on the outside door, "Enter Here;" and inside the door, "Exit Here." Also "Close Gently."

Air Conditioning

Temperature Adjustment
The San Antonio Hotel had an overactive air conditioning system. Half way through the afternoon, everyone in the room was so cold that they had removed the table cloths and were wearing them as shawls.

SEATING MATTERS

Temperature adjustment after lunch is typically set a bit below 72 degrees Fahrenheit in order to counter the stupor that follows lunch and competes with the meeting activity. If your room does not have a separate switch, then make sure the room is cooling over the lunch hour so that everyone starts fresh. Open an air wall to let in the chill from next door.

Presentation Backdrop

If at all possible, let your presenters know the color of the walls or of any backdrops arranged for their presentation. Wall and room color would be a welcome addition to the room charts, and information made available to the presenters.

Most meeting room charts say nothing about the color of the walls or wall paper. So, when the professional speaker showed up for the luncheon presentation in a champagne colored silk dress, she had obviously not been informed that she would be blending into the champagne colored wall paper.

Backdrops

One option would be to use a backdrop that provides a solid "ground" color against which the presentation can stand out. On occasion the backdrop is lit up and requires only a change of color of the lighting filter to change the background color.

Jay Leno used to do a skit with Mr. Brain, in which his head fairly floated against a dark backdrop. It was hilarious. But three panel members were not going for laughs when each wore a dark blue suit against a dark blue velvet curtain. They too floated on stage with only their faces and power ties showing.

Part IV.

Influence: Gaining Acceptance for Your Room Sets

Simple Question to Resisters
Should audiences be allowed to rotate their chairs toward the presentation? Or should they be required to rotate their heads toward the presentation in order to see?

Up until now, meeting participants, those who have attended various events, have had to assume an uncomfortable posture in order to see the presentation. The Greeks and Romans had it right millennia ago. How is it that only now there is some feeble return to turning chairs, ever so slightly toward the presentation. Not all the way, mind you, but somewhat more than before in the "modern" sets offered as state of the art by hotel brands. Remember, chevron is in many cases worse than straight row theatre style.

Understanding, Skill, and Commitment
Change does not occur without the coming together or introduction of contributing factors. And it won't happen in the meeting industry without your intervention. Therefore it is important that you be equipped with the necessary tips, tools and techniques to gain favor for the room sets you choose. It is not enough that you are committed to improve seating arrangements. You need also understand and be skilled first in setting rooms and creating environments that facilitate access, receptivity, interaction and learning for audiences. That is what we have dealt with leading up to Part IV.

If these room sets were all that we dealt with, you would be cut loose to do the best you can with the skills you started out with. And they may be sufficient. However, knowing some of the basics of effecting change by utilizing persuasion and influence helps. Then you are better positioned to guide the transition to improve meeting environments. Persuasion skills may further assist you in moving your agenda with meeting facilities, especially if you are employed within one.

In the following chapter we begin to focus more specifically on the process of influence, persuading others to be self-persuading regarding seating arrangements.

SEATING MATTERS

Chapter 12

Influence Issues: Overcoming Resistance

So, Why Do They Set It That Way?
While there is a great deal of staff turnover in the meeting industry, those with 30+ years experience in meeting planning or convention operations may well have accepted the room sets the way they were and continued to rubber stamp them into planning over the years. They were probably promoted based on their adherence to, and delivery of the standard room sets, mostly all straight row. No innovation, no surprises. But, reliable and consistent. Years later, they are likely the last to question the practices that got them their promotions. They continue to "dance with them what brung'em."

However, seating is set up by:
1. **Custom: This is how it has always been done.**
2. **Ease: Keeping it within the "perceived" capacity or skill level of the set-up crew**
3. **Accuracy: The straight row design printed on the carpeting, and**
4. **Capacity: The printed room capacity, which is assumed to be the way maximum number of bodies you can seat in the room.**

Seating set-ups are made with everyone in mind. But from cleaning, set-up, and banquet services are often given priority over the audience member, the end customer.

Arousing Their Survival Mentality
Whenever an individual is approached with the possibility of doing something new or different, fear arises at a subconscious level. The fear comes from the survival mentality. Those threatened think that change or doing things differently could put them at peril, either personally or professionally. Their ego starts up the inner chatter about threat. The reptilian brain emphasizes the importance of security, continuity, and survival. This will be but one of the unseen and unacknowledged resistance factors implicit in any change venture you undertake. Perhaps the threat is even more acute among meeting industry personnel who already have a sense of being stretched thin.

Part of the resistance will come from the nature and requirements of the meeting facility operation with tight turnaround times. Resistance also comes from those populating the meeting industry who prefer to have all fixed practices in place so that they have fewer variables and surprises. They have more predictability, less to decide and negotiate before each meeting. Their interest is in gaining efficiency and reliability by limiting options in certain aspects of the meeting. Typically they think they have enough to do negotiating and managing without adding another variable, room set.

State of the Art Seating Arrangements

SEATING MATTERS

Confronting the "Image of Competence"
Most people tend to feel less like a failure when they are unable to do something, as long as no one else can do it either. It is typically only when someone solves a problem, takes on an assignment and gets results, or introduces a new idea, that they may truly feel "incompetent."

A large carpet manufacturer in a southern state was rebuilding after a fire, when I offered to work with them to incorporate the curved row designs of Audience Centered Principles into their new carpet design. It would require simple adjustments in the software program that currently created designs, including the block patterns to facilitate straight row seating. I suggested that the company would benefit by offering color coding for different designs into the carpeting. That layout design would expedite and make efficient the set-up of curved as well as elliptical seating, saving the meeting facility time and ensuring accuracy in the sets. Providing these minor modifications would not add cost to the manufacture, but would add features and benefits that could be marketed. Value added. The response of the company representative was short and to the point, "You're creating problems for us." End of conversation.

Most people in the meeting industry, if not the entire nation, have been raised in an educational system and culture that values answers more than questions; rules, routine, and resoluteness over what Dr. Byron Nahser in his Corporantes approach calls "inquiry to discover the truth we don't know yet." So count on running up against many whose energy is invested in maintaining the "image" of competence. That is especially true in an industry which provides entry level labor in the convention operations arena. Those who rise through those ranks may tend to be more easily threatened and hold true to what they have been told, can predict, and control.

The "answer" or "truth" they currently hold is as far as they want to go. They accept it fully, unquestioningly. They feel more secure, more likely to survive, if their truth is unchallenged. That may be why much of the important work handled at organizational meetings is really done behind the scenes. Few are comfortable exposing their need to search, explore, or research the actual reality to arrive at the new "best answer." They would probably feel exposed in admitting they don't know and have to find out.

Individual professionals may think you are challenging their competence with new wrinkles in seating arrangements. They expect to have heard about everything of relevance and are likely to dismiss or resist what they do not know or understand.

Does the Meeting Facility Really Facilitate?
"To facilitate" or " make easy" is one definition of the purpose of a facility. And a meeting supposedly is a face-to-face interaction of two or more parties for a specific purpose. Generally, they come together at a meeting facility, often having traveled great distances specifically to get together. If the meeting itself is then marked by an inability to hear, see, or connect with those with whom the participant came to meet, does a meeting truly occur? And what obstacles or resistance might the facility itself present to such a meeting?

State of the Art Seating Arrangements

SEATING MATTERS

Industry Leadership:
Whose Job Is It To Initiate Improved Room Sets?

Ultimately, what will help bring about the improvement, even optimization, in seating arrangements will be meeting facilities personnel becoming knowledgeable and dedicated to providing the optimal learning environment, <u>the best in customer service</u>, for their participants. Since meeting facilities that improve their room sets will also benefit from an increase in capacity, one would think they would be the first to initiate the transition.

Perhaps, if brands realized that they may be turning away business just based on lower straight row capacities for their meeting rooms, they would be more receptive to not only give their participants the best seats in the house, but also realize an increase in capacity.

After all, the expense in time and lost business of knocking out walls or expanding a building is much greater than the efficiency and economy of introducing a room set that instantly gets greater capacity.

Chicken or Egg: Customer or Facility?

Facilities tell me they are customer driven and will change when the meeting planner or customer asks for it. However, that's not what I hear from meeting planners and speakers. They tell me that the facilities do not supply the room set that they have requested. Whether incapable, unskilled, or simply non-compliant is not clear. Resistance is obvious. No facilitation here. At some point, hopefully, we will get to a concern for the audience member and the overall success of the current meeting that will bring back repeat participants to future meetings.

Right now most facilities lack innovation in their meeting room set-ups.

Since the hospitality industry is driven by the latest fad such as "soap wars", pillow top mattresses, wiring rooms for the internet, or the cushiest bath linens, it will only take one major brand to start upgrading the meeting seating and environment – where most meeting guests spend the majority of their day – and the other major hotel brands will follow. As long as each and all remain traditional, and the customer does not ask, then no one seems deficient. Until someone adds these alternative room sets and does it well, no one seems incompetent.

At one point, the hotel industry was awaiting the results of one brand's upgrading of seating. The training was underway for 18 months. How would others be able to adjust? Yet, nothing really happened. The training text proved to be nothing more than photo copies of old texts on meeting rooms sets. What a fizzle! And for this the industry waited with baited breath?

SEATING MATTERS

Customers/Those Who Know Better
One facility claimed that alternative room sets would mean extra work for housemen, so why would the client promote these sets then have to convince her boss it is an improvement? Another facility said they were trying to inform meeting planners, but meeting planners were not listening. If the event were multiple days, the planners were afraid to deviate from the traditional menu.

Even so, the MPI 2008 Professional Education Conference – North America broached the subject of significant change in meetings design that found carry over in room design back home after the meeting according to one report. So, these major meeting industry associations may be the ones to promote this innovation.

One initial step in convincing the decision makers to at least allow variation in room set while reducing your own risk as the innovator, is to check with the stakeholders in advance of the meeting. Ask them what outcome they want from the meeting. Then frame your room sets in terms of the goals and objectives they have for the meeting.

You may have to search for the real "owner" of the meeting. It could be an established veteran of the organization who also holds a committee position or is on the Board of Directors. She may have been advocating better meeting outcomes for years. Contact that person, or persons, and have them describe the results, as well as the consequences they want from the meeting. Then set the room, and sell your room sets on that basis.

You First!
In the meantime, you will be more effective if you understand the different variables that ultimately have to be placed in motion to begin to optimize meeting seating and the learning environment.

First, know that you are raising awareness of the impact of seating on presentation, on meeting quality, and even on capacity. You will be resurrecting a meeting variable, a platform skill, ignored over time as inert, dead, and literally of no consequence.

Typical responses of those who have been exposed to curved row Audience Centered Seating™ include:
- *I never looked at it this way, and I have been a meeting planner for 30 years.*
- *It's all just common sense, something that is not so common.*
- *I never would have thought about this.*
- *What a difference it makes in comfort! This is marvelous!*

Customer Service: Anyone Can Improve the Presentation
Participants can assist by stating their learning needs, expectations, and posing questions to clarify the presentation and improve the interaction. But, essentially, anyone involved in the enterprise can contribute.

SEATING MATTERS

Steve Waterhouse, speaker, tells how a woman waiting tables at Dave and Buster's noticed that he was walking into the audience, but had only been given a wired microphone for the event. She, on her own initiative, found him an AV man who found him a wireless mike and switched it out for him immediately. Anyone can add value without increasing cost. When the audience has a better experience, or even the speaker does, they may recommend that venue for repeat business based on the better outcome of the meeting.

Presenters, Essentially, You are 100% Responsible
Presenters are not the only ones responsible. So, is the facility and its personnel, as well as the meeting professional. But, the presenter is ultimately the one who has to make sure the setup serves her presentation.

Michael McKinley carries rolls of masking tape with him to close off the back of the room and move people forward. If his room set falls short, he will change it himself. He even tapes off or removes chairs that have a bad sight line to his presentation. Steve Waterhouse will be in the training room at 6:30am to make any changes required to optimize his presentation. He would find step ladders, unscrew light bulbs that illuminated the projection screen, move chairs, clear sight lines.

You may have to mark certain light switches with masking tape in order to be able to direct anyone in the audience to go back and turn it off or on according to your needs during a presentation.

Those Facilities That Were Trained in ACS™
There has not been a big rush to get trained. [One person outside the meeting industry institutions drumming up business is no match for one recognized meeting entity considering, promising, or "threatening" to introduce something new. Then everyone has to have it to be up to standard.] With the rate of turnover in the meeting industry, even those facilities which have undergone ACS™ training may have retained few, if any, trained staff on their crews to carry on the practices. A refresher course is reommmended.

Grand Traverse Resort, Michigan
Following the 1998 training of this facility, the banquet manager and director of convention services made the following comments about audience response to their application of Audience Centered Seating principles:

We use it to max the room. We get increased capacities.
The customers love it. This truly is a quantum leap, a major breakthrough. And it requires such minor adjustments. The difference is incredible in terms of participant comfort.

We recently had a national group of 600 legislators from around the country. They are a well traveled group and have been to many facilities. We just went ahead and set the room in a semi-circular arrangement. The meeting planner was leery at first, but received so many compliments from the legislators that she was extremely pleased.

State of the Art Seating Arrangements

SEATING MATTERS

We arrange all our theatre style sets in the Audience Centered Seating™ manner. If we are asked about it, we reply, "Of course, this is how we set to optimize the learning experience. We know from experience it is the best set-up for this kind of meeting."

The Philadelphia Airport Marriott
The Philadelphia Airport Marriott contracted for the training the day before they opened the facility. We were taking the plastic off the recently shipped chairs and setting them up for the first time. We were determining the ACS™ seating capacity of each training room even while optimizing the seating.

Tom Antion noted years later that he was in his Marriott meeting room so early that he started setting it with curved seating from scratch. Then, one of the operations staff said, "I know how to do this. I had a course." Later a foreman came in with a great big ACS on his clipboard and was explaining audience centered seating. So, the training does stick. And Tom's meeting for the Philadelphia Chapter of MPI got high kudos from the program recipients.

These facilities cooperated in providing the ACS set ups requested.
Customer service is a valuable commodity in working with the facility. The following facilities provided that service in the way their convention operations staff pitched in and provided optimum room sets.

The Peabody Hotel - Orlando
The Peabody Hotel staff in Orlando were cooperative and customer service oriented in allowing their set up crew, mostly Guadalajara natives, to learn ACS as they set the ballroom in hosting the National Speakers Association national convention. The next morning, after breaking it down the night before, they initiated the re-set almost to perfection.

Opryland Hotel - Nashville
The Opryland Hotel in Nashville provided their evening crew to re-set and fine tune their major ballroom. They get honorable mention based on their collaborative partnering and service. And ASAE used the same set-up for their conference which was to follow NSA.

Benefits of Training
Unfortunately, at the rate of employee turnover, change in meeting facility management and brand, there are no guarantees that even these facilities mentioned above will better be able to continue to provide Audience Centered Seating without some tune up training.

Most facilities would profit most from full training of all their set-up crews, and then photo documentation of the room in fine tuned condition. Not only would this prove an effective training tool or guideline for future staff training, but it would also provide sales staff with hard copy of the best sets for the varying meeting spaces in their facility.

State of the Art Seating Arrangements

SEATING MATTERS

Once and Done! Provide Precise Designs with Seating Capacities
Various facilities purchase software seating design programs, which are then updated every so frequently. They may even get custom-tailored diagrams from the software that provides high accuracy for various room sets in their facility.

My own approach is to go into a facility and work with a cross section of their set up crews and foremen to train them in the variety of set-ups and how to fine tune them. I have them provide a photographer as well. Then, rather than having a diagram of questionable accuracy to show prospective clients and customers, <u>they have the actual room set with the very chairs that will be used.</u> If the customer has any apprehension, they can look at the photo and be re-assured of what is possible and the advantages of that set. Plus the staff will undertake the fine points of "fine tuning" the room for safety, comfort, line of sight, access, networking, …and capacity.

Now you have a trained staff as well as a precise seating design in the very space that will be rented out. Only a new space, new furniture of different size, or special needs would leave the meeting facility wanting for an accurate photo. And, even then, their staff is equipped to experiment with the set. You can inquire at <u>DrPaul@Thrival.com</u> regarding training for your facility, or for a facility you will utilize.

Certifying Facilities in ACS™
If you do not have someone in sales or banquet in these facilities who knows these seating principles and concepts, you may be starting from square one. And that is pretty much all the other meeting facilities in the world.

So, in order for the innovative room sets to catch on and gain full acceptance, all the stake holders in a facility need to know about these designs. Sales, Marketing, Convention Operations, and even upper management need to attend training to gain the understanding and skill to support their commitment.

Negotiating With the Facility: Capacity and Cost
Most meeting planners are ruled by a budget for their meeting, hence they contract for minimal space rental to accommodate their group. And when that comes down to asking the facility to maximize the number of audience members they can fit into a room, the assumed and unverified best solutions they are given is traditional straight row theatre style. The tendency for someone who already has a thousand things on her plate, and a potential budget buster in seating, is to stick with straight row offerings…. Unless, of course, she understands the core purpose of her work and also understands the importance of seating to the audience member and to the meeting.

State of the Art Seating Arrangements

SEATING MATTERS

Now that you know differently, you can request an improved room set-up for your meeting, and increase capacity.

- *Establish the room set as one of the fixed conditions of your contract, as of highest priority early in the requests you put forward to the meeting facility. If you inquire about any added cost for getting the room set you request, you have optimum leverage to get them to agree to your request without added cost.*

Remember, you can meet or exceed traditional straight row set-up room capacity by applying the tips, tools, techniques, and principles in this book. If they can get the required number of chairs in to straight row traditional theatre style, you can exceed that by up to 17% by curving the rows toward the presentation.

Industry Leadership

Since meeting facilities state that they are market driven, what will you have to do to get the sets you want and require to optimize your meeting? Since facilities have been openly reluctant to take cutting edge leadership, the initiative is squarely back on the meeting planners.

Planners feel they have to exhibit an exorbitant amount of initiative, bargaining power, or lay out extra money to get what they want from the facilities. This can be one more thing to negotiate, or not.

You, your organization, and especially your participants have the right to the best seating arrangement available. If they understand its importance to the meeting participant and the learning enterprise, a professional meeting facility would provide such a set-up as a standard part of their service.

Facility Resistance Point #1: Capacity

Facilities might counter any request for an alternative to straight row theater style or classroom with their own honestly held belief that they will lose meeting capacity. You know differently. Curving, or at least angling, rows, flaring aisles, spacing rows 17 inches apart will each and all provide maximum seating, safety, and comfort. You may have to insist on the set you want, or set it yourself in the wee hours of the morning.

As one way to reassure a production company that capacity would not be a problem when changing the general session set from straight row to curved row, I reset the front of the ballroom to assure the production company that the space would accommodate the numbers needed for the opening general session. Once they saw me bringing chairs up from the back of the room to fill in all the extra space remaining in the front, they relented and allowed the curved set.

SEATING MATTERS

Relationship is an important part of getting the set that works best for your group. In the case that follows, the veteran meeting planner was not available for consult about the room set when I arrived at the hotel. [Most meeting professionals do not expect to have a speaker who has an expertise in room sets. They pretty much think their approach is the best. And, ultimately, they are responsible for the meeting outcome.] He had retired for the night and blocked calls to his room. So, in consultation with the executive director of the association about the problem with the bowling alley set that distanced people and made it difficult for them to see, plus the expense of a long throw projector lens, he advised me to "set it up the way that worked best for my presentation."

Preceding my presentation was a brief panel presentation of five participants. I actually set the room up for their discussion, with only a simple and quick movement of table and lectern required to make adjustments for my presentation.

The transition went very well later that morning. However, the meeting planner was so incensed at the changes made without his approval that he would not speak to me and simply fumed off. In the best of all worlds I would have made a more specific request of set-up in the first place. With anticipation, I would have asked him about the room. Obviously he was surprised, and possibly felt a loss of control. Given the circumstances, I would still re-set the room and keep those in the back from being 93 feet away from the presentation. Optimizing the learning environment is still top priority.

Pay Attention to How You Get the Set-Up
Pay attention to the sensibilities of every one involved and impacted by what you do with seating. Should you decide to override someone in order to get the set that works best in your program, it is best to anticipate and seek to work with that person initially. It may then become obvious that the only way you will get the set-up is to override resistance.

Facility Resistance Point #2: Room Turnaround Time – Time to Set Up
Turning the room is a prime concern of the facility. They have to be up and running, and on time for your meeting. So, if they are unfamiliar with your room set or perhaps do it infrequently, then at first it will take them longer than it takes to do the familiar sets. But as they get practice, they can count on reducing set-up time.

One Minneapolis convention hotel reduced the time required to set their ballroom with 1800 chairs in a semicircular set, from 4 hours the first time, to 2.5 hours on only the second time. Practice and clear knowledge that they will be doing this set regularly brings down set-up time further, and could also reduce resistance.

Advantageous Set - Time Savers: General Session to Breakout in 2 Minutes
The illustration below shows a semi-circular room set for a large or general session. When this session is over, you can convert the larger room over to two small breakout sessions in about 2 minutes using only one convention operations person.

State of the Art Seating Arrangements

SEATING MATTERS

General Session To Breakout: 2 Minutes

The general manager of the Charlotte meeting property came to me with a grave expression and concern in his voice. To change over from the general session which would be set to the narrow end of the room, over to two breakout sessions would require 15 – 20 minutes and a full crew. He did not know if he could keep the meeting on schedule. So, I showed him the above design and explained how it would require only one staff person under two minutes to re-set the room for two breakouts. The same numbers were accommodated. Presto! Chango! It was done as promised.

Here is how:
- *Ask the audience for their assistance in clearing the room quickly.*
- *Pull out the chairs that are lined up in the track for the air wall(s).*
- *Separate the two platform components, angling them toward the new audience configuration, and separating them to allow for the air wall(s).*
- *Pull the air wall.*
- *Invite the audience back in for the next session.*

As meeting facilities recognize the benefits of various sets in efficiency, saving turnover time and staff required for the room turn, you will find greater receptivity. However, until you establish some interest, involvement and credibility, you will be up against inertia. Let's get the ball rolling for improved room sets that benefit audience and facility alike.

State of the Art Seating Arrangements

SEATING MATTERS

Preparing for Contact
As you approach your initial contact with whatever sites you consider, keep the purpose of a meeting first and foremost in your mind and among your decision making criteria for choosing the site. Make, clear, explicit requests for the specific seating arrangement that will serve your meeting purposes best. Make your request up front right from the start, together with your other up front service request priorities; and assume that the facility will be customer service oriented.

Beginning from the Ground Up
Here is what you are taking on as you start to revolutionize the world of meeting seating. Be aware that you are dealing with very limited tolerances as well as people's perception of change as a threat to their own survival when you bring new practices in seating to the table. But the work still needs to be done at the operations level, and then fed up the line to assure administrators.

It's All in How you Spin It
When I first began this work on seating I called the marketing directors of every major hotel chain in the United States. I asked each what they were doing in seating arrangements. A sampling of 1990's responses by Vice-Presidents of Marketing from major hotel brands – some of which I would call less than reassuring – follow below:

"Well, if it's worth doing, I'm sure we are doing it already."

"Our Director of Operations has been on the job for 30 years. I expect that he knows all there is to know about meeting sets."

"We have the most advanced set being used. We use the herringbone."

Very little has changed since the 1990's with respect to room sets, however beginning around December 2005, a resort conference facility in Mexico began advertising a semicircular room set in its advertising. The carpeting provided guidance with aisles woven into the design. Rows begin with 4 seats in the front and expand to more than 25 in the back row per section. With acknowledgement for what they are doing right, several problems are noted:
- *There is an aisle up the middle*
- *Break up long rows – more than 12 chairs – with single chair access lanes every 6th to 7th chair or so.*
- *Chairs are set up one behind the other as if ganged, creating a fan of heads.*

It is a good start. And I applaud their ground breaking offering.

Media Portrayals: "The Way" It's Done
Open any meeting industry magazine and you are met with attractive ads from one meeting facility after another. In most, there is a photo of a meeting room set-up. In almost all cases it is one of the traditional sets: U-Shape, Box Shape, traditional classroom, traditional theatre style, rounds. Surprisingly, about May of 2008, the ACS™ classroom design appeared in the ads of two different properties. A similar classroom set first appeared in

State of the Art Seating Arrangements

SEATING MATTERS

Convene magazine in 1988, so a 20 year lag time is not surprising between exposure and adoption.

Most of the other sets are depicted in ads as if they are the absolute best. For the smaller, board sized meeting, there are more pictures of boat shaped tables; fewer photos of rectangular tables. That is a step forward.

Ad preparation people do not get the message that they are portraying people who are obviously trying to adjust their posture to find some comfort in the seating arrangement. Are so few attuned to the pain inflicted by straight row seating that they arrange for their customers?

The problem in the portrayal may be that those pasting up the ads are not the ones sitting down, just as those choosing the seating arrangements do not have to sit in the room sets they design. So, that which inflicts pain and suffering in the audience member continues to be portrayed as not only acceptable, but the endorsed way to set a room.

A further problem with these depictions of room sets is that they reinforce the traditional sets <u>no matter how uncomfortable</u>, hindering in line of sight, or unsafe. Prominent reinforcement in publications assures the neophyte meeting professional that this is the way to set a room. They are less likely to experiment or go against the seeming grain. So, the straight row error gets compounded.

However, the reason this is being pointed out here is that you may very well be met by a facility, colleague, or someone within your organization that thinks the set portrayed is truly the best way to proceed. Find out their reasoning first before sharing yours with them.

I hope that you now see room setups differently as a result of this reading, and you are beginning to pay attention to how to optimize the learning environment. No one said change will be easy. However, in learning to deal with this effectively, you can also learn the process of persuasion and how to be influential. That can serve you the rest of your life.

I have been teaching How to Influence Decision Makers: Sell Your Ideas, Projects, and Programs, for over 35 years to such diverse groups as the Presidential Management Fellows Program, the Wall Street Journal Sales Department, and ASAE. The next chapter conveys some of the points from that course that will assist you in gaining acceptance for these highly improved alternative room sets.

Implementation Help

Meanwhile, should you experience difficulty in implementing what has been presented in SEATING MATTERS, please contact me at DrPaul@Thrival.com for consultation on getting the sets you request and dealing more effectively with facilities personnel, or even staff within your organization. We will make it an ongoing conversation. Always place all CAPS in the subject line and keep it brief, e.g. "ACS" as a way to differentiate from the unsolicited spam picked up by my filter.

State of the Art Seating Arrangements

Chapter 13

Optimize the Meeting Facility Experience

This chapter is intended for use in persuading meeting facilities to pay more attention to the service they provide within their meeting space. For, not only is this the main space occupied during waking hours, it is also the space that houses the main purpose of the meeting or event.

This chapter explores where participants actually spend their waking and sleeping time within a residential and a non-residential meeting facility. Once you realize how much of that experience is spent in the function room, and is therefore dependent upon the event, learning or meeting room environment, you will realize the importance of putting time, intention, and effort into optimizing that function room space especially. We will look at the use of space in terms of time spent in the educational enterprise. We will also engage in a brief overview of the temperament of those typically involved in meeting planning and logistics.

Focus on Your Meeting Space: Getting Beyond a Forgone Conclusion

The meeting space too often has been a foregone conclusion. It may have been pre-determined even before the committee, boss, HR, or the meeting department planned the meeting. The setup is arranged, irrespective of when the intent, purpose, agenda, and essence of the meeting is decided upon. So often the setup is out of step with the event.

When the room set is considered unimportant, a fixed non-negotiable item about which the facility knows best, those in the meeting industry tend to write off vastly improved choices about arranging their meeting space. Compared with other revenue centers, that space is considered insignificant, unimportant, or already being done the best way possible. I don't think so!

Choose Your Environment

Whether you are facility, meeting planner, or presenter, you cannot necessarily control who attends the meeting. However, you can make choices about the environment in which that person attends the meeting, and, in that way influence the behavior of the participants toward the results desired.

The Space Most Utilized: Optimizing the Meeting Environment

What is the benefit to the meeting facility of providing an optimal meeting set-up? Let's look at where the participant's time is spent in a residential meeting facility.

SEATING MATTERS

Time Spent and the Nature of Space Used

Many meeting or conference facilities are set up for residential programs. They have sleeping rooms. And the after hours informal gathering of participants is an important part of the meeting enterprise. So, here is a quick breakdown of potential uses of optimized space in, say, a hotel or conference center.

1. The Reception Area: Check-In and Check-Out

Participants form their initial impression of the service a facility provides beginning with the check-in procedure. The amount of time spent at this function should be infinitesimally small in comparison with sleeping, eating, and meeting room time. The more efficient the reception and check out goes, the better the first and last impression of the facility.

Inefficiency in this process bodes poorly for the first impression. Yet, many facilities function almost as if they are still going through opening week shakeout. They don't seem to know what to do with a sudden influx of new registrants. On-going quality improvement in this service is essential, especially since reception desk personnel tend to turnover or rotate through several jobs.

Preferential Treatment

Separate, preferential registration, for example, for one group over another when both are holding a meeting in the facility, does not sit well with those not shown preference. You have just flown across country all day only to arrive exhausted, and wait in line. When one group is obviously inconvenienced at the expense of another, it is a lose/lose for the lesser of the two groups. If you do priority registrations, then take them into another area where they can be processed, e.g. behind the first class curtain.

Late Night Arrivals

With airlines providing fewer amenities, including meals, more frazzled travelers are arriving late in the evening and famished. Providing a limited kitchen staff, or even a sandwich cooler, is a considerate, much appreciated service, rather than making a selection from a vending machine or mini-bar.

2. Sleeping Room

With the exception of one's morning routine or scheduled private meetings, few participants see the inside of their hotel or conference center sleeping room until the evening hours. While that room serves as a source of brief solitude during what can be an overwhelming day, most people are only in this room for 5-7.5 hours per day. And, if they are fortunate, most of that time is spent sleeping.

SEATING MATTERS

Additional Uses of the Sleeping Room
Business and internet connections for the guest may draw him back to his room for privacy in calls to clients, or to contact family, check lengthy e-mails, and stay connected to employees back home or around the world.

The sleeping room serves as the broadcast center for in-house television programming such as daily reports, and scheduling updates sent to the guest rooms. Industry newspapers reporting on their corporate or association event may be at their door in the morning.

And some may choose their sleeping room for exercise over the facility health club, or for their solitude, meditation, and spot to unwind. They may also order in for room service rather than meeting the group schedule for breakfast or dinner. This is a listing of the functions provided in the sleeping space, yet it does not indicate more sleep, simply more functions performed within the sleeping room.

3. Eating Function Rooms: Refreshment, Reception and Meal Break Space
The facility provides banquet and meal service in space converted from meeting general sessions, while refreshments are available in the halls during breaks, or in an area adjacent to or in the exhibit area. Eating function space can affect the meeting networking opportunities. Here logistics can be important as well. Consult the facility or a nutritionist on how they can assist you in maintaining the focus and attention of the participants through correct nutrition.

The refreshment and meal breaks may be planned to provide a seamless continuation of the learning session. Assignments might be given for completion before the next meeting. There may be an ongoing project that will be worked on in pre-selected or self-selected groups. Or, participants might meet at a table with a designated topic or expert consultant.

Attention to the nutritional aspects of the offerings can be essential to maintaining steady production of glycogen to the brain so that attention is maintained and people are at their best. This is done with protein and complex carbohydrates in the diet, rather than refined sugars and simple carbohydrates. The latter lead to sugar spikes in energy followed by a dip in energy, leading to a grab for caffeine or more sugar to get that buzz back. This bi-polar swing can be moderated in planning the menu.

Where refreshment breaks are set-up, the type of nourishment chosen, the design of the service and buffet table locations facilitate access to food and to each other.

So, easy shared access to the food service and dining tables allows those in conversation to grab something and go without a hitch. Meanwhile, standing in line for a buffet, for novel refreshments, or even at a reception bar can provide a basis for opening conversation between those in line based on proximity, the theme of the event, or the novelty.

State of the Art Seating Arrangements

Networking improves. So, how you set up a buffet line or refreshment table can impact networking and learning. And it is all part of the purpose of the meeting. For example, having buffet lines on both sides of a buffet table speeds the service and increases the likelihood that people on opposite sides of the table will meet and interact.

Architectonic Disposition
The term for this, "architectonic disposition," comes from early research of Leon Festinger, psychologist. It was conducted at a college housing complex in which, even though people were living and sleeping within 12-18 inches of each other, though they were separated by central walls that divided their apartments on either side of the building. What brought residents together, converging daily for a possible, incidental face to face meeting was the central placement of mail boxes. On occasion a snow storm would also bring them outside to help each other shovel their cars out in the shared parking lot.

4. Meeting Function Space
The meeting room itself is the most utilized space during waking hours. Yet, it is the most overlooked and least adapted or customized to ensure that people actually meet, especially under current standard straight row set-ups. All the other facility space we have considered involves meeting support: providing basic creature needs and sustaining quality of life. The meeting room space is a major focus for optimizing the learning environment. How the meeting space is arranged directly impacts the importance, value, and potential outcome of the meeting. Improving seating arrangements is a <u>value added</u> factor that immediately benefits those attending and the organization, at no additional cost.

The Facility Promotes Participant Focus
The participant's meeting experience is a function of time spent in congenial environment and challenging sessions. Give sufficient attention to comfort and access to the learning sources and presentation to allow the participant to focus fully on the task of learning, absorbing, refining, and finally, integrating the learning into her professional or personal repertoire for application in daily work and living. More than getting recordings for replay of meeting content on a TV channel in one's room, the live meeting situation is primary.

Optimally the meeting space should be designed to facilitate learning, comfort, safety, networking, line of sight. It should also be free of distractions, with all aspects configured to maintain the focus of the participants. The meeting space, to be congruent with its essential purpose, has to make it easier for people to get together, to meet, interact, and learn.

Meeting Facility Attention Getter: Gain The Seating Capacity to Host a Meeting
If you are a meeting planner or facilities staff member, room capacity may be a concern. You want to make sure you are accommodating the optimum number of participants.

SEATING MATTERS

Imagine a facility turning away your group or meeting because your current room spaces are a few chairs shy of the group requirement. Or, suppose you have been unable to book your event at a desired venue because your group has outgrown that facility, yet they are just a little short on capacity? Or suppose you have to limit late registrations and revenue because you are right at capacity for the facility. If you are that facility, consider the expense and loss of business as you are knocking out walls with commensurate dust and limited operations for months in order to boost meeting space. And you could have had immediate increases in capacity simply by setting the chairs more efficiently,…and effectively.

In the short run, at least, wouldn't it make sense to increase utilization of the space you currently have? Setting the chairs utilizing the five principles and several of the additional factors such as spacing between rows, will get you that increased capacity.

The Value Proposition
The Meeting Professional, and the Meeting Facility all need be attuned to the value of space utilization in facilitating the learning and relational dynamics of a meeting. That means conveying the rationale, value, service orientation, and basic principles of Audience Centered Seating™.

> *"The essence of etiquette, is to provide for the comfort and safety of your guests."*
>
> **HON. JAMES W. SYMINGTON, CHIEF OF PROTOCOL**
> **U. S. DEPARTMENT OF STATE UNDER JFK**

What would constitute adequate incentive for the meeting facility to look forward, even initiate providing a better alternative design of meeting seating? In addition to comprehending what is wrong with straight row seating, there needs be a basic desire to provide congenial and comfortable space utilization for the participant. How does one persuade them so that they become self-persuading, self-initiating?

State of the Art Seating Arrangements

SEATING MATTERS

What is the Pre-Disposition of Meeting Personnel to Serve?

I have been making presentations on Audience Centered Seating for well over 20 years. And frequently I run into a past participant, meeting professional or speaker. When I ask about that person's success with innovative sets, the response is through gritted teeth. When I ask what the problem is, the response is, "Your stuff is great. But when we try to get the facility to provide us with those sets, it is like pulling teeth. They are very resistant."

Even now, and every day, it is the basic disposition of those involved in the decisions and the implementation of improved seating that will be of concern to those who want rooms set in an audience friendly mode.

One of the biggest problems in effecting change comes with introducing innovation among those who think what they are doing is "right." Or, they consider it their professional responsibility, so your request might be viewed as a blow to their competence.

If they think they are the platinum standard and have all the answers, they are most difficult to deal with. Many cannot envision an alternative to their "best" set or standard set, for they think they then would be admitting to being "wrong." And, wrong has some unfortunate implications of being "inferior" or even worse, "bad." And no self-respecting individual wants to engage in activities that imply that he or she is bad. You have to find a way to demonstrate or show them without threatening or putting them down.

This may seem like an excessive focus on the mentality of the facility personnel. However, the more you know about what and with whom you are dealing, the more care you can take to get the results you want for your meeting. Some staff have to be buttered on both sides. And that may take some time. You may be preparing them to cooperate with you on your next meeting, not this one.

The Temperament of The Meeting Professional
The vast majority of those with whom you will deal in meeting facilities fall into two of the four temperaments on the Myers Briggs Personality Type Indicator. They are overwhelmingly sensate or left brained. This is not surprising, since some 75% of the US population is also left brained. There may be, and the assumptions is made here, of a disproportionate percentage in different job assignments.

It is helpful to understand the temperament typical of those in various aspects of the meeting industry. This does not mean that each person in the specified area will be of this temperament. But the vast majority will be, and it is important to understand what their perspective and motivations are.

SEATING MATTERS

Sensate Judger: The Temperament of The Meeting Professionals
The predominant temperament in the meeting industry for meeting professionals is the Sensate Judgers [SJ]. The SJ is future focused as a conservator of rules, standards, institutions, and organizations. And they approach time as something to structure and fill in advance. They do not want any surprises once they have planned and designed their meeting. They want to live to put on another meeting another day by playing by the seeming rules.

SJ's require organizational affiliation so that they can both <u>belong and work their way to the top</u>, where they will exercise power as they see fit. Enforcing rules and regulations give them security. They attribute "stone tablet status" to the rules, protocols, and established practices as if issued from a higher power. They may attribute the same degree of certitude to traditional room sets. You must remember this is their "ticket to ride," being rule followers, not upsetting the status quo.

Established Precedent
So much of the curving of seating, the facing directly toward the presentation has to do with ancient discoveries. There is nothing "new age" here. Remember the Greeks and Romans had the right setup from the start. Add to that concerns about lighting and acoustics to make it possible to fully attend to the presentation. Everything is demonstrable, or can easily be ascertained by checking with audience member or participants. A facility devoted to quality improvement will inevitably pick up on ACS innovations, if true customer service is truly on their radar.

No Surprises
Meeting planners have told me that they do not like surprises. Room sets, especially those in the facility sales brochure, are not viewed simply as a requirement inherited from an earlier context. The brochure and ad photos may be referred to as documentation, tangible proof of the "right" way to do it. So, the SJ temperament is likely to foster and promote the industry mindset without question: "the best way to max the number of people in a meeting room is with straight row seating." They accept rules and directions as if they came directly from the Creator, not from some mere mortal limited to pews or boards placed on barrels. They will follow that rule unquestioningly. So, if and when you question that established rule or mindset, or provide an alternative, red flags go up. Expect resistance, even an "it can't be done" statement.

Make Sure They Experience the Set
The SJ may relent and allow an alternative room set on their watch. But you have to get that person to follow through and actually sit in a straight row set to diminish their reluctance to change. And make sure to have them sit in the improved room set, so that they gain authority in that new set based on their own experience. You may want to point out the benefits while they are seated to assure that experience.

State of the Art Seating Arrangements

Revisit the purpose behind a meeting. Being customer focused, can lead the SJ back to basics where they review the purpose of a meeting and the seating. But, unless there is a concerted effort made to establish, get consensus on, and institutionalize the change, they will revert to the old accepted, "we've always done it this way" approach without apology. After all, "that's the way it's supposed to be." And supposed to means forever in the mind of the SJ.

I had just demonstrated the reset of the memorial service room in my home town funeral home. The funeral director, who had been in the business for 70 years, came in to sit down and get a sense of the new room set. "It feels a lot like the Congregational Church, he said, inclusive, comfortable." I called the owner at the funeral home to find out what had happened after I left. My friend, the owner, said, "After you left, he got up and immediately began rearranging the room back into straight rows."

The Temperament of Meeting Operations
Sensate Perceivers: The SP Temperament of Conventions Operations

A preponderance of those in convention operations seem to be action oriented, doers, executors. They go for all the gusto, focus on being mobile and in the moment. They are Sensate Perceivers, [SP's], the only temperament that is <u>not focused in the future</u>. They are all about getting the next crisis dealt with and checked off their list.

Their motto is "Git 'er done!" They are all about mobility and on the spot results. If you want to kill an SP, you give them nothing to do. Luckily, the continuing time crunches of room breakdown and set-up are right in keeping with their temperament to execute. "Do it now." Breast the tape. Meet the schedule. Keep the blood stirring.

Results, Not Consequences

They are focused on immediate impact – results - not on consequences. So, without a persuasive demonstration, they may not value what they are told. They have to experience things for themselves. However, SP's are particularly sensitive to being competent, or at least being beyond reproach. They do not take well to being "wrong." So, you may get through to them better by representing your new practice as something that is a "new alternative, designs that improve the function of a meeting for everyone," rather than implying they are wrong about the way they do it, and your way is right. That only invites fierce resistance.

One Practical Approach That Worked

Several participants who attended my course on set-up reportedly handled initial resistance from room set-up personnel by first talking to them about what they are trying to do. One of the conversations went something like this:

Speaker: "All the important people in this organization will be sitting in the front row. And we want to treat them as well as possible, make them comfortable, and make sure they can see the presentation."

Set-up Person: "Okay. That makes sense."

Speaker: "I'll show you what I mean. Would you mind going and sitting in the farthest chair, in the last chair in the front row?
[After the set-up man is seated] "Thank you."
"Now, this is supposed to be one of the best seats in the house. It's an orchestra seat that would cost well over $50 or more in most presentations. And you are a member of our Board. How would you feel about sitting out there for the next hour and a half?

Set-up Person: "I see what you mean. This isn't all that good."

Speaker: "That's why I'm asking that we set up the seats in a curved row, with each chair facing the presentation.

This kind of "walk or sit in my moccasins approach" can work very well to give facility personnel the experience you want them to have so that they become self-convincing about the usefulness of your seating set-ups and more cooperative. However, sometimes it is the mentality of the audience that can be just as concretized as that of the facilities staff.

Get Your Set-up When You Absolutely, Positively Have To

Essential Steps in the Process

Persistence and Insistence Work
There are undoubtedly several approaches to the meeting facility to guarantee that you get the seating arrangement that you request. Part of your lifelong learning in this endeavor is to continue to anticipate and cover variables and eventualities and explore effective avenues to getting the set you request even when you have been stymied.

Anticipate Contingencies
In your contracting discussion with Sales and Marketing, you will be assigned a facility contact person, usually someone from sales. However, knowing the amount of transience in the industry, you should try for two guarantees.

SEATING MATTERS

(1.) Get a designated backup for your sales person in case your primary contact person is unavailable or has moved on.
(2.) Get guarantees that the agreement you have reached will be honored in the event that the property is sold or taken over by new management.

Be Specific and Detailed in Your Request: Negotiate and Contract for it.
In many facilities, the communication between Sales and Marketing, and Convention Operations [or whatever set-up people are titled in your facility] may have little consistency or follow through. First off, you have to document the contract. Be very specific, detailed and precise in making a request for the room set that you want. If there is resistance, make the room set part of the early negotiation so that they don't see it as an insignificant add-on that they can easily ignore or dismiss because it is "inconvenient."

Leave Clear Directions
To assure the staying power of your request, leave one diagram of the room set, drawn to scale, for Sales and Marketing, and another diagram for the set-up foreman.

Follow Up Six Weeks Prior to the Event
Call in or visit the facility to assure that you are still scheduled for the very rooms for which you negotiated. On occasion, a facility will give you a space that is slightly more than your group requires. Then, as your meeting time approaches, they get a request from another group, that suddenly springs to top spot on their priority list. They change your group to a smaller or differently configured space. You are now being "fit in," whereas before you had plenty of space.

At this point, even if you have to redesign the seating for the new space, take or send the facility an updated design and make sure they acknowledge receiving it and know how to set it up. You have now left or sent them a minimum of three copies of the designs.

Two weeks prior to the event, call in to check if anything has changed regarding your meeting facility or the pressures that staff are under during the time of your meeting. If possible, speak to the foreman who will be setting up your room(s), Make sure he has received the last design you left. If not, get his address and snail mail, fax or e-mail it to him with USPS® Delivery Confirmation™.

You have now left or sent 4 copies of the desired room sets. But you cannot assume anything in this business. You will want to take two more designs per room with you. One you keep in your possession at all times as your major point of reference. The other you give to the head of the set-up crew for inclusion with that day's work orders. Check his work order to make sure there are no outdated designs or orders that could create confusion or countermand your request.

SEATING MATTERS

If necessary, check with the set up crew to find out when they will be setting up the room.

When possible, be there when the crew starts so that you know they are on the right track. Or at least show up part way through so that any corrections can be made, or you can direct the fine tuning required for a superb set.

The last minute may be when you discover a breakdown of communication, so it is essential that you have your own copy of the room design with which to illustrate what you want and guide the process.

The set-up staff may still think that your request is weird. So, once they have completed the work, have them sit various places in the room to demonstrate the functionality of the set-up that they have set. This builds repertoire in the staff and some degree of skill and authority for the next meeting room set-up that you request.

Your insistence and persistence on the importance of room seating will carry its own persuasive influence. But <u>your first concern, and the facility's responsibility in good customer service, should be with getting the set you requested</u>.

One Last Word of Caution

There needs to be communication between set-up crews. Morning crews have been known to quickly rearrange the room you have worked so hard to get set correctly between 5 and 6 am. When you walk in at 8 am, you find the room set switched to traditional theatre style. It may be that the new shift's work order for the day had the same errors as the crew before them, and it has not been corrected yet. Talk with the foreman, and bring a diagram along.

Once you get the room set the way you want, place a flip chart very prominently in front of the room, an overhead spot playing on it with the message:

> *"Do not change anything here. This is the requested 9 a.m. set-up."*

Sometimes you will have to use a whiteboard. You may have to place messages several places, and before the service door entry. Make the message short and concise. If necessary, write it in the language of the set-up staff. "No tocar." in Spanish. **"Don't touch!"**

State of the Art Seating Arrangements

Keep your sense of humor. You never know what will happen. You can't anticipate everything, but you can "head' em off at the pass" if you learn well from past experience. You may find yourself close to start time for your meeting and the room is not set the way you requested, negotiated, or require. You still have choices. While influence and persuasion requires a longer trajectory. You may have to revert to getting it done right now.

Last Minute Recourse
If the crew re-sets your room too late to change it back, all is not lost. You do have a course of action that could prove to be a valuable learning experience for everyone. In fact, it may work so well that you have the room set standard painful straight row theatre style just so that you can engage this icebreaker every time.

Use the re-setting of the room as an **ice breaker exercise.** Not only will it make your participants aware of how simple it is to give them a better learning experience, they will also get a sense that <u>you care enough to set the very best</u>. And they will gain authority on future room sets based on their own experience of the seating arrangement.

Caution:
Any physical movement of chairs and tables can result in bumps and bruises, so advise your participants to set their packages and purses out of the way. Usually they can put them up against the front or side wall where they can keep an eye on them during the presentation.

Check First
Your partnership with the meeting professional is important to the success of your meeting. Make sure that you check with the meeting professional in charge of the event. She may have a specific request for the next session in your room, or a limited budget for set-up crew reimbursement.

If the room ultimately has to be returned to its original set, as you begin your ice breaker you also mention that you will be working with them to return the room exactly as you found it before you all leave the session. However, you will be improving the room set, so ask in advance if you can leave it as you changed it to the benefit of the next session.

You May Have to Return to the Original Set-Up
Check with the presenter who follows you and invite her to preview the adjusted set. She may prefer it, okay it with the meeting professional, or even ask that it be secured for them. The meeting professional may also have to be shown the new arrangement, so invite that person in for a look-see to soothe her concerns.

Bringing in the meeting professional to see the changed arrangement can not only build credibility for you, but also provides the meeting professional with a new option should

SEATING MATTERS

she wish to use it for the next session or next meeting. Eyeing the set-up provides concrete evidence of the room set for any doubting Thomas.

If in spite of all your preparation, the room set still results in traditional straight row theatre style, then you can use it as an opportunity to improve group dynamics by introducing the following "ice breaker."

If All Else Fails…Use the Following Icebreaker Exercise

Begin by asking the audience if they would like to get a little more comfortable. Most will.

Ask them to set aside any cumbersome packages, refreshments, purses during the exercise. Usually placing their items against the wall works for a brief time. If they are concerned, tell them to place their items within view.

Failure to set aside items results in obstacles to smooth moving of the seating, tipped cups and glasses, spilled drinks, and some irritation among participants and the facility.

To begin with, ask those in the back to fill up the front rows for the presentation. Tell them it is essential that they are up front and participating in this demonstration. Once you have the front of the room filled, begin.

Ask those in the middle and back rows to move back the chairs behind them some 6-8 feet to make room for the new configuration. Then have those in back remain standing.

Tell the second row that they are going to engage in an activity called "dinner party" by seating the row in front of them, the first row. Ask the front row to stand up and form a curved row that allows each of them to face the presentation directly. Have the second row pull their chair back to give them room to form a curved front row in which everyone is facing the presentation. You may have to physically move the front row occupants around to get a more symmetrical curve. Actually move into place those who don't get it or are out of formation.

Choose two individuals from the front row to establish and maintain a minimum 4 foot wide aisle all the way back to the entrance doors as the other rows are forming. They have to start with the front row. There should be two main access aisles flaring off from the front row.

If need be, you can place masking tape on the floor to mark off the range of the presentation they will be viewing. For a stand still presentation, a simple 'x' marks the spot. For someone who paces back and forth in the front of the room, a more elongated area would be the central focal point.

Now, with the front row standing in a curved row formation, facing the presentation directly, ask the second row to seat the person in the row in front of them by sliding that person's chair

State of the Art Seating Arrangements

SEATING MATTERS

under the front row member. Make sure the aisle space is part of the front row, and that the two aisle persons are seated along with their front row.

As each individual is seated, you will probably find open slots in the front row. Fill them in by moving someone from the second row into the first row. Keep the aisles clear.

The second row participants now stand behind the first row, preserving the same basic shape of the formation and the aisles. Ask the third row to seat the second row. Move people ahead from the third into the second row.

Then ask each succeeding row to once again seat the row in front of them. Stay actively involved by shaping the rows, filling in gaps by moving people forward to be seated, and maintaining the aisle width. Broaden the aisles beyond a mere 4 feet in width as you move toward the exit in order to accommodate the accumulation of participants that will fill the aisle toward the back of the room.

The very last row has to pull the chairs they moved to the back, and seat themselves. You may have to direct them to do so.

Once everyone is seated check to determine if each person can see. If not, have those with obstructed views readjust their seating so that they are facing the presentation, can see, and are comfortable.

Ask the participants what they think of the curved row arrangement. Repeat their comments for the larger audience and the recording. Usually you can expect to hear – "comfortable,... see more people without effort,... clear view,... easy in and out." Draw them out, and make adjustments if anyone has placed himself in a worse position.

After one such reset, a participant complained that the place she had chosen to place her chair was worse than before. It was right behind the person in front, blocking her view. Curiously, she did not grasp that she was the one who re-set her own chair in the first place. She was reluctant to adjust her chair, and did so only after a certain amount of nudging.

This Chapter has dealt with several potential impediments to getting your participants set up in the way your request:
- o   Facility staff attitude toward arranging meeting space.
- o   The Temperament of facilities staff and set-up personnel
- o   Step by step strategy for ensuring the set-up you request.
        from the facility set-up crew
- o   An ice-breaker from your audience, if all else fails.

Now that we have considered overcoming resistance in the meeting space, facility personnel, and audience, the next chapter will deal with general, predictable resistance to innovative room setups.

State of the Art Seating Arrangements

Chapter 14

Influence

Getting Cooperation
Meeting professionals and speakers who have attended my workshop titled, "Get Your Audience the Best Seats in the House…and Increase Capacity," tell me that the biggest problem they have in getting the set-ups they want comes from the resistance of the meeting facilities. It's typically the staff that have been there the longest that are the most entrenched. They will even give you assurance that it can't be done. One question to pose then, with an air of objectivity is: "Does that mean that it is impossible, or that you will not do it?"

Charlie Fewell, a trainer who works mainly in the automotive industry, sends a template ahead to the hotel to get his preferred non-traditional straight row room set. The facilities often ask him, "What do you want that for? Aren't you going to 'teach'em'?"

Effective Persuasion Will be Required
This entire book is devoted to descriptions of seating arrangements that qualitatively will improve meetings, events, and learning. The presentation of these arrangements has been against a background of current practice and entrenched resistance in the meeting industry toward doing things differently.

Aspects of persuasion and influence are not just now being introduced in this book. Throughout each chapter you have been reading a litany of rationales for how the current practices are largely counterproductive if not dysfunctional. And, on the upside, you have already read numerous reasons for adopting improved room sets according to the five audience centered seating™ principles. You have already been armed with rationales, tips and methods for influencing decision makers, from conventions operations staff, through foremen, sales and marketing, as well as meeting professionals and facilities administrators. You already have a lot of content and procedures to rely on and call upon when you uncover or anticipate resistance.

Relationships are Everything in this Process
While the room set that you request is the result you want in the short run, it is preferred if you can get that result by gaining the cooperation and collaboration of those who can make it happen. Even better, orient those who will make improved room setups happen for you or your meeting so well that they literally carry the "baton" by becoming self-persuading. That way they are not only fully convinced and engaged, they have become advocates for these improved methods. They will continue to pass on their understanding, skill, and commitment to improve room sets far beyond your event.

SEATING MATTERS

Lifelong Learning in Optimizing Meetings
Once you become sensitized to the platform mechanics of a meeting, presentation, or production, you will never again attend or observe an event the same way. You will become a lifelong learner in how to stage events, together with initiatives you can take to optimize the environment, and maximize the benefit from that event. I have included much more than seating, but seating is a major place to start.

I have learned something new about optimizing the learning environment in practically every experience I have had whether attending meetings, speaking, working with the meeting planner, or meeting set-up staff. There is always something to pick up on. So, open your eyes and be prepared for a fascinating learning venture.

> *A participant in a recent meeting in Arlington, VA., arrived late at the opening general session. Entering by one of the side double doors toward the back of the ballroom, he hoped to slip in unnoticed and find a seat or stand at the back. However, this hotel had two lights beaming down from overhead immediately inside the doors. It was more like being the guest at his own surprise birthday party, than a late arriving participant.*
>
> *He was announced by the lighting, his entrance competing with the main stage for the attention of the nearest seating section. Personally I would opt for lighting strips in the floor. And if I were in charge of the event, I would check the fire code requirements first, and ask about the rationale for those lights. If possible, I would turn off the light over the door designated to open by unscrewing that light, or both. At least, turn off the light over the single entry door.*

Factors to Consider
Starting today, whenever you are in the company of people who are meeting or presenting, see what you can learn with them and from them. Ask them about their experience. How have they dealt with different situations? What works for them?

Pay attention to everything from:
- rationale and practices they have employed, to
- resistance they have faced and from whom, to
- details such as seating row shape and length,
- audience behavior [especially discomfort],
- access to seating during the presentation,
- blocked lines of sight, and especially
- your own experience as an audience member of
    - lighting and sound systems,
    - disturbances outside the room,
    - equipment malfunctions.

State of the Art Seating Arrangements

Rather than being an observer with a clipboard, start sitting down in the room set and see what vantage you gain; what you can discover. Only by operating with "beginner eyes" will you overturn your own assumptions.

You may be able to get the room set your way with a well-prepared argument. But there may be others involved, other stakeholders, who hold the final decision. So, you may end up having to manage up through a hierarchy, across or through departments, or executing the logistics yourself.

Exercise Discretion

And, even though it is easier to ask for forgiveness than gain permission, you have to exercise your own discretion in any and all of the matters introduced in this book. You choose your opportunities, what you will promote, how far you will go, and with whom. It has to be your choice, for you know the territory, the organization, the facility, the personalities and positions involved, the history.

Persistence is Part of the Persuasion Process

Often the process of influencing, persuading, convincing, is like dripping water on stone. It takes time to take effect. So begin at your earliest opportunity. Start the process in motion. You will have to exercise patience as well, for this is marketing, not sales you are engaged in.

For how long do you need to assert yourself? Promote your plan? Provide initiative in the matter of getting your room arrangements accepted? As often as it takes for as long as is takes.

The Art of the Long View

Influencing requires the art of the long view. It takes time. Forget immediate gratification. And just so that you understand how long it may take, the writings of Dr. James Prochaska lay out the process clearly.

Changing for Good

Changing for Good is a book on the process of awakening to one's responsibility that an individual undergoes before taking on the responsibility for dealing with an issue. Dr. Prochaska lays out five steps to help the change agent assess, understand, appreciate, and guide an individual through that process of adopting an innovation; and to assist in easing that person through to taking responsibility and initiative.

1. **Pre-Contemplative Stage:** The individual considers the innovation irrelevant or unrelated to their scope of concern or responsibility. Even the insinuation that seating, or the painful aspects of straight row seating are the responsibility of that position will be met with eyes glazed over.

2. **Contemplative Stage:** With time, as the issue gains consideration, soaks in, the individual starts to understand the relevance of seating to his or her role, choices, tasks, or function. It is no longer a matter of ignoring or denying relevance. The person is at least considering how it relates, musing.

3. **Planning:** Accepting that one's professional role encompasses this responsibility for the attainment of optimal meeting, learning, or event environment…even for audience comfort, the professional begins a conscious process of planning to implement. Initiative is taken in some aspect of the range of options and decisions that go into getting better seating and improving the meeting environment. This may involve discussion, assessment of impact, determination of capacity, costs in money or staff time, gaining authority or "sign off" to take on this operation, reassigning roles and tasks, getting buy-in and agreement from all those involved in the process.

4. **Implementation:** The plan is put into operation. Execution depends upon:
    a. how thoroughly <u>mutual planning</u> was engaged in by the immediate stakeholders,
    b. the anticipation, foresight, and initiative of everyone involved,
    c. the skills of those engaged in the implementation,
    d. inclusion of all parties who can implement or foul up the operation.

    There may be a series of subsequent attempts at implementation that provide self-correcting feedback or quality improvement in the operation undertaken. It is important to thoroughly plan with all stakeholders, lest they scuttle the implementation by finding their own stumbling blocks or excuses. There should also be a report back to those up the line who signed off on the innovation to solidify the rationale, efficiency, and on-going value of the process. That leads to the next step.

5. **Institutionalization:** The new procedures are now integrated and assimilated, made part and parcel of the organizational operation. If it is an organization holding a meeting, the meeting professional has the go-ahead to make this the operational mode, the way these matters are done in this organization. The meeting facility might adopt "curved theatre style" seating as the way they now do theatre style in their facility. They may now include it in their menu of room sets, or offer to set the room "the best way they know how," in the absence of any specific request by the customer. This stage involves true acceptance of the new practice.

> *People don't change.*
> *Things change. People transition.*

People Don't Change

One further elaboration on what it takes to introduce new practices is to look at the reality of human behavior. People typically do not make "cold turkey" choices to do things differently, and then actually do them. They generally experience some set backs, falling back into old habits, triggered by familiar circumstances, and revert to old behaviors. Think about those on diets to lose weight and the "yo-yo effect." The big difference here is that if you learn from those cases in which you were set back, you can find ways to counter a future setback of the same type. "Fool me once…" might be another way of underscoring the set back.

A transition looks more like a roller coaster. Pay special attention to the first rise. This is what often seems like early success to the person seeking to accomplish a behavior change or establish a new practice. This has also been called the "first love phenomenon." You make a decision to accomplish something, and set out to do it. Suddenly you are realizing the results as if your goal has been reached. Mission accomplished.

Not so fast. Now comes the undermining rebellion of all your inner selves that are not in agreement with what your leader self set out to accomplish. The insurgency can be subverting, but only if you are unrealistic and expect that it will not occur.

First Love Phenomenon

That first love phenomenon is the "head in the clouds" reaction of what appears to be early success. But just as your first love in life either dumped you, moved away, or lost interest slowly, you find yourself falling off the cliff and into the precipice. Only if you expect ideas that the embedding of new practices is a one shot effort that will stay in place like an industrial staple, will you be surprised or disappointed. But for anyone with a history and active brain, there are habits in place, routines, regimens, rituals. At some point, that formerly well established behavior will be triggered by some event and automatically be inserted into the process with the result that you experience a set back.

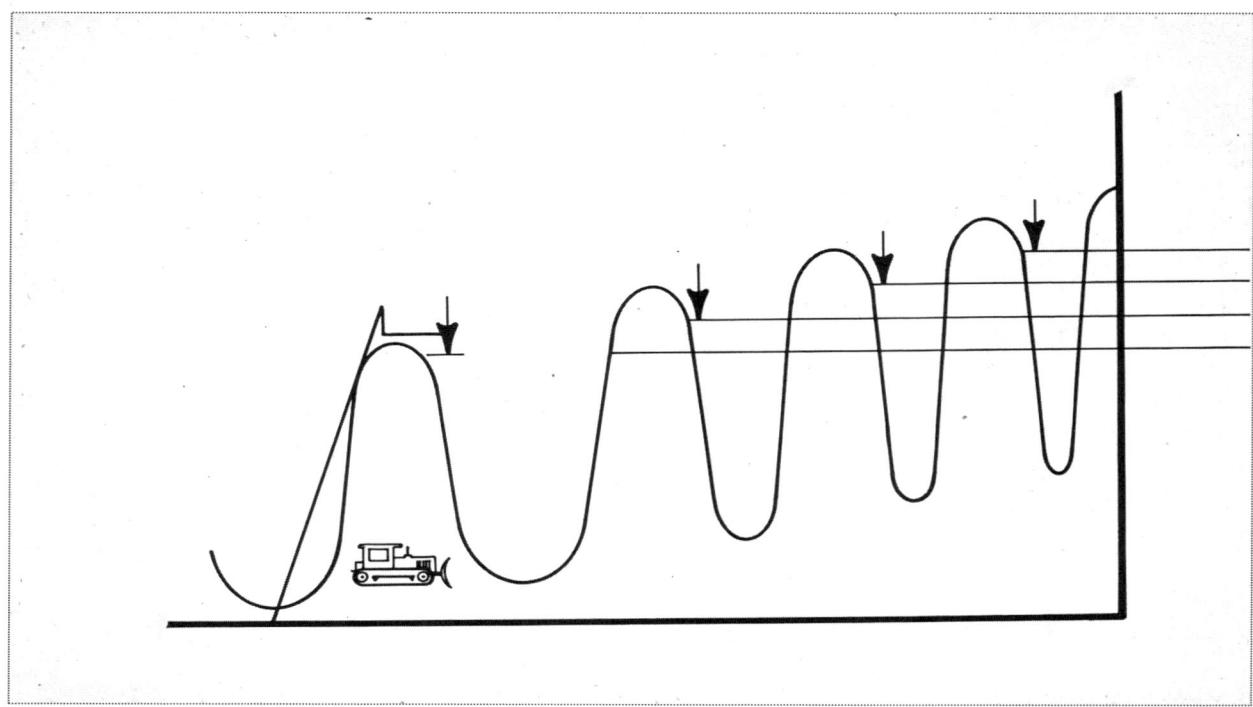

At that point, you can recall that your first success did require taking several steps up the ladder toward getting your goal. Then, with each succeeding setback, simply note what triggered the set back and develop counter measures to anticipate and offset the effects of that setback in the future. There will be plenty of things triggering the old behaviors. However, as you establish each counter measure as a new rung on the ladder, you gain the ability to approach your goal, advancing toward it with each step.

In some cases, the set backs you encounter may be from factors totally outside yourself. In those cases the resistance or triggers of your set backs are more systemic, entrenched in the facility you engage, or in the mentality of those designated to implement your preference.

Sorting Through the "Reasons Why Not"

Several planners claim that they made explicit requests for curved row sets, but facilities were not giving them what they asked for. "We send in detailed diagrams and they agree to do the set. But when we get down there in the morning to begin the meeting, the room is not even close to what we requested. Usually by that time it is too late. And the facility blames it on the night set-up crew that has already left."

SEATING MATTERS

You Will be Stalled, Stonewalled, Given Lame Excuses
It helps to know in advance some of the excuses and rationales presented for why you will not get the room set you request. But even being aware of the resistance doe not guarantee that your counterarguments will initially be sufficient to turn the tide to get your requested set. For example, by stalling, time may become of the essence and it is too late to get your setup. Once you are in the facility and four hours from the start of your event, your desires fall victim to the claim that "there isn't sufficient time to get that done." The amount of time preceding the event, setup crew availability, union rules, your relationship with the facility, may all be factors.

But, no matter what your first encounter, that failure to execute is an indication of where you are starting with that person, office, or facility. It's a benchmark. Once you get clear on that, you can begin the process of introducing those-who-resist-improvement to an alternative way of thinking and new practices in room setup. Begin dripping water on stone. Just remember, you have to exercise patience.

Rationales for the Bowling Alley Set-Up
If you should ever sit in a bowling alley set-up, you would know that it does not work at all unless you have a fairly high platform for the presenters. Even then, the bowling alley distances the audience from the presentation. If there is a general rationale for continuing to set it that way, it could be anything from, "It can't be set to the side," "we've never seen it set up differently," "this is the way it has to be set," or "I don't want to battle with the set up crew."

One colleague requested the curved set-up to the long side that I used in Indianapolis, and was assured by the meeting professional that it could not be done. He then went ahead and re-set the room by himself. When she returned to the room with the set accomplished, she refused to look at the arrangement.

The Importance of Predictable Sets
Remember that one reason the room is set in that straight row to the narrow-end-of-room way is that it is a safe, no surprises set and that makes the meeting professional [and the meeting facility staff] feel competent, therefore, comfortable. It requires predictable mechanical action by the meeting facility and does not disturb the working relationship by having required a negotiation or potentially obnoxious request. They treat setting your room as if they were setting pins in a bowling alley.

Dedicated Screen and/or Electrical Plugs Dictate the Set
Some facilities will point to the dedicated fixture of a drop down screen recessed into the ceiling in the middle of the narrow side of the room. They will use that as all the mandate they need to consistently set to the narrow side of the room. For some reason there is a tendency to set up for distance from the presentation rather than closeness. Perhaps it was prompted by early slide projector lenses that required a distance from the screen to cover even a 5 x 5 foot area. When you are dealing with an old historic property such as the

State of the Art Seating Arrangements

SEATING MATTERS

Albemarle Inn, Thomas Jefferson's own, in Charlottesville, Virginia, where a screen may be set in the ceiling, you can still bring in a portable screen. An extension cord can be provided by the facility, or you can bring your own.

> **Aside:** *Every portable projection screen I have ever set up has a triangular base. And the base is configured so that the back foot sticks straight back so that you cannot get the screen flush up against the wall, losing valuable setup space. There is no tight fit. And in a small room, that 18-24 inches of dead space behind the screen is not only wasted, it contributes nothing to the stability of the screen, and provides a smaller image in a small or a crowded room. It may also mean that you lose seating capacity to the side of the screen, since you can sit within about 22 degrees of the screen and see.*

Track Lighting is Set for the Narrow Side

A similar rationale for keeping the set-up to the narrow side of the room is the track lighting in the ceiling. However, many meeting facilities and customers seem as oblivious to lighting requirements as they do to the room set. I have been at numerous National Association Chapter meetings as well as at national conferences at which the track lighting went unused. It sat right up there in the ceiling, where it had been installed, right in front of the stage, and no one bothered to turn it on. Meanwhile, presenters took on a ghoulish appearance from the deep shadows under their eyes due to the overhead recessed lights, or their faces were barely visible.

Even without dedicated track lighting, it is easy and inexpensive to provide lighting in any part of the room. That is a poor reason to set to the short side. Set to the long side and adjust the AV and lighting to that long side set.

The Room is Set for a Later Presentation

Oh, does that mean that my presentation is not important? This room set for later may be nothing more than an excuse. The later presenter may have neither requested the set that is dictating dynamics for the day, nor had any discussion about it. Your Audience Centered™ set would probably serve the final presentation better than the standard set being used. This is where you have to take more initiative with those presenting in your designated room for that day.

You would do well to contact the final presenter of the day and discuss with her/him what would work best for all of you. Then take this solution to the meeting professional who is planning and coordinating the logistics. Usually, the easier you can make it for the logistics person, the better. And often these lame excuses come from an attempt to set the room and forget it. Check it off the list. And, under no circumstance incur more expense for setting it.

But it could have been set well once, for everyone, if only everyone involved had been consulted rather than handed a standardized set. And this could be a regular item for the

State of the Art Seating Arrangements

SEATING MATTERS

logistics planner to consider and consult with the presenters in the first place, even if it is an additional item. So, if after all your efforts to coordinate the resistance to a compromise set for the day persists, you may find that room environment is simply not considered important in the first place. And you may be perceived as complicating things, a troublemaker.

There have been occasions in which I have provided two of the four sessions in the same concurrent session room in one day, yet the room was still set for the last session of the day. What is it about that last session that takes precedence over all the others?

One Size Fits All
If you are discussing budget issues, it typically costs more to re-set a room during the day unless you made it part of the initial scope of work [or unless the facility is really into providing service]. Other wise, the meeting planner goes for a safe, one-size-fits-all traditional room design that fits all the anticipated events in that room throughout the entire meeting.

The Threat of Higher Cost
The Convention Liaison Council Meeting Handbook 7th edition, contains the warning: **"Be prepared to pay extra if you request a seating arrangement that varies from the standard room sets."** What a disincentive to the meeting planner for whom operating within the budget drives many of the meeting decisions.

When I wrote the 6th edition CLC Manual section on seating, I distinctly took out that highlighted warning. However, my exclusion was overridden by the editor, and it continued into the 7th edition. That warning alone will elicit an eye glaze response from the meeting professional when you suggest a different room set.

Anticipating the Unanticipated: Things That Come Up

Personnel Changes, Especially Your Contact Person
The person in sales from whom you initially requested room set services will already have been transferred to another job by the time the meeting occurs. Ask to be informed of any staff member substitutions, especially those on whom you ultimately count to carry through on requests. Anticipate and negotiate the room environment as far in advance as possible. Make the seating one of your priority requirements and then stand by your requirements. Be determined enough that you will do what is required for the session to be a success.

Why is This Important?
Many meeting logistics people are simply unaccustomed to discussing, let alone negotiating or accommodating anyone else's room request. They see this as their job, their

SEATING MATTERS

expertise, so they are the last word on it. And they consider their selection of "tried and true" traditional sets to be of refined, common usage, an offering with which you should be content. Or, they have just been at a conference from which they are introducing a set-up they thought would be "neat," but it proves not to be.

If you get someone to whom any alternative seating is a hassle, you might volunteer to change it yourself, thereby reducing the risk and potential cost to the planner. But make sure that you have the logistics person come in and view the room as you set it. Explain the rationale for what you have done. Then, make sure that person is present for at least part of your presentation. They need to see the participants in their seats, sense the energy and atmosphere in the room to assuage any fears, and derive their own rationale for using this set in the future.

The Crew Can't Do This Setup
You may even be told that the set-up crew "does not know how to do the set-up you are requesting." I overheard this statement from the meeting Sales office contact to the meeting planner for the event, while the Convention Operations person looked right at the requested diagram and said he could do it.

You are now in new territory. You could offer to teach their setup crew, or ask that they experiment with the set you request. Usually someone on the set-up crew does know how to provide your requested set up. And if that person does not know the setup you want, you need only provide him with the rationale and an overview of what you want, and he can approximate it. If he is open to it, you can guide or assist him. Or if he wants to do it on his own, then you can do the fine tuning necessary.

What is the Status of the Action Your Request?
There are three categories for actions or variables such as room sets. They may vary greatly between meeting facilities or meeting professionals. They are:
1. **Fixed**, as in dedicated seating. It would take a major renovation in order to change the way the room can be set.
2. **Negotiable** as in open to discussion and variability depending upon the persuasiveness, skill, and willingness of each party.
3. **Choice** as in you merely ask and your wish is their command, or you execute your choice yourself.

Make The Room Set Non-Negotiable

Begin With the Initial Phone Call
Your leverage is greatest when the facility is still trying to get your business. Of course, it helps if it is a buyer's market. But there will be more "yes's" on the phone in response to your inquiries just to get you into the sales office then there might be if your wait till you are in the sales office to begin making your requests, or demands. It is up to you to follow

State of the Art Seating Arrangements

through on your seating requirements from the outset. Let them know you mean it. You are serious. Seating matters.

First Qualify The Facility
Is this a facility you want to explore further? What is the facility's understanding, acceptance, and track record with your request? Have they hosted meetings with similar requests in the past? Ask for references. Were the conditions different? What pressures do they anticipate could complicate your request?

Lead Off With a Room Set Request
Negotiation may be required, the earlier you handle it in your discussion the better. Get ready to get the facility's attention and deal with it. They have not dealt with speakers, education specialists, human resources professionals or other customers who have specific requirements beyond the menu of traditional meeting facility offerings. And you have little way of knowing their intention or strategy in keeping control and ultimately stonewalling you, if at all.

In one case the meeting logistics person for a facility claimed that my room setup requirements might result in injury to his staff due to their having to move heavy tables. He said that the professional speaker preceding me required those tables for his presentation. My "translation" of his resistance was that my setup request was inconvenient and he would rather not have to deal with it.

The truth was that <u>the professional speaker preceding me had not even been secured</u> at that time. The logistics person had established what he wanted and expected me to accommodate to his set-up. However, my full session included a demonstration of seating arrangements which would have been impossible with those tables in place.

When the speaker preceding me was finally secured, he and I discussed his actual set-up requirements. He said that his presentation would go better without tables and with my set-up. [He had not been asked what he required by the logistics person.] So, we moved the tables out during an earlier break and it became a non-issue.

However, the logistics person did not enter the room for any part of my seating presentation, so at no time did he observe the importance of the requested room set or learn from it for his organization, which continues to utilize many of the dysfunctional room sets we are seeking to replace.

Taking Initiative
You have to take the initiative and persevere in advocating for your requirements, priorities, and preferences in seating. So, be ready to
1. persist in tracking down the facts and stakeholders;
2. contact, coordinate and team with speakers and presenters; while adapting to the capabilities of the facility and facility personnel.

SEATING MATTERS

Remember that most professionals consider the long-standing practices to be the best way, tried and true. They have been doing it, the industry has been doing it, this way for a long time. That is pretty much all they have seen. And since joining the meeting industry, they have not sat through anything but their own organization meetings. So, what they set is not only acceptable, it is considered "state of the art." And safe.

Who is the "Customer" in Your Meeting?
While one would expect customer service to reign supreme in the room setup enterprise, you have to determine who the facility considers "the customer." Frequently it is the person who writes the check, or who makes the requests – often one and the same person.

The audience has no real voice in the meeting logistics except an occasional complaint or suggestion during the meeting, and comments on the meeting evaluation,
- if there is an evaluation,
- if it is read, and
- if any weight is given the evaluation.

On occasion, an exhausted staff and volunteer committee, together with an outgoing association president will lament having produced a poorly received convention, and then not subject themselves to further critique by ignoring the evaluations. "Why learn from the mistakes. We know it was a disaster."

In many cases it is the meeting professional that is treated like the customer and the budget is perceived as one limiting factor. Since seating is considered a limited choice, a standard offering, it is more of a check-list item than something that is spelled out and negotiated in the planning. So, even during an essential part of the early familiarization trip to the facility consider, "Can they provide the optimal learning environment for your group? And, will they?"

Any Effective Agreement Requires Mutual Accord, Planning and Execution
Many people think that because they have a signed agreement, that the requested performance is ensured. However, <u>the agreement is not complete until it is executed</u>. That is why you have to have mutual agreement on the initial terms and results, but also need to mutually work out the particulars in planning and execution. Then you are more likely to attain the results.

Get Advance Agreement Rather than Agreeableness
In the crucible of mid-meeting pressures and concerns, your early room set priorities and request are not as likely to be honored. They can give way to an insufficient number of facility staff to make a timed room re-set. One of your designs might be omitted from the meeting master book. A staff person might be out of the loop and just set it "regular."

To avoid slippage, you have to plan ahead, get real agreement, mutual planning and execution in advance, not in mid-meeting. Learn to distinguish "agreeableness" from true agreement and commitment on the part of the facility. You don't want to discover that you had no true commitment in the midst of the meeting maelstrom. At the last minute, no

State of the Art Seating Arrangements

matter who fails to execute the contract or complete the assignment, shortage of time or concern about other priorities means that the seating does not get set correctly.

Make The Room Set Part of the Contract
Use the word, "contract." An agreement does not carry the weight of a contract. "Contract" says mutual responsibilities and accountability, even liability for non-performance. And even though an "agreement" is intended to have the same full force of law, contract goes to the core of the performance issue more directly.

It could be that the convention operations shift:
- came on at 2 am and actually came in and re-set the ballroom, which was
- already set correctly for the next morning's 8 am start time by an earlier shift,
- the shift did not have the designated diagram on their work order, or,
- they came in and completely ignored the diagram, so they reverted to the standard straight row theatre style.

Be Ready to Negotiate Up Front
You will probably be one of the first customers that makes a request, or brings to the facility's attention that seating can be done differently and better. In fact, you may wish to share this book with them or purchase one for them. Facilities may wish to purchase the book for clients to share how they can best set the rooms.

Give Them a Copy of SEATING MATTERS. Let the Book Do The Persuading
Share this book with the facility. The printed word and illustrations carry a certain persuasive power. Getting the innovation accepted does not all need to depend upon you. Flag those sections of the book that make the points you wish to convey and hand it over to the facility.

Go Forth and Optimize Your Meeting Environments
You are now equipped to determine, design, request, set, and obtain the room set that will best serve your meeting. You will have challenges, but few that you have not been prepared for. Remember, you will learn something new in every meeting you run, setup, plan, present at, or attend. You simply need to keep your eyes open and your body and mind tuned to what is going on.

Should you have questions about these sets or any of the assertions of this book,, wish to have your facility set and photo-documented in the various fine tuned Audience Centered Seating designs; please contact me at DrPaul@Thrival.com. Put ACS in all caps in the subject line, nothing more, so that it can be distinguished from spam.

What follows in Appendix A, is a section of full sized room designs, from the large general session to the small group and board room meeting, an application of the five principles.

I wish you much good fortune, and even more persistence and perseverance, in optimizing your meetings and events. Remember, **SEATING MATTERS!**

State of the Art Seating Arrangements

SEATING MATTERS

State of the Art Seating Arrangements

Appendix A – Room Diagrams

> **Limited Permission for Use**
>
> This folio of Audience Centered Seating™ arrangements is offered under the following licensing agreement for the exclusive use of the owner of this book. Use of these diagrams, which are the intellectual property of the author, is permitted under the following conditions:
>
> **Local Use:** If a meeting facility is the owner, then use is restricted to within that distinct facility, not extending to other franchises, part, or all of the brand. Other facilities under the same brand or management are required to obtain their own copy in-house to utilize this folio in-house.
>
> If use of a diagram or diagrams is required to request a specific event or meeting room set, then those diagrams may be copied for that use. Transmission, however, must be by fax, snail mail, or hand transmission.
>
> **None of these illustrations or diagrams is to be placed on or transmitted by the internet, zip file, or in any electronic method other than facsimile. Doing so is a violation of copyright law.**

Training and Certification in Audience Centered Seating™ Arrangements is available to associations, corporations, organizations, and meeting facilities. This training involves an overview of the process, followed by hands on instruction in setting and fine tuning the meeting or event room. An on-site photographer is engaged for the purpose of documenting the capacity and design of the various set-ups in the very room in which the set will occur, with the in-house equipment employed for that setup.

SEATING MATTERS

Angled ACS™ Straight Row Theater Style
Audience Centered Seating™ Principles:

1. **Set to the long wall** for closeness to the presentation.

2. **Curve the seating to face the presentation. No Straight rows.**
   Even the most intransigent facilities person has to see some merit in this setup. You get the very same capacity as the more typical straight row seating. It is still straight row seating. Some facilities convention operations staff have indicated that this set-up is easier than the regular straight row set. Participants will be more comfortable and track the presentation more easily.

   This setup is a half-way application which utilizes only a few of the 5 principles. Rather than curving the row, simply **angle the seating, pivoting each chair to face toward the presentation – <u>more than in the illustration</u>**. The pivot point is the back leg of the chair nearest the presentation. It remains exactly where it would be in a traditional straight row theatre style setup. In this case, keeping the row straight is essential to your argument of equaling straight row capacity. When an audience re-sets to angled seating, they tend to bow the row slightly.

3. **No center aisle. Flare aisles off the end of the podium to the back doors.**
   Space two aisles just outside the podium according to the diagram. They will generally be straight rows and parallel to the sidewalls and perpendicular to the podium. That lines up the center section dead-on to the platform or podium. Make sure the stage is high enough for them to see over a fan of heads. Those in the outside sections can pivot or angle their chairs toward the podium. Usually it does not require more than 3-4 inches rotation for the front legs to face the stage.

4. **Face each chair toward the presentation.**
   You will come closer to honoring this principle by angling the chairs than by keeping them facing the front wall. The chairs are already placed in the straight row. Face them toward the presentation, while they remain in the straight row.

5. **Cut single-chair veins or access lanes into long rows**.
   Every middle or seventh chair is removed to assure ease of access and egress. No one need walk in front of more than 5 chairs in order to get to a seat – generally only 1-3.

6. **Set the last row on the back wall.** Leave aisle space in front of the last row for ease of access and exit, primarily exit. If this session is set for a break-out or concurrent session, and if the registration allows for each registrant to attend any sessions without prior registration, then setting on the back wall will depend upon whether you wish to leave room for grazers to come and go, and to optimize the room capacity. If you anticipate a heavy contingent of grazers, leave open space in the back, including putting the water table out in the hall.

State of the Art Seating Arrangements

SEATING MATTERS

State-of-the-Art Theater Style

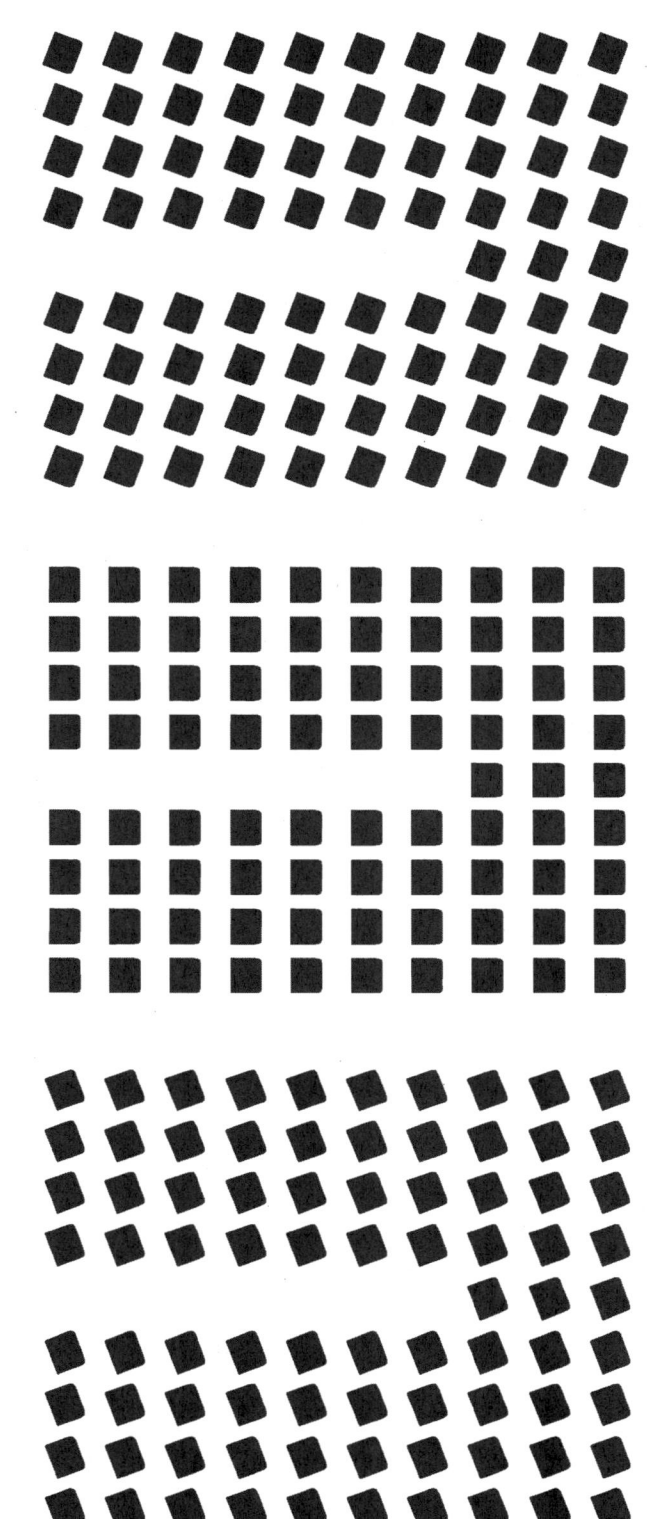

State of the Art Seating Arrangements

SEATING MATTERS

Angled ACS™ Herringbone/Chevron

This setup is also a half-way measure, utilizing only a few of the principles. Still it is superior to traditional chevron and solves the line of sight problems of chevron. The latter part of Chapter 2, details the problem with straight row herringbone, with visibility worse than theatre style.

Audience Centered Seating™ Principles:

1. **Set to the long wall** for closeness to the presentation.

2. **Curve the seating to face the presentation. No Straight rows.**
   Even the most intransigent facilities person has to see some merit in this setup. Certainly you can get the very same capacity as the more typical straight row seating, so that argument doesn't work as resistance. Plus, participants will be more comfortable. But this setup still violates the pure principle of no straight rows, which is why it is a half-way measure.

   We simply **angle the seating, pivoting each chair toward the presentation.** The back leg of the chair nearest the center of the room is the pivot leg, remaining exactly where it would be in a non-angled herringbone or chevron setup. In this case, keeping the row straight is essential to your argument of equaling straight row capacity and being within the setup crew's ability.

3. **No center aisle. Flare aisles off the end of the podium to the back doors.**
   Space two aisles just outside the podium. As per the diagram, they will generally be straight rows parallel to the side walls and perpendicular to the podium. That lines up the center section dead-on to the platform or podium. Those sitting on the aisle of the side sections can pivot or angle their chairs toward the podium – usually not more than 2-3 inches rotation for the front legs.

4. **Face each chair toward the presentation.**
   You will come closer to honoring this principle by angling the chairs than by keeping them facing the front wall. The chairs are already placed in the straight row. Face them toward the presentation, while they remain in the straight row. In some cases, depending upon the initial slant of the outside section of the chevron, you may have some of the angled chairs in the same row, pivoting left toward the presentation, those chairs in the middle staying straight, and those toward the other side pivoting right in order to "face" the presentation more directly.

5. **Cut single-chair veins or access lanes into long rows.**
   Every seventh chair is removed to assure ease of access and egress. No one need walk in front of more than 5 chairs in order to get to a seat – generally only 1-3.

State of the Art Seating Arrangements

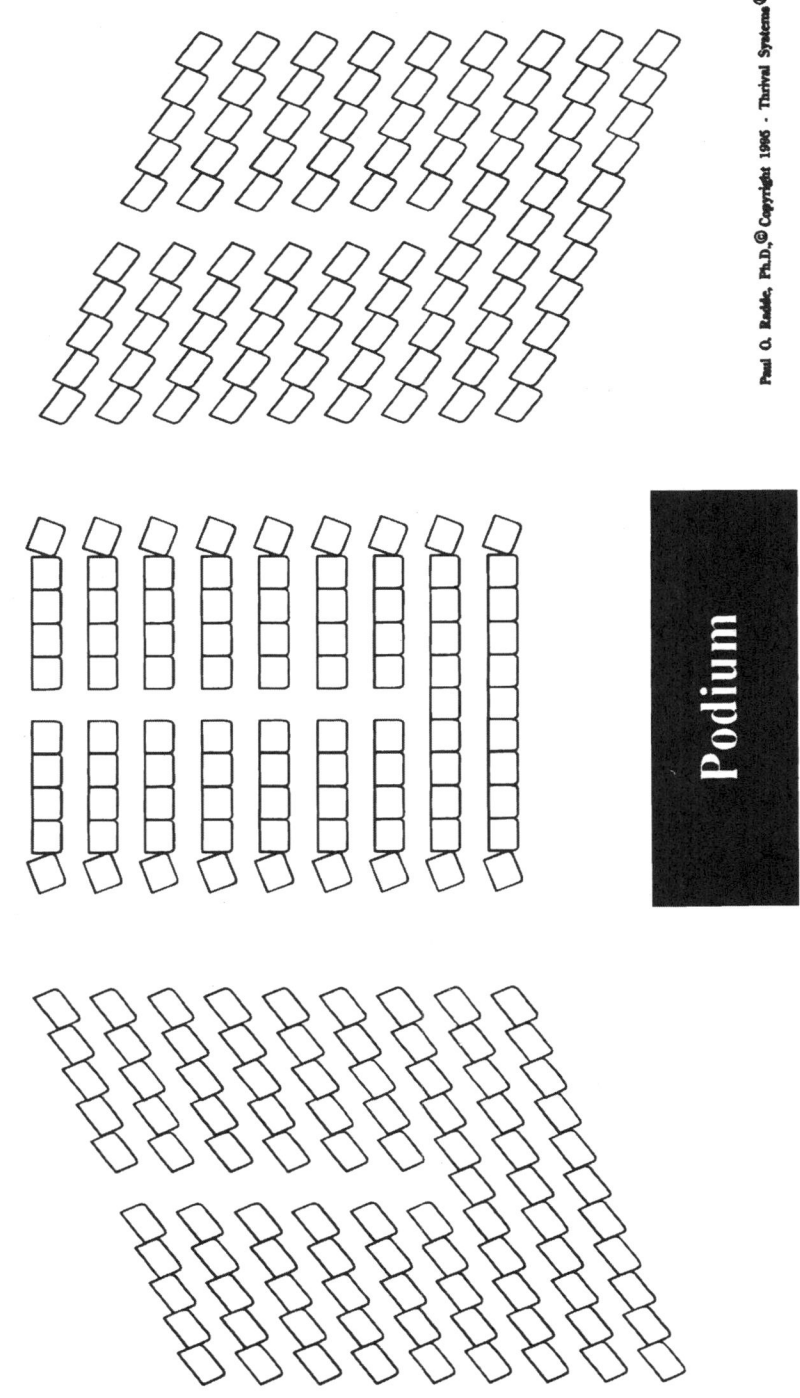

SEATING MATTERS

Curved Row ACS™ Theater Style
Audience Centered Seating™ Principles:

1. **Set to the long wall** for closeness to the presentation. <u>Set the front row within 6-9 feet of the stage, closer than is indicated in the illustration.</u>

2. **Curve the seating to face the presentation. No Straight rows.**
   When designing this room set, especially when using a stencil or compass, the central dot in the illustration - between the "d" and "i" in Podium - will indicate the focal point for the presentation. A fixed point presentation is delivered from a single position such as behind a lectern. If this is not a single point presentation, then the focal point might be expanded to a focal range as shown in the first illustration in Chapter 11, but the seating is generally disposed in the exact same direction.

3. **No center aisle. Flare aisles 45 degrees off the end of the podium to the exits.**
   Space two aisles from the front corners of the podium. As per the diagram, the aisles will generally track directly toward the exits, widening out toward the back doors to accommodate increasing volume of traffic and those who want to schmooze around the doors. This angle of the aisles may be 45 degrees, but that is a general rule. **The better rule is to draw a line directly from the corner of the stage toward the exit.**

4. **Face each chair toward the presentation.**
   This principle is redundant with principle 2, since the focal point is fixed.

5. **Cut single-chair veins or access lanes into long rows.**
   Every seventh chair in from the aisle [or the middle chair in rows numbering from 9-13 chairs] is removed to assure ease of access and egress. No one need pass in front of more than 5 chairs in order to get to a seat – generally only 1-3.

6. **Set the last row on the back wall.** Use only in smaller groups, under 350. Leave aisle space in front of the last row for exiting. In larger spaces, you can gain capacity by setting from the back wall forward, as long as that section does not impede traffic flow for those from other seating sections.

   Again, if the registration is oversubscribed, or allows for each registrant to attend any sessions without prior registration, then setting on the back wall will depend on whether you wish to leave room for grazers to come and go, or to optimize the room capacity. If there is a heavy contingent of grazers, leave open space in the back of the room by taking out additional seating rows. Also, take the water table out in the hall.

State of the Art Seating Arrangements

SEATING MATTERS

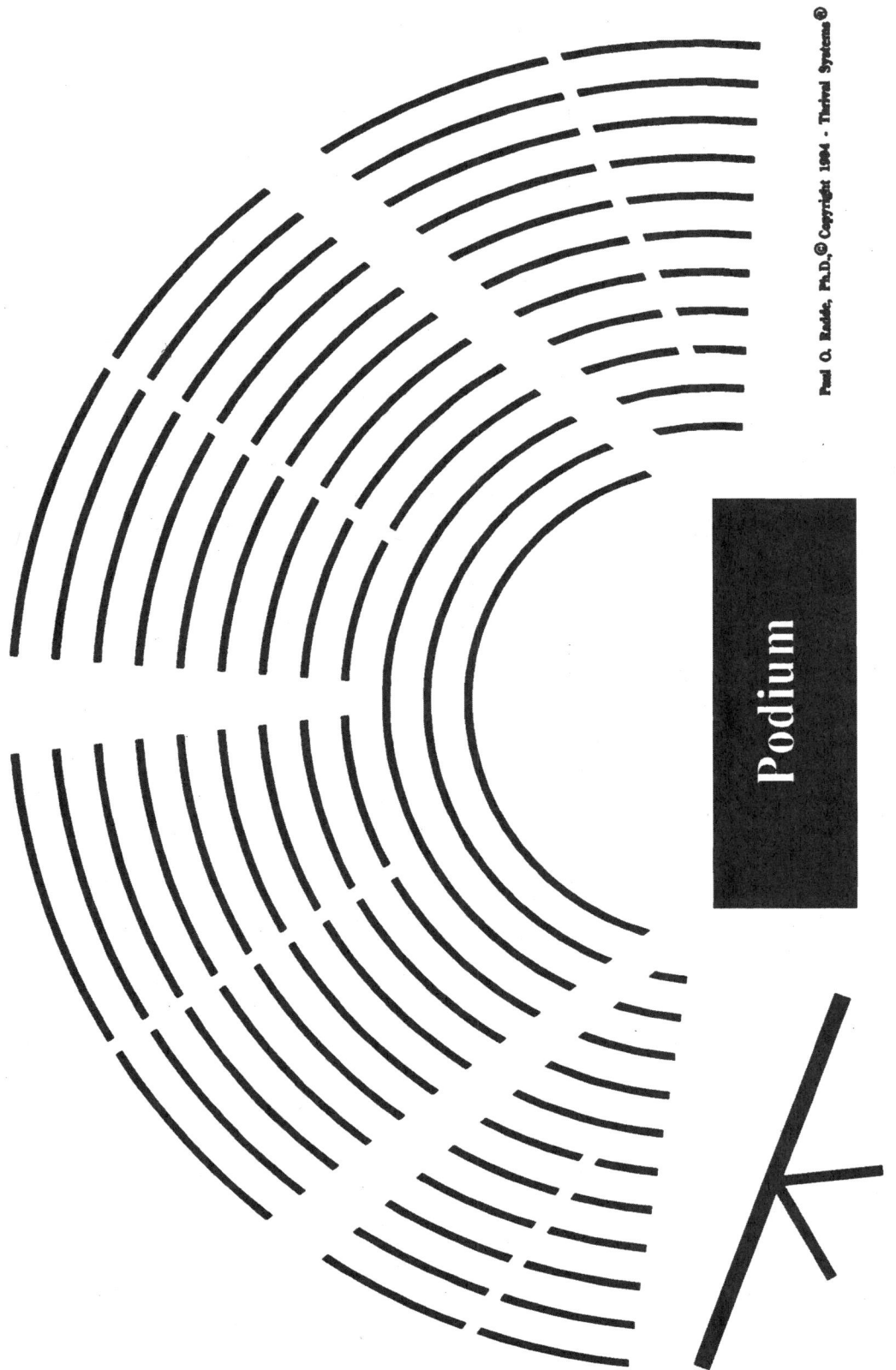

ACS™ Ellipse for Wide Ranging Presentations
Audience Centered Seating™ Principles:

1. **Set to the long wall** for closeness to the presentation. Set the top of the arc of the front row within 6-9 feet of the front of the stage unless the area in front of stage is required for other activity.

2. **Curve the seating to face the presentation. No Straight rows.**
   When the presenter will range across the platform, shape the rows in an ellipse. Use a stencil for the ellipse with a standard ¼ inch per foot, for the facility diagram. Utilize the area up around sides of the podium. You may place chairs as close to the front wall as the area even with the back of the oval, as long as each chair is facing the presentation.

3. **No center aisle. Flare aisles off the edges of the platform at a 45 degree angle, or toward the exits.** Do not use a center aisle, for it tends to drain energy from the presentation.

4. **Face each chair toward the presentation.**
   This is somewhat redundant with principle 2.

5. **Cut single-chair veins or access lanes into long rows every 7th chair.**
   Every seventh chair is removed to assure ease of access and egress. No one need walk in front of more than 5 chairs in order to get to a seat – generally only 1-3.

6. **Set the last row on the back wall.**
   This principle applies only to breakout sessions and would not usually be applied in a smaller breakout session utilizing the ellipse.

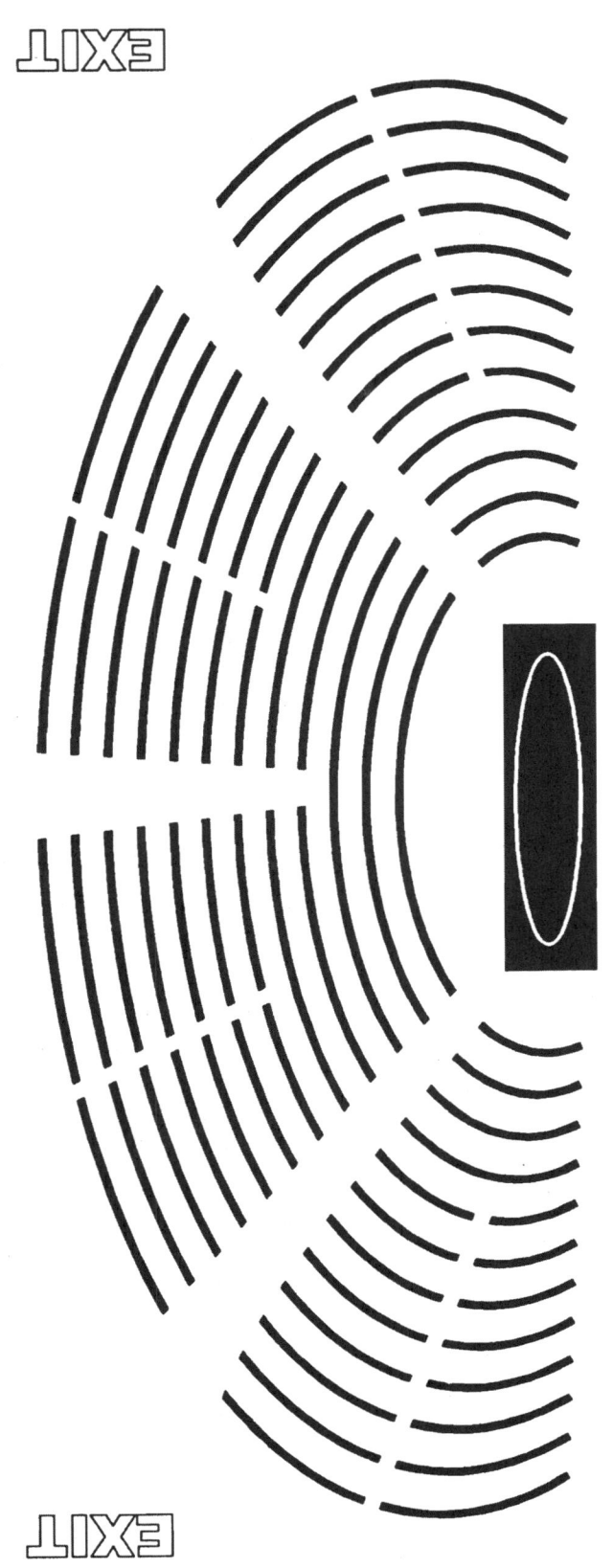

SEATING MATTERS

Audience Centered Seating™ - Rounds
Audience Centered Seating™ Principles:

1. **Set to the long wall** for closeness to the presentation. Set the top of the arc of the bowed front row within 8-10 feet of the presenter as long as sight lines for A/V can be preserved and it rounds out the table configuration for the front row.

2. **Curve the setting of the rounds to face the presentation.**
   Even though this curving is accomplished naturally at each table, curving the set of tables allows those at other tables to see each other. This promotes an improved dynamic at the meeting. Even if the rounds are set up straight across, many will still be able to see each other, but the curving of rounds allows more individuals to see each other and contains the room energy.

   At each round, under set the tables of 10 by 3 [less 2 if part of a meal], and tables of 6 by 2, so that everyone can more naturally and initially be oriented toward the presentation or facilitator when breaking from a group discussion. Eight is about the upward limit for time limited group discussion or a split table of two groups of 4 – 5 each when the table is filled. Pay attention to what table numbers result in side discussions, thus splitting table participants and damaging inclusiveness.

   If individuals have migrated around the entire table, you will have to be most specific in insisting that they then turn their chair completely around in order to see the presentation or participate in the program. The facilitator or MC can give advance notice, and then simply not start until everyone complies.

4. **Face each chair toward the presentation.**
   This is somewhat redundant with principle 2, and will require clear direction following small group discussion at each table, i.e. to turn one's chair and face the presentation.

If you are having discussion interspersed with presentations from the front of the room, or a program that follows a meal, you have to be very direct and explicit to get audience members to face their chairs toward the presentation. Many would twist their necks and bodies rather than turn their chair around. Other are reluctant to give their back to anyone at their table, even though they are showing their back to many others in the room.

Consider opening aisles from the front stage in between the first and second tables on each side, or the second and third, depending upon which provides the straightest line to the back entrances. Rounds with aisles up the middle severely divide the audience, due to the space the tables occupy. They can become a major challenge to the presenter and drain energy out of the meeting. A participative presenter using the middle aisle will have to make major sweeping moves to see everyone. And the rounds may make interaction more difficult for the presenter due to the space required by the setup.

Illustration courtesy of 3M Visual Systems Division, from the book Mastering Meetings, 1996.

State of the Art Seating Arrangements

SEATING MATTERS

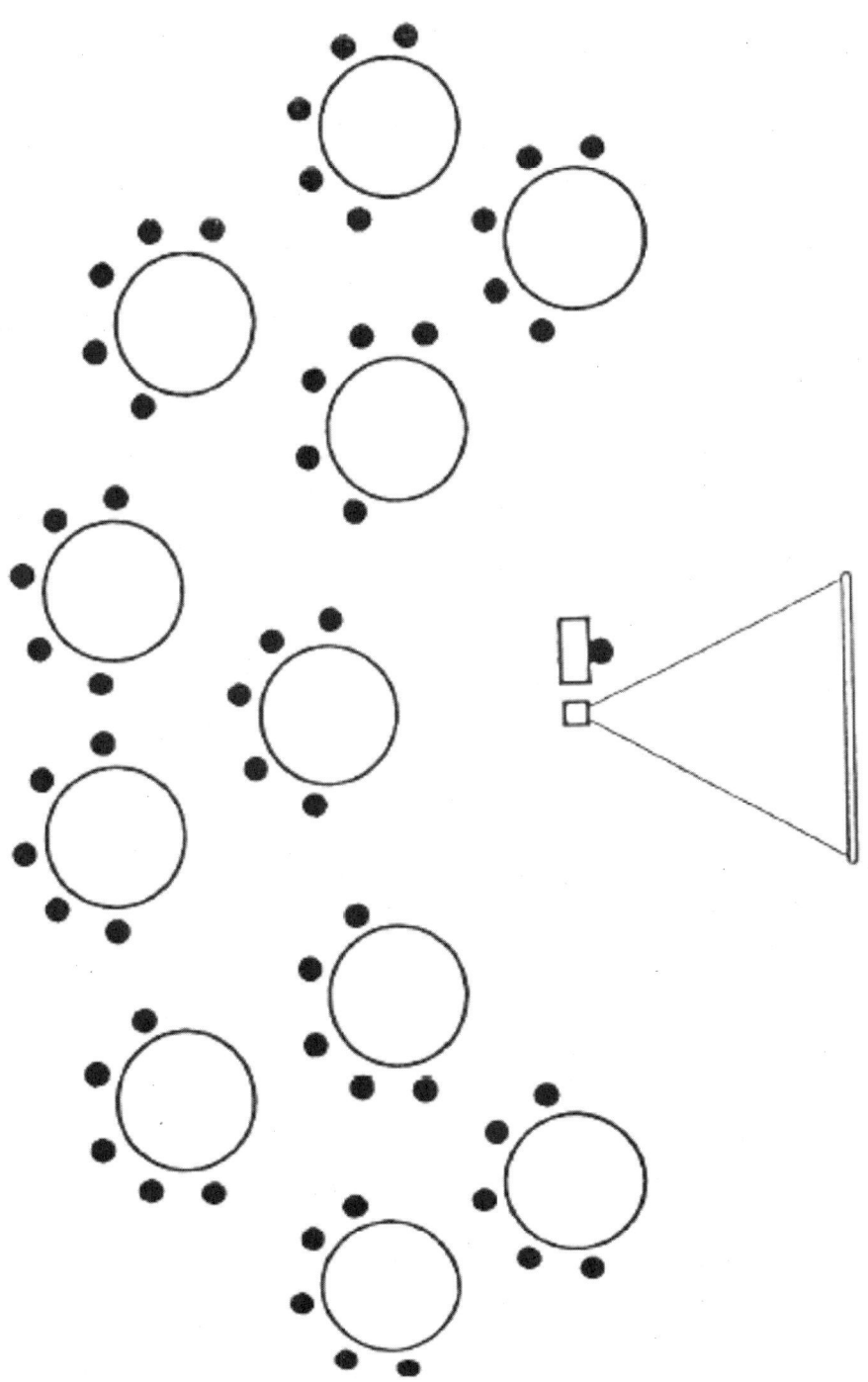

State of the Art Seating Arrangements

SEATING MATTERS

Audience Centered Seating™ - Starburst

Audience Centered Seating™ Principles Applied:

1. **Set to the long wall** for closeness to the presentation, more intimate and greater capacity than rounds, even when using 3' x 6' tables. There is less space in the middle of the table to distance participants from presentation and presenter. Less space is required between tables in order to allow access around those seated. Movement within the audience is facilitated with straight rows, for participants are less likely to spread out, as opposed to those around rounds.

2. **Curve the setting of the rectangular tables to face the presentation.**
   Treat the tables like arrows, and aim them directly at the presentation. Curving the set of tables allows those at other tables to see each other, promoting an improved dynamic at the meeting.

3. **Flare any aisle off at 45 degrees from the front corners of the podium.**
   Leave sufficient room in between each table so that those facing the presentation will have sufficient space to the next table so that an individual can pass between them.

4. **Face each chair toward the presentation.**
   If you are having discussion interspersed with presentations from the front of the room, or a program that follows a meal, you have to be very direct and explicit to get audience members to face their chairs toward the presentation. Some would twist their necks and bodies rather than turn their chair around.

This room is set for team work, small group discussion, attention to presentations, and possibly a meal. Each table can accommodate 6-8 persons, depending upon whether binders are in use, by adding one chair at the end toward the presentation and one on each side. The table size used in this diagram is outsized at 28 inches by 76 inches. For that reason, I have overlapped the chairs with the table. Use a 30 inch wide six foot table for this work – wider is better for these numbers. Capacity of this 25 by 40 foot room is 75 set 5 per table, and can be increased to 90 by adding one chair to each of the 15 tables. Six by three foot tables generally are better. No specific aisle is noted, although that can be determined according to the room and the location of the exits. Participants may also be advised to push in chairs during breaks in order to facilitate egress and access.

Caution!

n.b. *Leaning chairs forward against the table, a customary way of reserving a table spot, leaves protruding chair legs out in the aisle-ways where people walk. Those legs can easily inflict bruises and gashes in shin bones. Another way to reserve that very seat would be to pull a napkin through the top loop or slat of that chair, and push it right up to the table.*

SEATING MATTERS

State of the Art Seating Arrangements

SEATING MATTERS

Audience Centered Seating™ - Classroom
Audience Centered Seating™ Principles:

1. **Set to the long side to be closer** to the presentation, more intimate. Set the top of the arc of the first row of tables within 6-9 feet of the front of the stage in order to still allow for rounding out the table configuration.

2. **Curve the seating and table to face the presentation. No straight rows.**
   Treat these tables like "bows" by grasping the front of the table, facing the presentation focal point, palm down. Aim the bow/table directly at the focal point for that presentation. Then place chairs on the far side of the table facing the presentation. Place 3 participants on an 18 inch by 6 foot table when little work space is required. Place 2 participants at each table when 3 ring binders, notebooks, or some other paper work is required.

   Participants may be placed within 22-23 degrees of a screen on the front wall in order to see the full picture. And additional capacity is gained by placing side tables as close to the front as the front wall. However, setting depends upon unobstructed line of sight.

3. **Flare the aisles off 45 degrees from the front corners of the platform, or toward the exits.** No center aisle, for it drains energy from the presentation. In this design, there is some slight wiggle room to pull the tables on the left of center section back a foot or so, thereby clearing more room for the aisle.

   Also, the front two center tables, shaped in a V, can be removed for more space for the presenter. Or, an additional table could be placed in the same configuration as the tables behind in order to increase capacity.

4. **Face each table and chair toward the presentation.**
   This is redundant with principle 2, and will require clear direction following small group discussion at each table, i.e. to turn one's chair and face the presentation, especially if additional participants have joined with the table residents and are facing away from the presentation as the result of an exercise.

   This room is 25 by 40 feet. The table size illustrated is 18 inches by 6 feet. There is no water table in the diagram, though there is room for one to the right of the right back exit, and to the left of the back left exit. Preferably, set a 3 foot square table placed in the corner with a small water tank.

State of the Art Seating Arrangements

SEATING **MATTERS**

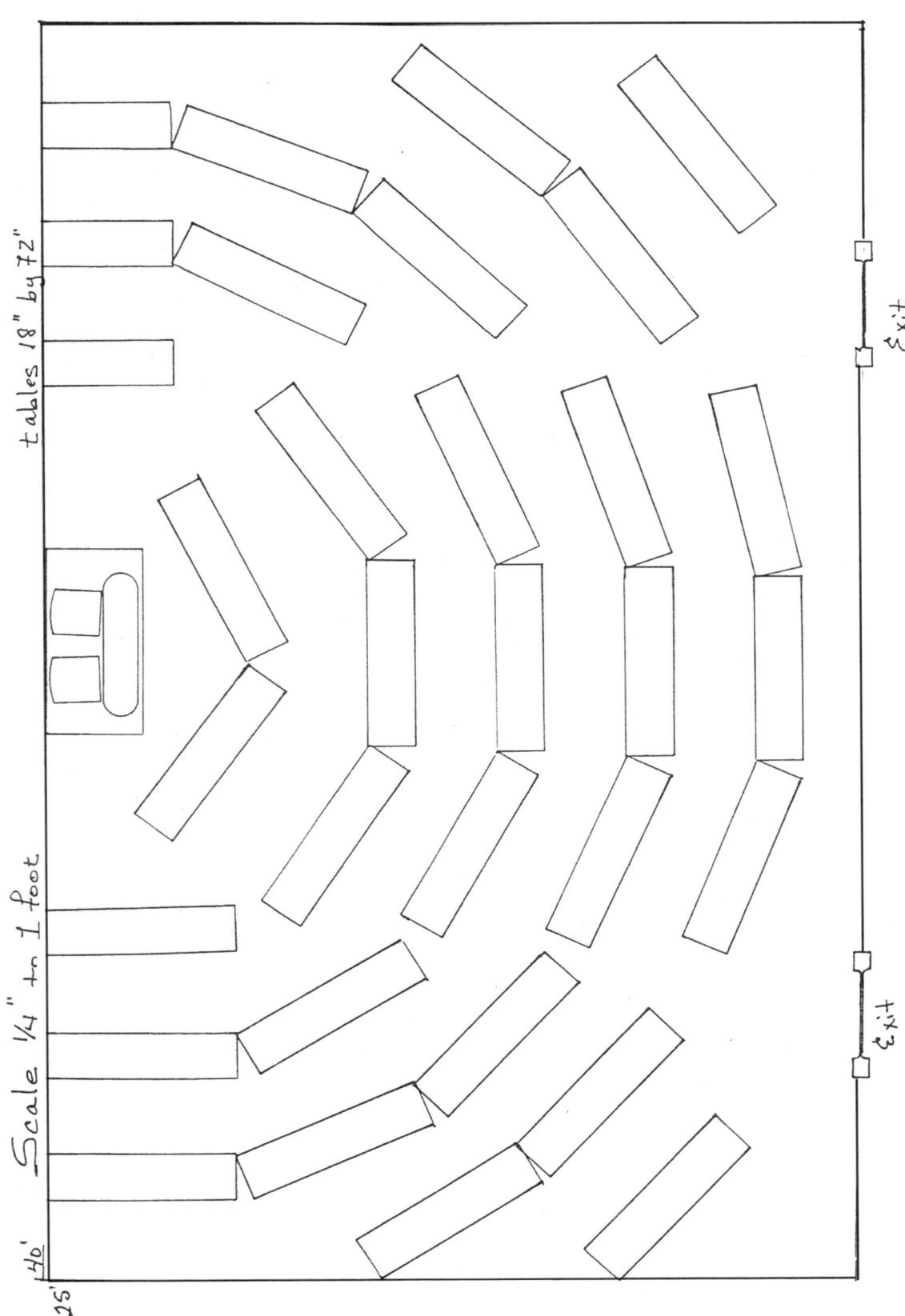

State of the Art Seating Arrangements

ACS™ J Shape for Narrow Long Rooms
[Especially for subdivisions of ballrooms.]

Audience Centered Seating™ Principles Applied:

1. **Set to the long side to be closer** to the presentation, more intimate. Set the top of the arc of the front row within 4-9 feet of the presentation.

2. **Curve the rows so participants can see each other.**
   Participants can be placed within 22-23 degrees of a screen on the front wall – see right front row - in order to see the full picture. And additional capacity is gained by placing chairs as close to the front as the front wall. However, setting depends upon unobstructed line of sight of the presentation.

3. **Flare the aisles off 45 degrees from the front corners of the platform, or toward the exits. No center aisle**, and especially not when there is no door in the back. These sections of ballrooms and other narrow rooms have exits flared off from the front edge of the stage. Hence, it is important to design the exit aisles directly, or angled, toward the exits from the front stage for efficient egress, and also to safely maintain the highest capacity for the room.

4. **Face each chair directly toward the presentation.**
   Focus the room set predominately toward that aspect of the presentation that will occupy the most time as shown in the first illustration of Chapter 11. For example, if power point will only last for 15 minutes, the stage should be the focal point for the entire presentation. Do not set toward the screen, for most people can tolerate neck twisting for 15 minutes or less. Those awkwardly seated can stand against the back or sidewall for a few moments.

5. **Cut single chair access lanes** into longer rows, every seventh chair or for access in more distant reaches of a narrow room as needed to facilitate access.

6. **Place last row on the back wall. Leave more aisle exit space in front of the last row.** This is the very type of situation in which this principle serves best.

If there is no ceiling mount for projectors, place it on a 6' stack or elevated platform in place of one of the back row chairs most directly facing the screen.

State of the Art Seating Arrangements

SEATING **MATTERS**

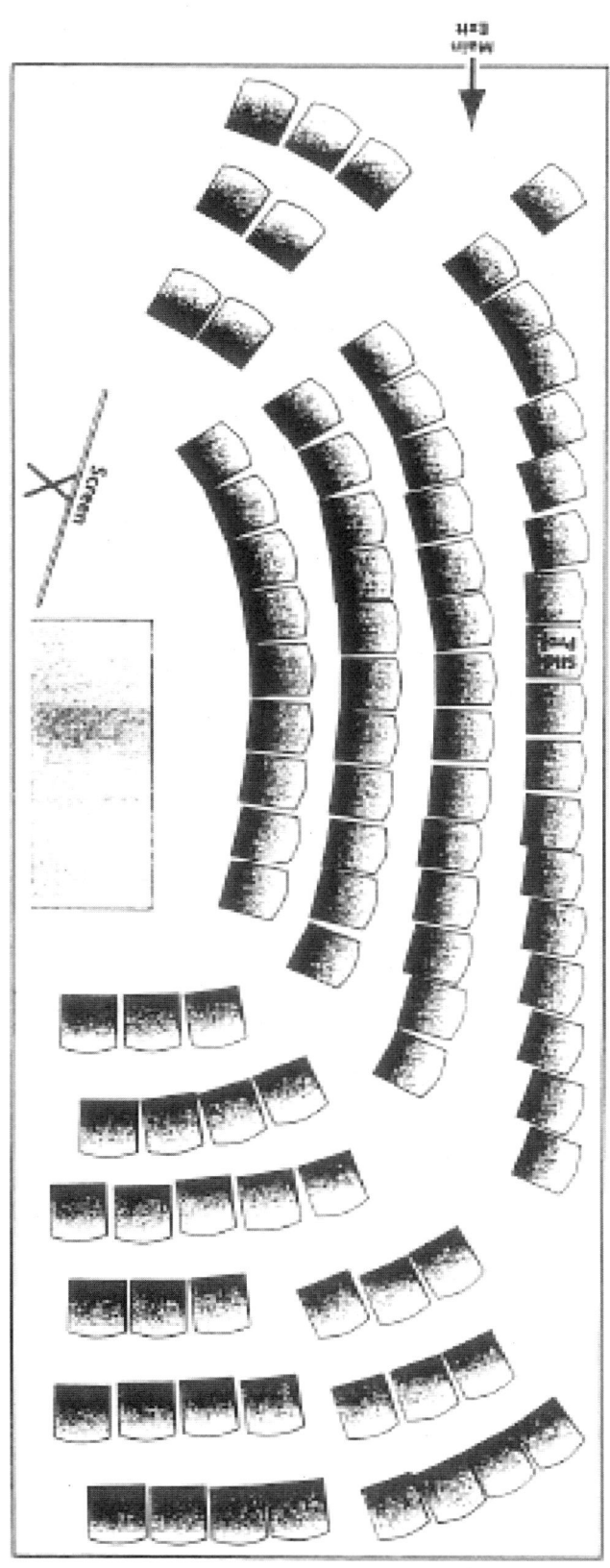

State of the Art Seating Arrangements

SEATING **MATTERS**

ACS™
True ACS™ Horseshoe

This is a small meeting set-up with tables. This particular configuration accommodates 24 or more. This is a true horseshoe, unlike the so-called U-Shape, which is nothing more than a Hollow Square with one side removed.

This is an excellent board room set. The horseshoe is a high energy, highly interactive setup that affords participants easy viewing of each other, and allows for presentations and facilitation as well. Each table is set separately – no overlapping of table cloths. Six foot by 18 inch wide tables are preferred.

Those in the front two tables would simply swing their chairs around for easy viewing of AV at the front. or when not in small group discussion at their tables.

The facilitator or presenter in this setting may get a high level of energy from the group, and would be well forewarned to be grounded.

Audience Centered Seating Principles Applied:

2. Curve the seating in order to assure that each participant will be able to see every other participant. No straight rows.

    Drape the table individually so that they can be moved in quickly, and moved around more easily.

    The best configuration here is to continue rounding so that the tables form a horseshoe. That configuration is shown on the next page.

Seating Per Table
The actual number that are best accommodated at each table will depend upon the materials in use – e.g., a binder of papers, folder, or spreadsheets would comfortably accommodate 2 participants per table. Absent the materials, each six foot length of table will accommodate 3 each.

Illustration used by permission of 3M© Visual Systems Division. From the book Mastering Meetings, 1996.

SEATING **MATTERS**

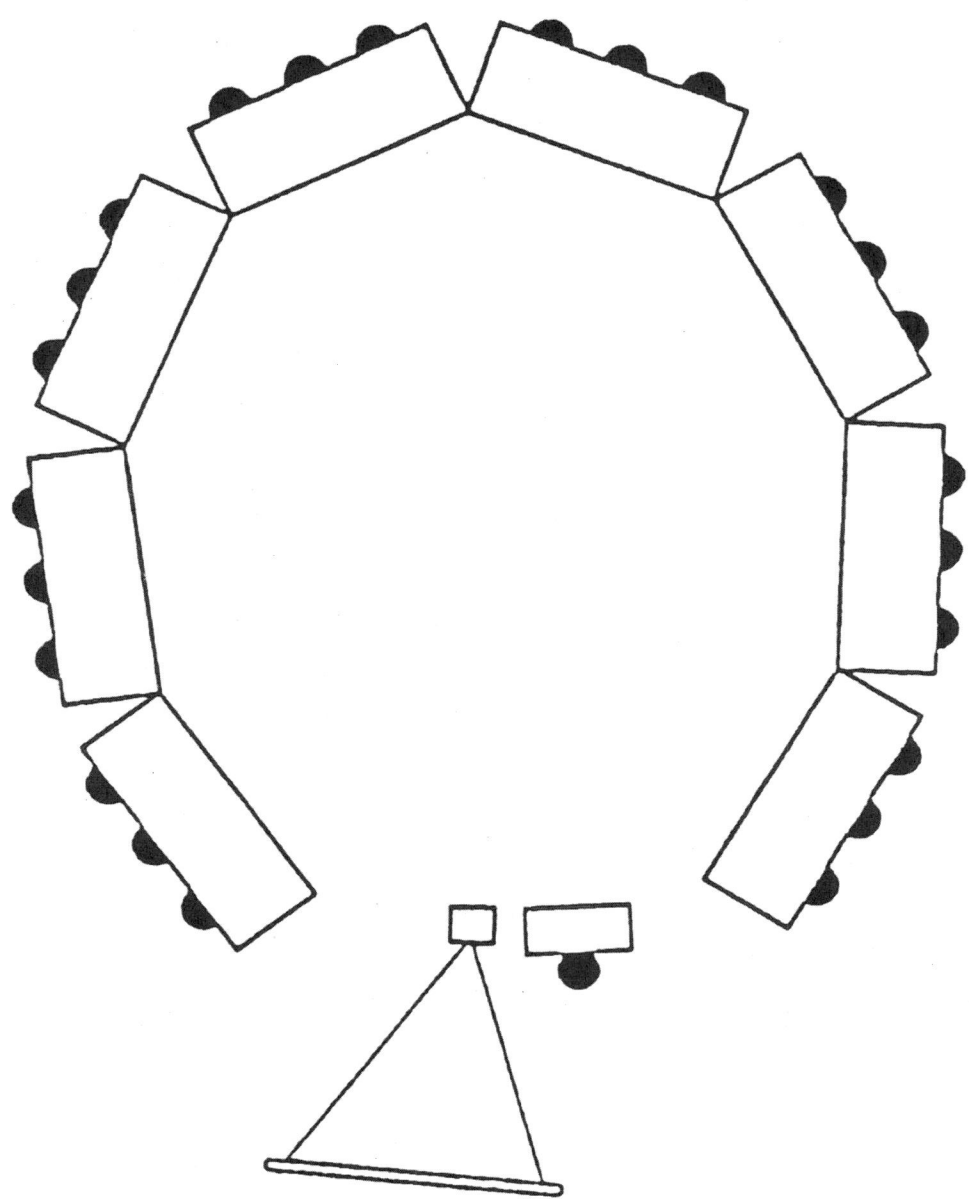

State of the Art Seating Arrangements

Acknowledgements

I wish to thank Shirley Bird Perry, former Director of the University of Texas Student Union and her Assistant, Sue Wagnon Clagett, for their support in my first experiment with alternative conference seating for the 1968 Challenge Colloquium general session program, "I the Starting Point."

Over the years, the following have played a role in keeping me going through their interest, writings, and have made this venture sustainable. My thanks to them all, and those who might have slipped my mind in the past 26 years. Joan L. Eisenstodt, Ed Scannell, CMP, CSP, Susan Sarfati while at ASAE and now the Executive Vice President of the American Program Bureau, Dr. Joe Jeff Goldblatt, founder of ISES now at the University of Edinburg, Scotland, Ilse Whittemore of HSMAI Affordable Meetings, Tom Antion, Andrew Silver, Immediate Past President of SGMP in Michigan, Orvel Ray Wilson of the Guerrilla Marketing Group, Carol Weisman, CSP, of Board Builders, Denise Cavanaugh of Cavanaugh, Hagen, Pearson, and Mintz, Marjorie Brody, CSP, CPAE, Kevin O'Sullivan, Jim Rhode, CSP, Naomi Rhode, CSP, CPAE, Sheila Murray Bethel, Pennsylvania Credit Union Cooperative, James M. Radde, S.J., Frank Briganti, Ed.D., Dr. DeWayne Woodring of RCMA, Dominick Chiappetta, who provided early art work, Jerry Tapley of 3M Visual Systems, Leslie Stephen, my long time and excellent editor, and Beth Ricciardi graphic artist.

Many entrenched elements of resistance to Audience Centered Seating™ have surfaced over time. They have been excellent teachers about effecting change and transforming mindsets. This book is intended to foster more safety, comfort, ease of viewing, access, networking and …capacity for events worldwide.

Author Biographical Information

Dr. Paul O. Radde is a keynote speaker, organizational consultant, and practicing psychologist. An executive coach to association executive directors, and the American Red Cross Quality Assurance Division; he has consulted to the World Bank, major health care associations, and information technology companies. Dr. Radde has presented on 4 continents, to 24 federal agencies, Fortune 50 corporations, and over 100 state and national associations. Paul taught at the University of Texas at Austin and Georgetown University. For 25 years, Dr. Radde lived and practiced in Washington, D.C.

Paul is most noted for bringing out the best in people at all levels and walks of life, helping them capture the "richest experience of their lives." Dr. Radde gives people the tips, tools, and techniques to spiral up. He leads his audiences from the endless struggle of survival to Thrival!, the inner joy that defies circumstances, through his custom-tailored speeches and seminars on:

- **Thrival! Sustaining the Positive Charge of Success,**
- **Advanced Leadership,**
- **How to Influence Decision Makers,**
- **Collaboration and Team Building, and**
- **Creating Self-Managing Employees.**

The founder of The Thrival Institute, Dr. Radde is an Ahead of the Curve™ big picture thinker, visionary, and researcher. He is currently exploring

- **Lifelong Self-Care as a Solution to the Health Care Crisis;**
- **Progress Measures in Human Development Programs; and**
- **Top Down/Power Over → Side-by-Side/Power With,**
  a major paradigm shift.

Paul currently lives in Longmont, Colorado, the headquarters of Thrival Systems® and The Thrival Institute, where he plays racquetball, skis, hikes, bikes, and enjoys the Rocky Mountains.

Find additional information on Dr. Radde's presentations and a streaming video at www.Thrival.com.

Training in "fine tuning" the meeting room is now available to meeting professionals and facilities.